Centres and Peripheries

Centres and Peripheries:
Metropolitan and Non-Metropolitan Journalism in the Twenty-First Century

Edited by

David Hutchison and Hugh O'Donnell

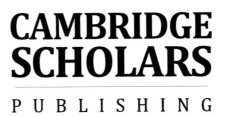

CAMBRIDGE
SCHOLARS

PUBLISHING

Centres and Peripheries:
Metropolitan and Non-Metropolitan Journalism in the Twenty-First Century,
Edited by David Hutchison and Hugh O'Donnell

This book first published 2011

Cambridge Scholars Publishing

12 Back Chapman Street, Newcastle upon Tyne, NE6 2XX, UK

British Library Cataloguing in Publication Data
A catalogue record for this book is available from the British Library

ISBN (10): 1-4438-2671-5, ISBN (13): 978-1-4438-2671-6

TABLE OF CONTENTS

Introduction
David Hutchison and Hugh O'Donnell 1

The Changing World of News
Tom Thomson 6

The British Isles

From The Periphery to the Core: Post-Coloniality and the Celtic Tiger
Farrel Corcoran 16

Those Post-devolution, Falling Revenues Blues: A Political Economy
of Northern Ireland's News Media
Greg McLaughlin 27

What's News in Wales? Welsh-language Journalism Today
and in Historical Context
Glyn Mon Hughes 42

"Postcode Lottery": The Future of Cross-border Media in Post-devolution
Wales
Simon Gwyn Roberts... 53

To the Periphery of the Periphery: The Regional Press, Micro-news
Agendas and Local Identity
Andy Price 65

Regional Television News and its Audiences
Samantha Lay and Deirdre O'Neill 76

Paying the Price? Sustaining Regional Television News in Britain
Sue Wallace 90

Knowing Me, Knowing You: White but not Quite Right
Marc Stanton 105

Local Journalism in a Peripheral Area: Newspapers in the Scottish
Highlands
Mike Cormack 118

Eòrpa—Taking Europe from the Periphery to the Core?
Douglas Chalmers 128

Provincial Insiders or Metropolitan Expatriates? The Strange Case
of Scottish Journalists in London
David Stenhouse 149

London Rules—The Myth of a National Media
Howard Tumber... 161

European Perspectives

Journalism in Contemporary France
Raymond Kuhn.. 172

Journalism in Catalonia: Creating a Perspective on the World
Enric Castelló 184

Structural Shift and Functional Stability: German Journalism
in the "Berlin Republic"
Siegfried Weischenberg, Maja Malik and Armin Scholl 201

"The Island of Loneliness"? Literary Journalism from the Azorean
Periphery
Isabel Soares... 215

Beyond Europe

Abandoning the Country: The Failure of Centralized Ownership
and Control of the Canadian Media
Christopher Waddell... 226

Journalism in the USA: The National, the Local and the Online
Challenge
Michael Parks 239

The Alhambra Project: A Theory-based Strategy for the Construction
of a Citizen Journalism Website
Nancy Nien-Tsu Chen, Sandra Ball-Rokeach, Michael Parks
and Jin Huang 255

Someone Else's Periphery? Journalism in New Zealand
Linda Jean Kenix 271

Afterword
David Hutchison and Hugh O'Donnell 286

Contributors 291

INTRODUCTION

DAVID HUTCHISON AND HUGH O'DONNELL

This collection of essays had its origin in a conference held at Glasgow Caledonian University in the spring of 2009. The conference attracted speakers from continental Europe and North America as well as the British Isles; most of these were academics but a significant number were journalists or former journalists. Subsequent to the conference, when the decision to publish was made, we sought additional contributions in order to broaden the scope of the book. We do not claim for a minute to have covered the globe, but, in addition to chapters concerned with the United Kingdom and Ireland, there are several which address the situations in Spain, Germany, France, and part of Portugal. There are also chapters on the United States, and the former British dominions are represented by Canada and New Zealand.

The centres/peripheries relationship has been explored in a number of contexts.[1] Most obvious is the political one where the development, for example, of the European empires can be viewed in that light, the colonial powers seeking to centralise decision-making in, say, London, Paris, Lisbon or Madrid, with Ceylon, Algeria, Brazil, Peru and other possessions in subservient positions. Closely allied in the history of empires is the centre/periphery economic interaction, where the central power sought to use the wealth of its colonies to maximise benefit to itself, whether through the exploitation of a colony's natural resources, the development of markets for industrial goods produced at home, or the imposition of tariff regimes designed to ensure that the colonial power remained a net beneficiary, even when economic development in the colony started to accelerate. And within former colonies, a similar analytical framework can be used to account for the way in which, for example, the fur trade in North America produced a centre/periphery

---

[1] Johan Galtung's 1971 essay is often cited in discussions of centre/periphery relationships. He distinguishes five types of imperialism "depending on the type of exchange between Center and Periphery nations"—economic, political, military, communication and cultural.

relationship not only between France—later Britain—and Lower Canada but also between the trading centres of Lower Canada and the fur trapping parts of the country.[2]

In many countries today the argument continues about the relative power of the economic centre(s) and the more peripheral regions which, to take a couple of examples, can manifest itself in discussion about whether the south east of England is successful at the expense of the north east and north west, and whether the relative backwardness of the former East Germany continues because of the excessive economic power of the former West Germany.

Our concern here is with the cultural aspect of the centre/periphery relationship but, while empires may have disappeared in the political sense, the economic strength and reach of powerful countries continue to constrain the behaviour of other countries in many spheres including the cultural. Within that domain we are concerned with the media, and within the media we have chosen to focus on journalism. In a liberal democracy it is largely through the work of journalists that as citizens we are enabled to understand what is going on in our societies, to participate in public debate in an informed fashion and ultimately to make political choices. This is perhaps to describe an ideal situation which can sometimes be more of an aspiration than a fact, and journalism can often be concerned to entertain and divert as well as inform us. Nonetheless, for a great deal of the time much journalism does exactly what it is supposed to do in democratic societies: informs, asks awkward questions and promotes public debate.

Centre/periphery relationships in journalism are about power and perspective. Do the metropolitan newspapers and broadcasters in any particular country dominate in terms of circulation and viewing figures, to the exclusion or weakening of the media in peripheral areas? How do peripheries sustain their own identities and perspectives? Do metropolitan media construct views of their societies and the world which are very geographically centred, even parochial? How do the different regions of a country, or the distinct nations within a particular state, know and understand each other? Because we are Scottish-based academics we hear these questions being asked constantly and we sometimes ask them ourselves. But similar questions are raised in many other parts of the world, as will be clear from the essays which follow.

An important topic to emerge in a number of the contributions is that peripheries are not only constituted in the ways mentioned earlier: they are

---

[2] The classic study in this area was published by Harold Innis in 1930. Innis went on to write *The Bias of Communication*, one of the "founding texts" in the communication studies field.

also constituted in and through discourse. The existence of such a discursive dimension carries with it the inevitable potential for contestation, a refusal to accept the status of periphery assigned by others, even for attempts to bring about a reversal of established centre-periphery discursive positions. A number of the chapters discuss such "self-centring" or "recentring" strategies, themselves invariably part of larger power struggles.

***

Readers might be struck by the fact that, although there are a couple of chapters in the book concerned with Gaelic and Highland Scotland, there is no extended discussion of the Scottish situation overall. That is largely because the Scottish media have been fairly thoroughly analysed in print recently; however it might be worth briefly summarising here the position in the country, since it was the starting point for our conference and ultimately this volume.[3]

As is the case in other parts of the British Isles, indigenous Scottish newspapers compete with English ones, many of these editionised with content aimed exclusively at the Scottish market—in local parlance "north of the border". In the last twenty-odd years the editionising has increased, as has the number of homegrown titles. Currently five Scottish dailies and four Sundays compete for readers with London titles, some of which like *The Sun* and the *Daily Mail* editionise heavily, while others such as the *Daily Express* and *The Guardian* do less so, or scarcely at all. The establishment in 1999 of a devolved parliament in Edinburgh notwithstanding, Scottish produced papers now account for 43% of daily sales and 56% of Sundays; in the mid seventies they had well over 60% of both markets.[4] These losses in market share have combined with the overall slide in sales, which has afflicted the press throughout the Western world, to significantly lower revenue and journalistic resources.

BBC Scotland and STV (formerly Scottish Television) are both major news providers, but the latter, in common with other ITV companies, has indicated that the provision of a regional news service is no longer financially viable—an issue which is discussed in relation to Britain as a whole in two chapters in the book. So the likelihood is that in the future it is to the BBC, on air and online, that Scottish viewers and listeners will

---

[3] See for example Blain and Hutchison (2008) for several essays on the historical and contemporary situations.

[4] These figures are derived from circulation data available from the Audit Bureau of Circulation (www.abc.org.uk).

look for a comprehensive news service, since the commercial radio stations offer only limited provision and the service provided by the digital Gaelic television channel, BBC Alba, which began broadcasting in 2008, is targeted principally at speakers of that language, currently less than two per cent of the population. The output of Radio Scotland, a stand-alone service comparable to similar services in Wales and Northern Ireland, has a high journalism content, the opt-out television programming (roughly five per cent of what is seen onscreen on BBC1 and BBC2 north of the border) a smaller one. Arguments about the allocation of resources to BBC Scotland are long running and focus on the cash available for programming intended for Scottish consumption and the commissioning of programming destined for the national networks. The Nationalist government which took power in Edinburgh in 2007 established a Scottish Broadcasting Commission, which in 2008 recommended that a publicly financed digital channel should be established, and that it should have at its heart a news service, in order to ensure that there would be an alternative to the BBC if the commercial channel opted out of that kind of provision (Scottish Broadcasting Commission 2008). At the same time as the Commission was established, the BBC, under pressure from other parts of the United Kingdom as well as from Scotland, committed itself to greatly increasing the shares of production generated outside of London: currently the Corporation intends that the Scottish share of network production should by 2016 reach nine per cent, which is almost triple the present figure.

The BBC has become very sensitive to accusations of metropolitan bias in the allocation of resources and in the way in which the nations which make up the United Kingdom are represented in news output originating in London. In 2007 the BBC Trust, the quasi-independent body which oversees the Corporation's operations, commissioned an academic report on the matter (BBC Trust 2008). What is at issue in Wales, Northern Ireland and Scotland is the extent to which, post-devolution, these nations have fallen off the radar of the metropolitan media (newspapers as well as broadcasting), a question which is explored in one of the following chapters. Similar arguments take place elsewhere in the world, as will be seen from several other chapters. How we come to know and understand each other within particular countries, never mind how we relate to other countries, is an extremely important issue.

**

Conference organisers anticipate that a call for papers will elicit proposals which cover areas of interest which the theme inevitably suggests but also that there will be "outliers" at a slight angle to the theme, but fascinating nonetheless. Both kinds are represented here.

The book begins with a general overview of the challenges facing journalism in the digital age which is provided by the current managing editor of one of the leading Scottish publishers, who draws on his previous experience as managing editor of Reuters. There follow chapters which explore aspects of journalism in Wales, Ireland, the English regions and the Scottish Highlands, which take account of both historical context and contemporary practice.

The focus then shifts to Europe and thereafter to North America—Canada as well as the United States—and finally to a country which sometimes thinks of itself as being on the periphery of a periphery, New Zealand.

Themes distinctive to different geographical locales emerge but so do others which are common across oceans and continents. We shall discuss some of these further in our Afterword. Perhaps it might seem as if the structure we have chosen creates its own centre/periphery relationship but that is certainly not the intention and of course readers can navigate whatever journeys they please through the book.

Works Cited

Blain, N. and D. Hutchison, eds. 2008. *The Media in Scotland*. Edinburgh: Edinburgh University Press.

Galtung, J. 1971. A Structural theory of Imperialism. *Journal of Peace Research*, 8(2): 81-117.

Innis, H. 1930. *The Fur Trade in Canada: an Introduction to Canadian Economic History*. Oxford: Oxford University Press.

Scottish Broadcasting Commission. 2008. *Final Report*. www.scottishbroadcastingcommission.gov.uk/news/finalreportnews. html. Accessed 2 September 2010.

The BBC Trust. 2008. *Impartiality Report: BBC Network News and Current Affairs Coverage of the Four UK Nations*. www.bbc.co.uk/bbctrust/assets/files/pdf/review_report_research/ impartiality/uk_nations_impartiality.pdf. Accessed 2 September 2010.

THE CHANGING WORLD OF NEWS

TOM THOMSON

The news media industry is at a crossroads, struggling to make sense of a world where there are no longer any certainties. Newspapers are folding, or going web only, or making big staffing and spending cuts. At least 12,500 jobs have gone in print journalism in the United States in the past two years and hundreds in the British regional press.

We are facing a revolution, when the old order collapses and something new and unthinkable takes over. Many of us want reassurance that old systems won't really break before a new, orderly world is in place, that career paths we have assumed since we began in the business are not going to just vanish. The whole business or profession or trade of journalism is facing pressures and stresses almost unthinkable a decade ago. Part of the change is certainly cyclical, caused by the global recession, but a large measure is structural as the internet and connectivity change the very way we live.

The business model which has sustained journalism for decades is no longer valid—being able to generate audiences in a way that no one else could and then selling these audiences to advertisers, while giving readers what we thought they should get. We must now fight and innovate to survive, not sink, as is so easy in an industry in crisis, into a managing decline mentality. There is a continued and critical role for journalism to play in safeguarding democracy and public debate, however that ends up being delivered and funded. We all saw the internet coming and for a while we thought we had the answers. We could charge for content in walled gardens like AOL, we could rely on the copyright laws, micropayments were the way forward or we would be saved by advertising on the Web. But it all went horribly wrong. Gardens were forced open by users keen to experience the whole World Wide Web, copyright was largely swept away, micropayments nobody liked and web ads make little money. And to compound our problems, almost a quarter of internet users in the US say they stopped their subscription to a printed newspaper because they could access the same content online for free.

The Background

The background to these developments is well known:

- Newspaper circulation in most of the developed world (with a few special exceptions like the *Financial Times*) is in long-term, potentially irrevocable decline. There appears to be no way to turn that around using conventional thinking and tweaking content at the edges. The Scottish indigenous press for its part faces unusual challenges in competing with what are essentially very large national UK competitors in the print market, the so-called "tartanised" editions of the London-based titles which can cut cover prices and provide a richness of columnists, business and foreign coverage with which it is very difficult to compete.
- Print advertising revenue has fallen at an astonishing rate. The recession hit the industry hard as car and house sales stalled and recruitment was affected by the economy. But the decline is also structural since advertising spend is moving to channels which are cheaper or free or have better targeting or functionality. The threat of slabs of public sector advertising moving online is merely one example. This is heady stuff with pessimists predicting that the cyclical recovery, when it comes, will be offset by the structural decline and we may never again reach pre-recession levels.
- Web audiences are growing but in an environment where it is accepted that general information and news is free, not least with the dominating presence of the BBC and its great digital ambitions fuelled by a £500 million news budget. In a search-dominated Web, readers also prefer to read selected parts of the news agenda. This leads to the commodification of the Web and increasingly fragmented audiences, so with diminishing audiences advertisers want to pay less. The growing Web advertising revenue thus goes largely into paid search controlled by the likes of Google. Again there are exceptions, like *The Wall Street Journal*, where content is protected and must be bought but this is only proven of real money-making value in niche areas.
- Web advertising is low yield and diluted across so many outlets with everything from social networking sites and blogs competing with newspapers for advertiser spend. New threats are emerging—Google for example announced recently it would put ads on *Google News*. It can do this with a degree of targeting regional news firms will never achieve, using its

sophisticated monitoring of users, and thus it is reasonable to expect they will appeal to local advertisers seeking a very finely filtered audience. Local authorities are moving recruitment to their own websites. *Craigslist* has devastated the American newspaper industry's classified advertising sector. Britain has not been gripped by free ad sites to the same extent but that may come.

Some people in the industry are giving up. Some, like the *Seattle Post-Intelligencer* are going Web only (and watching page impressions fall).

The way forward

It all comes down to this. How do we quickly get growth in our digital revenue to outpace the downturn in our print revenue?

Engagement, involving readers in the digital world, is certainly a key part of it. Our readers want to do stuff with the content we produce whether to share it, Tweet it or blog it. Serious news sites must establish a more personal relationship with their readers. We've had letters to the editor since the late 19th century but journalism's relationship with readers has been one-sided. We need to create a feeling that they are missing something if they are not part of our sites.

There is hope emerging in our industry and the tide may be turning. Rupert Murdoch, the doyen of newspaper publishers, has decided that his British newspaper titles—*The Sun, Times* and *Sunday Times*—will charge for their content online and must do so to survive. Murdoch used *The New York Times* as an example of an online paper that, he believes, has a great website but is not covering its costs with online ad revenue only.

He has advocated a change in publishers' relationships with Google and other aggregators: "Should we be allowing Google to steal all our copyrights? Not just Google. I think if you've got a brand like *The New York Times* or *The Wall Street Journal* you don't have to do that" (interview on SkyNews Australia 6 November 2009).

Mathias Döpfner, chief executive of Axel Springer, believes it is time for new copyright laws in Europe to prevent all of the value of content being extracted by the aggregators, who make money by displaying search advertising around news material (*Financial Times*, 13 April 2009). Axel Springer publishes *Bild*, by far Germany's highest-selling paper and the highest-circulation tabloid in mainland Europe with daily sales of more than three million. Döpfner wants a proposition where Google contributes to Axel Springer's costs if it is going to use its content.

The Associated Press says it would take "all actions necessary" to pursue websites that use its members' content without paying (AP press release, 4 June 2009). The aggregators say they promote material and bring traffic to websites but traffic per se is becoming a devalued commodity, with a sudden belief emerging in quality of readership and not volume. This is quite a turnaround after years of seeking large numbers of users and measuring digital success by traffic alone.

The new iPad and iPhone operating system allows media companies to charge for some or all content, Kindle users seem to accept that you get newspapers if you pay a monthly fee, and mobile device users do seem more amenable to paying for content. Payment mechanisms are becoming much more unobtrusive, which is a really simple but important element in customer acceptance of paying. The iPad may well have a transformational effect on readers in terms of their willingness to pay for content. Other manufacturers are poised to introduce low-cost tablets which could well transform this into a mass market for newspaper-formatted paid content. This is an area to watch very closely.

Journalism Online is an interesting new start-up company that is offering to work with news publishers to address the growing cry to make online readers available as newsreaders. It's a company that is more an intention than an operation at this point, but it has an impressive pedigree for stating that intention.

Its progenitors, Gordon Crovitz, former publisher of *The Wall Street Journal*, and Steven Brill, a serial entrepreneur who founded both *Court TV* and *American Lawyer*, have been talking through various paid content models, the need for a flexible, modern news-centered e-commerce platform, and how such a system might work.

Their initial concept envisions four potential roles for the company:

- Creating a password-protected portal with one easy-to-use account through which consumers can buy annual or monthly subscriptions, day passes, and single articles from multiple publishers. The password-enabled payment system will be integrated into all of the member-publishers' websites, and the publishers will have sole discretion over which content to charge for, how much to charge, and the manner of charging.
- Establishing all-inclusive annual or monthly subscriptions for those consumers who want to pay one fee to access all of the JO-member publishers' content. A royalty pool would pay publishers based on usage.

- Negotiating wholesale licensing and royalty fees with intermediaries such as search engines and other websites that currently base much of their business models on referrals of readers to the original content on newspaper, magazine and online news websites.
- Providing reports to member publishers that identify the strategies and tactics that achieve the best results in building circulation revenue, while maintaining the traffic necessary to support advertising revenue.

Or it could be a paid and free model. *The Wall Street Journal*, for example, earns more than $60 million a year from one million online subscribers. At the same time, its "freemium" offers pull in an additional nineteen million unique users. They get to *Journal* content through various entry points, and are monetised through advertising.

It may well be that acting as an agent for news publishers with the search engine aggregators may rise to the top of the list. It doesn't require technology (though publishers adding intelligence to their content through better tagging and tracking is clearly a part of a successful future) so it could be acted on sooner rather than later.

The role of Google

The time is overdue for a reckoning of the news industry suppliers' relationship with Google. Here, too, though, *Journalism Online* faces an uphill battle, making the case that it is best positioned to be the lead negotiator. AP has made that case, and many news companies have preferred to go it alone in the past.

Google CEO Eric Schmidt is worth listening to. He's keen on mobile which he sees as being a fundamental change in the way people get information. There will soon be something like one billion smart phones in use.

He thinks we'll end up with a number of business models.

There are free television, over-the-air television, cable television and pay television. And they have smaller markets as you go from free to more highly paid. And that structure looks roughly the structure of all of these businesses. The reality is that in this new situation, most people will likely only deal with the free model. So we will be forced, whether we like it or not, to have a significant advertising component, as well as a micropayment and an additional payment system.

Schmidt proposed three layers of revenue for news content, similar to that of the TV business: a free model which would make up the bulk of a news website, a subscription model which would allow access to all articles, and a micropayment system for specific articles, priced at a few cents.

We also need smarter publishing—so that a digital newspaper knows what is new to groups and individuals, for example. But the industry must move the thinking beyond "fair use"—is search engine and other usage "legal" or not? —to "fair share". In basic business terms, the news industry is a supplier—and an important one—to Google and the other search engines. While a handful of key suppliers—Associated Press, Agence France Presse and others—have secured Google licenses and are getting paid for their content, individual newspaper publishers are not. They need to band together, testing here not just "fair use" but "anti-trust" (a concept that seems out of another newspaper age at this point)—and act like suppliers, demanding a fairer share of the pie.

The response of the press

But what of newspapers? They have to change. They have to accept that in a far more profound way than radio or television ever brought about, most people now know what has happened long before they pick up a print newspaper.

We talk constantly in the industry about newspapers adding value—the question is how. We could do no better than consult a road map for how newspapers can live alongside new media that was drawn up more than 50 years ago by Bernard Kilgore. Kilgore had remarkable judgment early about the journalistic issue of our day: how readers use old media, new media and both. When Kilgore became managing editor of *The Wall Street Journal* in 1941, he inherited a business model that technology had undermined. Founded in 1889 to provide market news and stock prices to individual investors, the *Journal* lost half its circulation as this basic information became widely available.

Kilgore observed that then new media such as radio meant market news was available in real time. Some cities had a dozen newspapers that had gained the *Journal's* once-valuable ability to report share prices. The *Journal* had to change. Technology increasingly meant readers would know the basic facts of news as it happened. He announced, "It doesn't have to have happened yesterday to be news", and said that people were more interested in what would happen tomorrow. He crafted the front page "What's News " column to summarise what had happened, but focused on explaining what the news meant.

On the morning after Pearl Harbor, other newspapers recounted the facts already known to all the day before through radio. The *Journal's* page-one story instead began, "War with Japan means industrial revolution in the United States". It outlined the implications for the economy, industry and commodity and financial markets.

Kilgore led the *Journal's* circulation to one million by the 1960s from 33,000 in the 1940s by adapting the newspaper to a role reflecting how people used different media for news. His rallying cry was "The easiest thing in the world for a reader to do is to stop reading".

Business and financial news is different from the general news focus of city newspapers, but in 1958 the owners of the *New York Herald Tribune* approached Kilgore for help. The *Herald Tribune*, he wrote, is "too much a newspaper that might be published in Philadelphia, Washington or Chicago just as readily as in metropolitan New York". Kilgore urged the "compact model newspaper". Readers valued their time, so the newspaper should have just one section, with larger editions on Sunday when people had more time to read.

His advice was clearly ahead of its time. The owners didn't heed it, and the *Herald Tribune* went out of business in 1967. But his observations on what readers want from city newspapers may be even more true in today's online world. Readers increasingly know yesterday what happened yesterday through websites, television and news alerts.

Indeed, at a time when print readership is declining, *The Economist*, with its weekly focus on interpretation, is gaining circulation. The *Journal* continues to focus on what readers need, growing the number of individuals paying for the newspaper and the website.

If readers would prefer more compact city newspapers, a less-is-more approach could help cut newsprint, printing, distribution and other costs that don't add to the journalism. Newspaper editors could craft a new, forward-looking role for print, alongside the what's-happening-right-now focus of digital news.

A role for government?

Print media are very important for democracy. Whether holding politicians to account or reporting councils. Who's going to do that?

The Web is just forty years old, public use twenty years, and using the internet as a normal way of life is less than half that. We're still in the revolutionary stage and revolutions are messy and chaotic. What seem minor diversions at the time—it could be Facebook or Twitter—can later be revealed as fundamental turning points that change our lives.

Where will journalism take us? It's likely to be an overlapping mesh of amateurs and professionals. There is a risk that cost-cutting and a focus on packaging and processing will increase the reach and power of PR companies and those who can afford to disseminate a positive message and a weakening of the rightly cynical editorial filter.

Can government help? It may have to. The Labour administration which lost power in the UK in 2010 promoted the idea of Independently Funded News Consortia as a way to state-fund ITV regional news, which the Channel 3 companies argued was no longer financially viable, and generate the kind of reporting that a converged world will need. This could bring together the regional newspaper groups with broadcast news providers and output good quality video news, whether delivered by terrestrial broadcast or the internet to television receivers along with multimedia content on web sites viewed on televisions, PCs or mobile devices, along with print products. The Conservative Party, which formed a coalition with the Liberal Democrats after the 2010 election, rejected subsidies outright, preferring instead a network of city television stations that would rely heavily on volunteer staff but whose business model is unproven.

The new UK culture secretary, Jeremy Hunt, announced that he backed a combination of significant deregulation of the television advertising market to allow the private sector to generate more revenue, combined with either the abolition or drastic easing of local cross-media ownership restrictions to allow rationalisation and cost cuts.

The one certainty is that a new media landscape will emerge in Britain under the coalition government. How precisely that will look remains uncertain until the fine print is examined and the industry decides how to respond.

Everyone accepts, though, that the current model is broken.

The BBC's independence from government seems to be generally accepted—top-slicing the BBC's licence fee or providing other tax revenue to maintain a diversity of news in Britain does however seem an acceptable way of preserving a core of high-quality journalism, and a quoted figure of £100 million per year would go a long way to making broadcast consortia feasible.

Getting the future right, however, will not be easy.

It's a particular concern for a company such as the Herald & Times Group, whose heritage goes back to 1783. It has met the challenges of hot metal, web offset, colour and a host of other technical advances. Can it get it right in an internet world?

It won't be plain sailing but we, like the rest of the British media industry, work constantly to adapt. We do need to stick with our core values and our belief in quality journalism. But if we do, the new distribution channels now opening up offer audiences larger and more globally distributed content than our greatest fans could have dreamed of even ten years ago.

THE BRITISH ISLES

FROM THE PERIPHERY TO THE CORE: POST-COLONIALITY AND THE CELTIC TIGER

FARREL CORCORAN

That there is a catastrophic dimension to Irish history is not in dispute among historians today, despite the various revisionist currents that have run through Irish historiography since the Troubles erupted in the late sixties. One historian sums up the record of the past as "seared by successive waves of conquest and colonisation, by bloody wars and uprisings, by traumatic dislocations, by lethal racial antagonisms and indeed, by its own 19th century version of a holocaust" (Bradshaw, quoted in Gibbons 1996, 6). To give an adequate account of centre-periphery relationships in contemporary Irish culture, one must take into account the historical dimension of how the Irish aspiration to independence has been defined against British claims to rule in Ireland. For a very long time, the colonial structures controlling print maintained an uneasy relationship with the indigenous culture based in the Irish language, which retained its own separate identity quite apart from the dominant print culture, until the dawn of the 20th century. In contemporary Irish society, the cultural position of the old colonial power has waned in inverse ratio to the quickening of the forces of cultural globalisation, shaping new trans-national information flows, including the increasing hegemony of neoliberalism. We follow Ashcroft et al. (1995) here in seeing the post-colonial aspect of contemporary societies as designating a historically situated set of cultural strategies that refer not only to the period after colonies becomes independent, but the totality of cultural practices that characterise post-colonial countries from the moment of colonisation to the present day.

News and Nation Building

Print was first introduced as part of the Tudor project to extend the reach of the English Reformation, as the medium of religious conversion and colonial administration, making Ireland one of the very late adopters of print among European countries. Gaelic Ireland never developed its own print infrastructure, as this ancient culture did not have what Braudel (1981) calls an "accelerator", or what Winston (1998) terms a "supervening social necessity" to embrace the new technology. Its power was based on a network of traditional bardic families, whose scholars and poets were guardians of a vibrant oral culture, supported by collections of manuscripts in Irish and Latin. As an incipient appetite for news and a public sphere began to emerge a century later, the oppositional role of print was still clear. The first newspaper in Ireland, the *Irish Monthly Mercury*, was produced by the Cromwellian army and published in Cork in 1649, demonstrating the new awareness of contemporaneity that was driving the development of news in London and beyond. But news gathering and distribution depended on the entire apparatus of a reliable postal system— safe roads and sea lanes, horses, riders, inns, ports, supply lines—and Ireland did not have a reliable system until much later. So towards the end of that century, newspaper readers in the coffee houses of Dublin had quite a skewed informational map of the world. Reports from faraway European cities were frequent, but news from around Ireland was rare and unreliable, with little more credibility than rumour. Over the course of the next century, dozens of newspapers appeared in Dublin, some destined to last only a few months, many of them linked directly to the colonial administration in Dublin Castle (Morash 2010).

The first stirrings of resentment against domination from London came from an unlikely quarter: the descendents of the Anglo-Irish who had settled in Ireland during the preceding century. Nurtured in the saturated news culture of the Pale, they began to appropriate the idea of a "native" culture at the heart of a new "nation", and to argue for greater Irish self-determination. Local newspapers began springing up at the end-point of major postal roads—Belfast, Limerick, Sligo, Galway, Cork, Waterford, Kilkenny—many of them to last into the middle of the 19th century. This regional press reinforced local loyalties but also helped forge the basis for conceptualising a shared, all-island consciousness.

Benedict Anderson was one of the first scholars to theorise how the development of news in colonial situations began to transform the cultural relationship between periphery and core areas of the world. Central to his account is the ephemeral popularity of the newspaper, a "one-day bestseller, obsolete tomorrow, yet creating an extraordinary mass ceremony: the simultaneous consumption ('imagining') of the newspaper-as-fiction, performed in silent privacy" (Anderson 1983, 35). Something similar was happening in Ireland in the 18th century. Morash (2010, 51) notes a new sense not only of national culture in the Irish Volunteer newspapers that appeared in the 1780s, but also a new ability to imagine Ireland's place in an international informational order. Earlier Irish newspapers had carried news from North America under the heading "Plantation News", but the press of the Volunteer movement, deeply influenced by the American Revolution, remapped the world to include America as a republic and a model for Ireland. Like the Volunteer movement, the United Irishmen also insisted on the centrality of the press to their political project in the 1790s. They had links to the United Scotsmen, who also aimed to end the relationship with England (Curtis 1994). Print was becoming the foundation of a new national culture, especially the flood of new populist political writing, often orally performed for those who could not read (Williams 1996). In the editorial stance of newspapers like the *Northern Star* and the *Press*, there was a deliberate attempt to create a cosmopolitan public sphere, with the boundaries extended to North America and Revolutionary France, where modern republicanism was being shaped. This new political press soon triggered a crackdown, as the colonial government struck back. Soldiers smashed the printing press of the *Northern Star* in Belfast in 1797, confiscating information on the movement's organisers and circle of sympathisers. New legislation enacted in London made it more difficult to obtain a licence to set up a paper after this.

When a distinctive Catholic press finally emerged in Ireland in the early 19th century, the agitation for Catholic Emancipation turned the courts into a kind of alternative parliament. Newspaper editors were increasingly prosecuted for sedition, and courts, immune from prosecution for libel, became platforms for public debates about justice, legislation and free speech, their records preserved and amplified in newspapers. Printing in Irish was still minimal, mostly confined to evangelical groups, until the Gaelic League initiated its major printing project in the 1890s. But periodicals in English proliferated, with up to 4,000 titles extant at several points in the 19th century. As the Great Famine loomed in the 1840s, the Young Irelanders, drawing their inspiration from revolutionary movements then sweeping Italy, Switzerland, France and Germany, called for complete independence from England, by force if necessary. Their newspaper *The Nation* had the largest circulation of any Irish newspaper of its time and claimed to be a truly national medium, though one driven by a cosmopolitan vision of a non-sectarian, bilingual country, in which native and settler would prosper (Curtis 1994). Ironically, the infrastructure of the imperial state to which *The Nation* was implacably opposed, was being used in a very deliberate way to create a unified, national informational territory and sustained the growing sense of a shared geographical space with a shared history.

Towards Independence

In the second half of the 19th century, as emigration to North America increased in the wake of the Great Famine, yet another geography of information was emerging, one that would later parallel, if not replace, the old core-periphery relationship with Britain. As early as the 1850s, the decade that saw the laying of the first trans-Atlantic telegraph cable, Ireland was becoming what one commentator called "the eastern shore of America" (Morash 2010, 84). The growth of electric communications, as the 19th century advanced, had the practical effect of diminishing space as a major factor in human affairs, of making geography irrelevant (Carey 1989). The more Ireland became part of the new information order, the more difficult it was to suppress the idea of nationality. Even news generated outside Ireland could be seen as a threat to the British imperial order. In 1868, for instance, the owners of a Dublin-based newspaper were charged with "seditious libel" for reporting Fenian meetings in the United States. The Irish diaspora, increasingly interwoven into the fabric of American culture, developed strong nationalist views in its enforced exile, providing Irish cultural nationalism with a dynamic that led eventually to the ultimate break with Britain in the War of Independence.

The relentless misery of the Great Famine, and the waves of emigration that followed, had a major impact on the Irish language, driving it into steep decline, and it was not until the full flowering of the Gaelic Revival at the end of the 19th century that material written in Irish began to be published with increasing frequency. With cultural nationalism now in the ascendant, the old culture of Gaelic civilisation ceased being peripheral, as it had been since the birth of print, and took a new direction, becoming the focus of an idealised Irishness, with traditional music as its purest form (O'Flynn 2009). The Gaelic League forged a close affinity between language and national identity as an essential value of the decolonisation project, elevating Irish language, music and games as potent emblems of a new Ireland. Its president, Douglas Hyde, in his famous essay *The Necessity for de-Anglicising Ireland,* argued for the need to be rid of the central Irish ambivalence of imitating England yet apparently hating it, resulting from the erosion of Irish over the course of the 19th century, an ambivalent attitude which left people "ceasing to be Irish without becoming English" (Browne 1985, 55). Echoes of the cultural politics of the Gaelic League can be felt in contemporary Ireland, as public opinion surveys regularly indicate that a large number of people place considerable value on the symbolic role of the language in national identity and support broadcasting in Irish (Corcoran 2004, 177-195).

The Free State

An independent Ireland came into being at the same time as the new medium of radio arrived and one of the first tasks of the Free State government, as soon as the Civil War ended (May 1923), was to develop a national radio service. In the Treaty which had established the Free State, the British negotiators, keenly aware of Ireland's position in the scheme of imperial defence, had insisted on a clause restricting the right to broadcast outside the national territory without prior British agreement. The US already had hundreds of radio stations, all competing in an unregulated market, and while the BBC model of licence fee funding of a single service was attractive, there was a pragmatic recognition that Ireland's smaller, poorer population would have a radio station only if it was funded—and tightly controlled—by the Post-Master General (a title borrowed from the British administration).

In the decision to establish the national radio service 2RN, the major policy dynamic was both to emulate the BBC and to rival it. The cultural power of British broadcasting spilling over Irish borders had to be forestalled by developing an Irish station. As the Postmaster General put it in 1924, Ireland risked surrendering Irish broadcasting to "British music hall dope and British propaganda", to which a Unionist critic retorted that "if we are to have wireless broadcasting established on an exclusively Irish-Ireland basis, the result will be *Danny Boy* four times a week, with variations by way of camouflage" (quoted in Horgan 2001, 15-16). In fact a lot of Reithian discourse on public service permeated the final report of the Dáil Committee on radio and John Reith himself actually sat on the board to appoint the first Station Director for 2RN.

Similar policy constraints were in evidence decades later, when Ireland had become a nation very much secluded from the outside world. The long debate throughout the 1950s about setting up a television service was spurred by the opening of BBC Northern Ireland in 1953. The fact that television sets south of the Border could receive British television signals from Belfast created a dilemma for a Dublin government that still officially claimed jurisdiction over the six counties of Northern Ireland, the nation's lost "fourth green field" (Savage 1996, 24). As with radio, BBC television was both admired for its Reithian philosophy and feared as a potential source of renewed colonial influence on Ireland.

The early development of censorship in the Free State was also a post-colonial development. Major British newspapers still had substantial circulation in Dublin, but the new government was quick to seize newspapers arriving off the ferry from England if it did not like what was being published in London about the Irish Free State. (Horgan 2001, 10). Moral as well as political censorship was in the air. A Catholic group, the Vigilance Association, was formed in 1911 to protect public morality from the incoming tide of newspapers, magazines and motion pictures, but had little success in lobbying the British administration. After the Civil War, their influence increased. Catholic activists saw the media primarily in patriotic-moral terms and railed against what they saw as the soul of the nation being steadily destroyed by smut coming in from England. Clerics in some parts of the country were busy confiscating and publicly burning British magazines. In 1923, legislation to censor films was passed. At the urging of Catholic bishops, a "Committee on Evil Literature" was set up to protect the population against "unhealthy" imported publications and its report laid the foundations of the Censorship of Publications Act (1929), a piece of draconian censorship that remained in place until the late 1960s. In its first decade alone, the Censorship of Publications Board banned 1200 books and 140 periodicals. This urge to censor—books, periodicals, films—assumed hegemonic proportions in Irish cultural life for the following half century and produced high levels of alienation from the state among a whole generation of Irish intellectuals and writers whose work was also often banned. The ground was well prepared for the political censorship in Irish broadcasting of the IRA and a range of other paramilitary groups that lasted through most of the Troubles (Corcoran and O'Brien 2005).

Towards Internationalism

The conservative, Catholic political culture that became entrenched in Ireland soon after Independence set out to resist the evils of "internationalism" by utilising the power of the state to implement a strong set of strategies: censorship, raising tariffs against the importation of English newspapers (with their agendas of crime, sex, contraception and anti-Irish prejudice) and fostering alternative Irish media: radio, film and Irish-language printing. In contrast with Britain, however, American soft power, especially in cinema, was received more benignly. Because of emigration flows across the North Atlantic over the previous century, the US had become culturally closer than Britain, the focus of many dreams and longings in the Irish imaginary, therefore not so vehemently denounced for the alien values of its popular culture. When television arrived in 1961, the economics of programming dictated that while the BBC showed relatively little American content, US networks supplied approximately half of everything broadcast on Irish television throughout the first decade. Heavy viewers in Ireland were in a sense far more Americanised than viewers in England or Northern Ireland.

This tentative opening to international culture took another stride in 1958, as a major change of economic direction took place which would later become part of the dominant narrative of the provenance of the Celtic Tiger, infused with the notion that the country's engagement with neoliberalism would be exceptional, that its embrace of globalisation would be cost-free. Under the leadership of Sean Lemass, economic policy was radically redrawn to emphasise international trade and inward investment (Horgan 1997). Major changes in the old core-periphery relationship with Britain were set in motion with the opening up of the economy to American investment and the setting in train of negotiations that would lead to Ireland joining the European Economic Community. It was clear that Ireland could no longer live within its own buttressed little media world, its insularity and prudery dominated by conservative Catholic forces. The change was foreshadowed as de Valera handed over power to Lemass. At the launch of Teilifís Éireann (later RTÉ) on New Year's Eve 1961, a gloomy de Valera confessed to the nation that "sometimes when I think of television and radio, and their immense power, I am somewhat afraid. Like atomic energy, it can be used for incalculable good, but it can also do irreparable harm ... it can lead through demoralisation to decadence and dissolution" (Savage 1996, xi). Sean Lemass, on the other hand, emphasised that:

> Irish people are citizens of the world as well as Ireland ... The reasonable needs of the Irish people ... would not be satisfied by programmes of local origin ... Events in all parts of the world and new ideas and developments everywhere ... can be of direct and immediate interest to our own people (Morash 2010, 171).

While London had been the metropolitan centre throughout four centuries of Irish print culture, coloniality and peripherality were being fiercely rejected in the 20th century. But it now appeared that new centres were emerging in the global mediascape, exerting from a distance a slow, gravitational pull on the Irish public sphere, as a new geography of knowledge, first glimpsed in the debate in the 1980s about deregulating radio and television, began to take hold.

Cultural Globalisation

Changes associated with globalisation reduced the lingering sense that, because of its colonial history and geography, Ireland had to remain insulated from the rest of the world. Irish culture was now becoming increasingly cosmopolitan and porous, no longer divided between two languages. As the expanding Irish economy in the 1990s was in the process of attracting immigrants in large numbers, the long debate on setting up a television service in Irish finally reached a resolution of sorts, with the opening up in 1998 of Teilifís na Gaeilge, later called TG4 (Corcoran 2004, 177-195). This debate had centred on a number of issues: whether broadcasting in Irish should be integrated into existing public service channels controlled by RTÉ, or given an independent existence, which might generate an alternative programming policy but risk ghettoising the language; whether a new channel should cater for a nationwide audience or address the more specific needs of the Irish-speaking Gaeltacht; whether the main objective was to initiate yet another measure to revive a dying language or to respect the minority rights of those using what EU terminology refers to as a "lesser used language".

Parts of the long debate drew on arguments first presented by the Gaelic League long before the television era, about connections between language-based cultural self-confidence and economic success. Declan Kiberd (1996) for example, argued that the cultural confusion, diminished sense of enterprise and stagnation due to a lost sense of self-belief, all of which characterised the generation living in the early decades after independence, despite their successful dislodging of a mighty imperial army, could be traced in part to the experience of losing Irish. This post-colonial argument contrasts sharply with antagonistic views about broadcasting in Irish, articulated by some of the newspapers owned by Independent News and Media (INM) throughout the 1990s, expressing what some critics called "a post-colonial shame more appropriate to the mid-1800s post-Famine trauma than to late 1990s confident multiculturalism based on economic prosperity" (Corcoran 2004, 189). The significance of TG4 is that it functions as a means of public debate and entertainment for those using Irish as their first or second language and has not become the "tediously worthy museum of folk culture ... the tabernacle of Irish nationality" that its critics feared (Morash 2010, 217).

The old centre-periphery tension between English and Irish media is finally loosening, as Irish-language culture now explores innovative forms of information and entertainment in the context of an increasingly globalised society. British media are, of course, still widely available in Ireland. In television, for instance, digital cable and satellite systems (terrestrial is due to launch in 2010) bring in a cornucopia of channels to two thirds of Irish homes from across the world, though audiences tend to be loyal to national broadcasters. Of the top twenty programmes in the

Nielsen ratings for 2009, nineteen were broadcast by RTÉ and seventeen of these were home-produced. Irish channels between them have close to a 60% share of peak time audiences, while the main British services together—BBC1, BBC2, UTV, Channel Four—enjoy a 16% share of peak time viewing (RTE 2009).[1] British newspapers fare considerably better in circulation figures, controlling 42% of the total circulation of Sunday titles and just under 50% of daily titles (NNI 2010). Concerned opposition to any signs of colonial legacy that might be inferred from these figures, however, has given way to considerable enthusiasm for cultural mixing in the media of the Celtic Tiger.

In 1998, *Foreign Policy* magazine initiated a series of surveys to measure the level of globalisation in different societies—defined as integration into the world political and economic system. Ireland reached first place in 2000 and maintained that position for several years, with high levels of imports, exports and inward capital investment flows, high telephone volumes with the rest of the world, and impressive levels of investment in information technologies by some of the behemoths of the ICT world: Intel, Microsoft, Google, eBay. The statistics of globalisation were impressive. Ireland was the largest recipient of foreign direct investment in the OECD in the decade from 1993 to 2003. The country's labour force expanded by 43% in the same period and complaints were common that there were not enough people coming in to fill the jobs. Rising prosperity brought about significant demographic change, as a whole new generation of immigrants—from China, Brazil, Nigeria, Central and Eastern Europe—became a large, visible part of Irish society, establishing new social networks and linking in to new transnational media networks. The census showed that the population increased by 7% from 1996 to 2002, and again by a further 8% in the four years to 2006 (Hegarty 2009).

The Celtic Tiger was well and truly on its way, realigning Ireland with new metropolitan centres of influence. This time, however, clear geographical lines of power, to mark out centre and periphery relations, were not so important, despite the popular political and journalistic trope of getting the country to choose "between Boston and Berlin". The drivers of the boom were EU transfers for investment in infrastructure, a liberalisation of capital movements in the form of massive foreign direct investment, especially from American-owned multinational corporations, and increased private sector local investment, heavily weighted towards property. Institutions such as the American Chamber of Commerce and the

---

[1] However, the UK soap operas *Coronation Street* and *Emmerdale* are both simulcast on TV3. *Coronation Street* currently attracts over 350,000 viewers.

international ratings agencies Moody and Standard & Poor, though hardly household names, assumed a new power over the Irish economy (Cooper 2010). Foreign investment was happening in the media sector too, with businesses from Canada and the UK (Canwest, Scottish Radio Holdings, the Johnston Group) buying Irish print and broadcasting media, while the Irish media conglomerate INM bought into media in the UK, South Africa, Australia, New Zealand and India.

Probably the most significant metropolitan force impacting on Ireland in this period was the growing hegemony of neoliberalism, underpinned externally by transnational institutions and capital flows, but also co-produced at the national level through the successful control of ideological assumptions in the public sphere by national political, business and media elites. This was expressed in what Phelan (2007) calls "euphemised" neoliberal discourse, which deliberately disavowed the antagonistic kinds of sharp distinctions associated with the founders of "transparent" neoliberalism, Friedrich Hayek and Milton Friedman, and disseminated in the 1970s by Margaret Thatcher and Ronald Reagan. An important aspect of the Celtic Tiger, as a collective image of rapid but benign transformation, was its reliance on notions of Irish exceptionality and the dream of a people blessed by the collective disposition to harness cost-free globalisation (Titley 2009, 158-9). The confident claim of the Tiger years that "we are cosmopolitan now" suggested that all signs of colonialism were well and truly behind us. It became a soothing sign of both progress and control of our own destiny, securing for the Irish people the ambivalences of globalisation, until the crisis of late 2008, when the dream turned to nightmare and all sense of control over Irish destiny seemed lost.

Works Cited

Anderson, B. 1983. *Imagined Communities: Reflections on the Origins and Spread of Nationalism.* London: Verso.

Ashcroft, B., G. Griffiths and H. Tiffin, eds. 1995. *The Post-Colonial Studies Reader.* London: Routledge.

Braudel, F. 1981. *Civilisation and Capitalism 15th-18th Century: Volume 1.* New York: Harper and Row.

Browne, T. 1985. *Ireland: A Social and Cultural History.* London: Fontana.

Carey, J. 1989. *Communication as Culture: Essays on Media and Society.* Boston, Unwin Hyman.

Cooper, M. 2009. *Who Really Runs Ireland: the Story of the Elite who led Ireland from Bust to Boom and Back Again.* London: Penguin.

Corcoran, F. 2004. *RTE and the Globalisation of Irish Television*. Bristol: Intellect Books.

Corcoran, M. and M. O'Brien, eds. 2005. *Political Censorship and the Democratic State: the Irish Broadcasting Ban*. Dublin: Four Courts Press.

Curtis, L. 1994. *The Cause of Ireland: from the United Irishmen to Partition*. Belfast: Beyond the Pale Publication.

Gibbons, L. 1996. *Transformations in Irish Culture*. Cork: Cork University Press/ Field Day.

Hegarty, S. 2009. *The Irish and Other Foreigners*. Dublin: Gill and Macmillan.

Horgan, J. 1997. *Sean Lemass: the Enigmatic Patriot*. Dublin: Gill and Macmillan.

—. 2001. *Irish Media: a Critical History*. London: Routledge.

Kiberd, D. 1996. *Inventing Ireland: the Literature of the Modern Nation*. London: Vintage.

Morash, C. 2010. *A History of the Media in Ireland*. Cambridge: Cambridge University Press.

National Newspapers of Ireland (NNI). 2009. Circulation Figures. Available from www.nni.ie. Accessed 23 April 2010.

O'Flynn, J. 2009. *The Irishness of Irish Music*. Dublin: Ashgate.

Phelan, S. 2007. The Discourses of Neoliberal Hegemony. *Critical Discourse Studies*, 4 (1): 29-48.

RTE. 2009. Annual Report. Available from www.rte.ie. Accessed 23 April 2010.

Savage, R. 1996. *Irish Television: Political and Social Origins*. Cork: Cork University Press.

Titley, G. 2009. Celtic, Christian and Cosmopolitan: Migrants and the Mediation of Exceptional Globalisation. In *Transforming Ireland: Challenges, Critiques, Resources*, edited by D. Ging, M. Cronin and P. Kirby. 157-173. Manchester: Manchester University Press.

Williams, K. 1996. *Tree of Liberty: Radicalism, Catholicism and the Construction of Irish Identity*. Cork: Cork University Press.

Winston, B. 1998. *Media Technology and Society: A History from the Telegraph to the Internet*. London: Routledge.

THOSE POST-DEVOLUTION, FALLING REVENUES BLUES: A POLITICAL ECONOMY OF NORTHERN IRELAND'S NEWS MEDIA

GREG MCLAUGHLIN

In *The Propaganda of Peace*, McLaughlin and Baker (2010) identify two media narratives for explaining Northern Ireland's transition from war to peace. The first, explicit narrative tells the story of conflict resolution between two warring sectarian tribes, providing continuity of the dominant media frame used for explaining the conflict since 1968. The second, implicit narrative is based on a much deeper, ideological framework, telling the story of Northern Ireland's departure from barbarism to what Tony Blair described as "the civilised world"; and from decades of being a heavily subsidised, economic basket case to a new era of private, inward investment, property development and entrepreneurialism. The problem now, just as devolved government is beginning to function somewhere near to "normal", is that this new dawn of civilisation and venture capitalism has suddenly darkened. The financial crash of 2008 and the ensuing economic downturn have hit Northern Ireland hard and while the local news media have reported the fall-out in grisly detail they too have suffered.

Yet ominous signs were apparent for some time before this. A chronic decline in readerships and audiences in the last decade has brought with it a slump in advertising revenues and operating profits, closures, sell-offs and inevitable job losses, while the commercial broadcasting sector has seen a reduction in local news and current affairs. An optimistic, industry perspective might see these trends as inevitable and desirable in a regional media sector too saturated for the relatively small population of just over 1.5 million. It will point to improvements in newspaper content, including the provision of international news from a local perspective; a thriving and expanding public service broadcast sector; competition-driven innovation in print technology and page design; and local as well as inward investment in new media businesses. A more critical, academic position might accept all this up to a point but express concerns for the future of journalism in a region that is now experiencing, for the first time in its history, something approaching "normal politics" and the potential for a more representative public sphere (McLaughlin 2007).

It is from a political economic perspective, then, that this chapter surveys the state of print, broadcast and online journalism in Northern Ireland as we move into the second decade of the new century. The current trends and outlooks described below are broadly in line with current research into the regional and local media in England, Scotland and Wales (see Franklin 2007; McNair 2007; Thomas 2007; Dekavalla et al 2010). Except where otherwise stated, all newspaper circulation figures are sourced from the Audit Bureau of Circulations.

Print journalism

Newspaper readers in Northern Ireland can choose from a wide and diverse range of daily newspapers published locally, and in Britain and the Republic of Ireland. The region has three daily newspapers (Monday–Saturday), all published in Belfast: the *Irish News*, the *News Letter* and the *Belfast Telegraph*. There have been others but they failed due to lack of demand and/or advertising. The *Daily Ireland* launched in 2005 but closed eighteen months later in 2006 with sales of under 10,000 copies per day, while the daily Irish language newspaper *Lá Nua* ("New Day") closed at the end of 2008 after 24 years in publication. The briefest experiment of all must be the *Daily View*, which Johnston Press launched on 4 April 2005. It made a virtue of its non-political editorial content, with an agenda devoted to "bread and butter issues"—health, education and employment among others—and to human-interest and consumer stories that might appeal to readers alienated by sectarian politics and a crisis-ridden peace process (McDonald 2005). However, despite its avowal to cover "real issues of the 21st Century, not the 17th Century", the *Daily View* struggled to compete for 21st Century readers and advertising revenues; it closed just a month later, on 6 May (McLaughlin 2007, 87).

The future of the three surviving dailies, all of them integral to the history and politics of Northern Ireland, is less than certain. Figure 1, below, charts their circulations, in six-month periods, from January 2006 to December 2009, and compares them with those for the *The Sun* and the *Daily Mirror,* now the biggest selling daily newspapers in the region and the only British titles that publish Northern Ireland editions. It should be noted here that the circulations for these two titles are publishers' estimates and that figures for July-December 2009 were, at time of writing, unavailable.

Figure 1. Daily newspaper circulations in Northern Ireland, 2006-2009

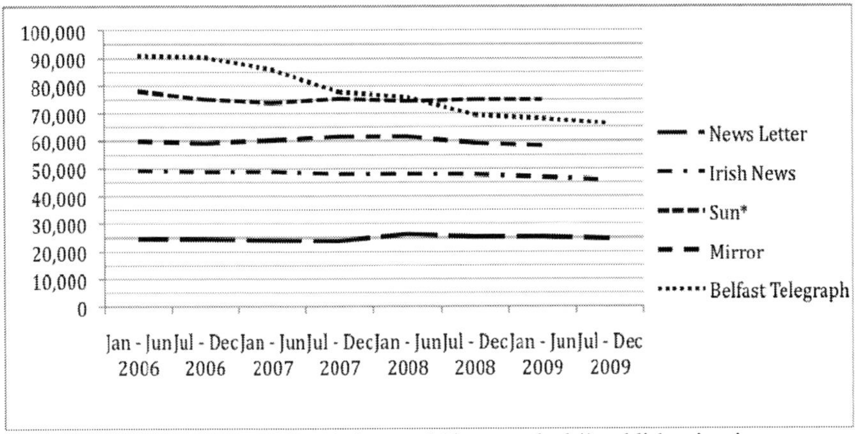

Sources: Audit Bureau of Circulations and (those marked *) publishers' estimates.

While the nationalist *Irish News* has maintained fairly steady daily circulation, its unionist rivals, the *News Letter* and, most dramatically, the *Belfast Telegraph*, have experienced decline. Looking at the latest figures in abstract, it would be easy to conclude that all three dailies are losing out badly to *The Sun* and the *Mirror,* which have circulations of 74,935 and 58,202 respectively. Although in the past four years these papers too have been losing readers, their eclipse of the Belfast daily titles is significant. As with other regions of the UK and the Republic of Ireland, it suggests a critical shift in newspaper readership in Northern Ireland away from the specific content of regional titles to the more general content offered by the major metropolitan titles based in London. The opposite applies to broadcasting, where a significant majority of viewers and listeners still prefer local services. The following analysis of what has happened in the local print and broadcast media in the last decade may provide some insights into these contradictory patterns of consumption.

The *Irish News* is a morning newspaper with a daily circulation of more than 45,667 copies at the end of 2009, down 7.3% from January-June 2006. Privately owned by the Fitzpatrick family, its editorial line is broadly supportive of the policies of the moderate, nationalist Social Democratic and Labour Party (SDLP). In 2005, the paper changed from Berliner to compact tabloid format and invested in advanced printing technology to reproduce brighter, cleaner page design with full colour capacity. Although it continues to deliver strong political news content, the *Irish News*, much like many British "quality" newspapers, employs populist strategies to broaden its appeal to the affluent youth market, including a human interest oriented page three, daily entertainment and lifestyle supplements, extensive sports coverage and popular holiday offers.

The *News Letter*, also a morning paper, has experienced a dramatic collapse in political influence and circulation in the past sixty years, falling from more than 100,000 copies, post-Second World War, to just 24,555 by the end of 2009, down 2% from January-June 2006. The paper has changed ownership three times since 1996 and is now owned by the Scottish media group Johnston Press. The title's daily freesheet version, the *Belfast News*, has fared much better with a circulation of 49,418 in the period Jul-Dec 2009, but is still down 2.7% from the period January-June 2006. As well as claiming to be "the world's oldest continuously published English publication" (est. 1737), the *News Letter* was and still is the voice of official Unionism in Northern Ireland so its troubles have been of obvious political significance. When it was sold for the second time in December 2003 by Trinity Mirror to the venture capital firm 3i, BBC Radio Ulster's *Talkback* programme conducted a vox pop at the Connswater Shopping Centre on the unionist Shankill Road in Belfast. The general response was revealing. Most people interviewed professed no real concern about the newspaper or its sale to new owners. In fact they admitted that they had stopped reading it because it did not provide them with the kind of sporting and entertainment news on offer in *The Sun* and the *Mirror*, both of which avoid editorial commentary on politics in Northern Ireland.

However, of the three dailies, it is the *Belfast Telegraph* that gives most cause for concern. The paper is owned by the Dublin-based, Independent News & Media (INM), which bought it and its associated titles for £300 million from Trinity Mirror in 2000. While it is moderately Protestant, unionist in editorial policy, it also appeals to a Catholic, nationalist readership by virtue of its campaigns on issues such as education, health and public accountability, and its weighty advertising and consumer content. Once a multi-edition, evening broadsheet, it underwent a major revamp in 2005, launching an additional, compact tabloid morning edition in a bid to compete head-to-head with the *News Letter* and *Irish News*. Its contract printing plant in Belfast gives it full colour capacity and a look as sharp and modern as any other city newspaper in the UK; by 2009, all editions were published in compact tabloid format.[1] If this revamp was designed to halt falling sales, the strategy appears to have failed. In the period January-June 2006 its daily bulk circulation averaged 94,000 copies, falling to 66,242 by the end of 2009, a 27% decline. The Belfast Telegraph titles, which include the *Sunday Life*, returned operating profits of just £3 million in 2009, a drop of 86% from £21 million in 2000 and a figure that excludes revenues of £7 million from its contract printing operation (McCaughren 2010). Inevitably, advertising revenues have also fallen by 30%, a global figure that includes a 44% decline in public recruitment advertising, a lifeline for a newspaper serving a region still so highly dependent on the public sector (Sweney 2010). With INM recording losses of £144 million in 2008, the NUJ accused the company of leeching on the *Belfast Telegraph*'s profits to subsidise its loss leader titles, the UK based *Independent* and *Independent on Sunday*, a claim that INM has always denied (Plunkett 2008).

Newspaper readers in the region also have access to a wide selection of Sunday papers but, as Fig. 2 shows below, the local market is in steady decline. There are three locally produced titles—the *Belfast Telegraph*'s Sunday counterpart, the *Sunday Life* (60,057), the Ulster edition of the Dublin-based *Sunday World* (62,423), owned by a subsidiary of INM, and the Derry-based *Sunday Journal* (2,616), part of the Derry Journal newspaper group, owned by Johnston Press. The figure for the *Sunday Life* represents a 22.8% decline in sales since January-June 2006 and mirrors the failing fortunes of the *Belfast Telegraph*. As with the dailies, the Northern Ireland Sundays compete with regional editions of leading British titles such as the *News of the World*, *The Observer*, *The Sunday Times* and the *Sunday Mirror*. Historically the biggest selling title in the region, the *News of the World* has sales of 75,998 copies although that represents a fall of 14% from January-June 2006. The *Sunday Mirror* records a modest 37,999—a slight decline of 0.8% from January-June 2006—while the Northern Ireland edition of *The Sunday Times* (not included in this sample period) sells an estimated 35,000 copies.[2] Northern Ireland editions of the Dublin based *Sunday Tribune* and the *Sunday*

---

[1] In 2007, INM opened another, more advanced plant in Newry, County Down, and won for both plants a series of lucrative printing contracts from major newspaper groups in the UK (including the *Daily Telegraph* and the *Sunday Telegraph*, *The Independent* and *Sunday Independent*, the *Daily Mirror* and the *Daily Record*) and in Ireland (including the *Irish Star*, the *Sunday World* and the *Sunday Tribune*).

[2] Sales of the *Sunday Times* are not included in the principal survey period, 2006-09, because of unavailability of data.

World also sell well, the *Tribune* with its major breaking political news and the *Sunday World* with its focus on local crime and sex scandals.

Fig. 2. Sunday newspaper circulations in Northern Ireland, 2006-09

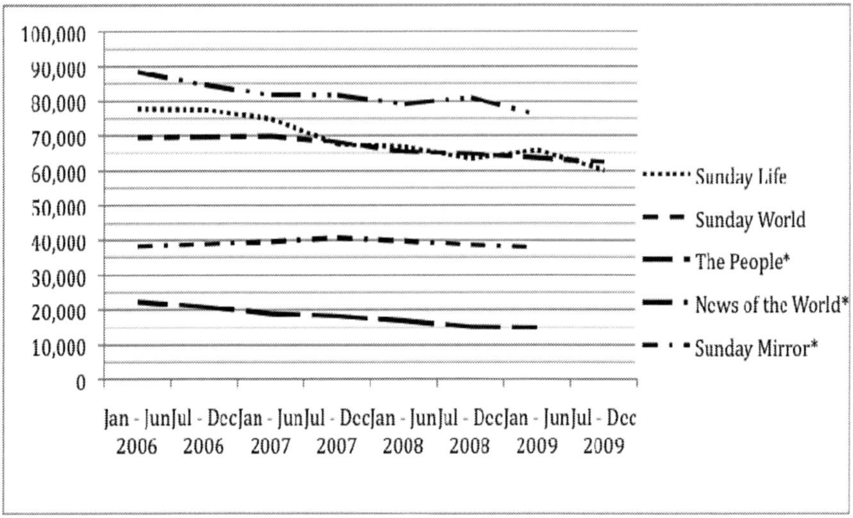

Sources: Audit Bureau of Circulations and (those marked *) publishers' estimates.

In addition to its dailies, Northern Ireland has a saturated weekly/bi-weekly newspaper market of over 70 publications.[3] This is in part a legacy of the sectarian, political history of the region, with many large towns having both a unionist and nationalist weekly newspaper; but there has been the trend in recent times for some of these to publish localised editions for neighbouring towns. For example, the *Derry Journal* (Johnston Press) publishes bi-weekly editions for Derry city and for its hinterland of county Donegal in the Republic of Ireland; while the *Coleraine Chronicle* (Northern Ireland's Alpha Newspaper Group) publishes local editions for neighbouring Limavady, Ballymoney and Ballycastle.

Very few of these weeklies serve a mixed, nationalist and unionist readership or compete directly with each other for readers, surviving on restricted sales and advertising markets. New entries are rare and they find it hard to challenge the local monopoly. In Derry city, the launch of the

---

[3] For a comprehensive index, see the Northern Ireland section of British Newspapers Online: www.britishpapers.co.uk/category/n-ireland.

Derry News in 2001 challenged the position of the *Derry Journal*, one of Ireland's oldest newspapers. It sparked a bitter newspaper war, with the *Journal* resorting to quite ruthless tactics to quash its upstart competitor, although the fact that sales of the *Derry News* fell well short of the *Journal* might suggest a degree of arrogance on the part of the larger newspaper and a determination to protect its long-standing monopoly of the local market. Indeed, its editor was forced to defend the company's position against the criticisms and concerns of local commentators who feared for the quality and integrity of local journalism in the city (McLaughlin 2006).

It is uncertain how much longer the weekly newspaper market can sustain this level of saturation but the arrival of Johnston Press in 2005 offers an ominous clue as to how things might work out. Its strategy right across its newspaper portfolio in the UK and Ireland appears to be rationalisation and cost reduction. In some cases, this has led to closure of titles or industrial action such as at the *Derry Journal* in 2009.

As well as newspapers, a small number of monthly magazines are published in Northern Ireland but only *Fortnight* and *Ulster Business* qualify as current affairs journalism.

Explaining the decline

The decline of Northern Ireland's unionist dailies, the *News Letter* and, most dramatically, the *Belfast Telegraph*, is symptomatic of general market trends in Britain and Ireland over the past decade. The print news media are struggling to survive in the digital age, regardless of the relative success of their online ventures. Readers are turning increasingly to the diverse range of sources on television or online for their news, entertainment and classified ads (once a unique selling point for the *Belfast Telegraph*). But there is also a political dimension to this problem in that it coincides with the collapse of unionist hegemony, unassailable up until the 1990s and the peace process. Since then, the Ulster Unionist Party's affluent, liberal middle class voters have been abstaining in increasing numbers, while its more conservative lower-middle class base has shifted allegiance to the Democratic Unionist Party (DUP). More recently, both parties suffered setbacks at the 2010 Westminster election; the UUP failed to return a single MP and the DUP's leader, Peter Robinson, lost his once safe seat in the wake of serious allegations about his financial dealings. The local media drew their own conclusions: the results represented nothing less than the "decapitation" of Ulster unionism (BBC NI, *Hearts and Minds*, 13 May 2010). While there is no direct evidence to suggest cause and effect here, political developments like these can only have eroded the editorial and institutional authority of the unionist dailies.[4]

Although there has been a similar realignment of politics on the nationalist side, with Sinn Féin overtaking the once dominant Social Democratic and Labour Party (SDLP), the *Irish News* appears to have adapted much better than its unionist counterparts. When it endorsed the 1998 Good Friday Agreement and urged readers to vote "Yes" in the referendum, it did so with regard to the strong nationalist-republican consensus in favour of the Agreement.

Broadcast journalism

As with other regions of the UK, Northern Ireland is served by its own local broadcast media, with television the preferred source of local news for 47% of the population compared to 28% for newspapers, a statistic slightly lower than the UK average (Ofcom 2008).

With an annual budget of £60 million, BBC Northern Ireland (BBC NI) provides an extensive news and current affairs service on television and radio (Radio Ulster and, in Derry, Radio Foyle). As well as its daily peak time news programme, *News Line*, the BBC broadcasts a daily public access programme, *Talkback*, on Radio Ulster; and, on television, weekly programmes such as *Hearts and Minds*, *Live at Stormont*, *The Politics Show*, and the investigative journalism slot, *Spotlight*. It was *Spotlight* that revealed the personal and financial scandal surrounding Peter Robinson, Northern Ireland's First Minister and DUP leader, and his wife and MP, Iris Robinson, in early January 2010. The programme went out first on BBC NI but was also networked on BBC1 as a special edition of the current-affairs programme *Panorama* ("The MP and the Whistleblower", 11 January 2010).

In the commercial sector, Ulster Television (UTV), an independent company and part of the ITV network, mirrors the BBC's local news provision but it has also established a large audience in the Republic of Ireland by virtue of its majority content of light entertainment programming. It commands a 8% lead over BBC NI in average audience share for peak-time, early evening TV news programmes (Ofcom 2009), but it has only one current affairs programme, *Insight*, and falls far behind the BBC in terms of in-house production of original programming. Apart

---

[4] The newspapers' unqualified endorsement of the Good Friday Agreement in 1998 seemed to confound significant opposition to the Agreement among nearly half of unionist voters (McLaughlin and Baker 2010, 19-34).

from these two major players, the community-based Northern Visions Television (NvTv) serves the Belfast area and is part-funded by the Northern Ireland Film and Television Commission (NIFTC). The commercial Channel 9 in Derry ceased transmission in 2007 after just 11 years in operation but there are plans to relaunch and rebrand it as C9TV.

Seventy-one percent of television viewers in Northern Ireland can receive up to four Republic of Ireland based television channels, terrestrially or by cable/satellite: RTÉ1, RTÉ2, TV3 and the Irish-language station TG4. An Ofcom survey on media consumption in Northern Ireland reported that "almost a third" of respondents watched RTÉ1 and RTÉ2, the most popular stations, every day, while "another 40%" claimed to watch either channel "at least once a week" (Ofcom 2009). The reception of RTÉ services, then, is obviously important to a significant minority of the viewers and listeners in Northern Ireland, most of whom would consider themselves Irish rather than British citizens. However, unlike the rest of the UK, the impending digital switchover (2012) presents them with political and cultural concerns, not just technical or consumer challenges, because the transition to digital in the Republic of Ireland somewhat lags behind the UK. It threatens their commitment to TV news, current affairs and entertainment from Dublin—as important to them, if not more so, as programming in these genres from London. Thanks in part to the intergovernmental structures set up under Strands 2 and 3 of the Good Friday Agreement, the relevant broadcasters and policy makers have taken note of the problem. In a submission to Ofcom, in 2008, RTÉ committed itself to work to ensure continuation of its service in Northern Ireland after the UK switchover (Ofcom 2008a); and, in 2010, the Irish and British governments agreed a memorandum of understanding to this effect.[5]

The commercial radio sector in the region is similar in profile and content to the rest of the UK with an emphasis on music and light entertainment rather than journalism. There are ten stations in existence, six of which are owned by the Northern Media Group, essentially a franchise network operation with local variations. The remaining four stations—Cool FM, Downtown, Citybeat and U105—operate in Belfast.[6]

---

[5] Memorandum of Understanding (MOU) Between Ireland and UK on Digital Switchover and the Provision of DTT Services in Northern Ireland and Ireland, 1 February 2010. http://www.digitaltelevision.ie/National+DTT/Digital+Switchover.htm. Accessed 2010.

[6] Cool FM is the clear market leader with 340,000 listeners per week, followed by Downtown (226,000), U105 (143,000) and Citybeat (112,000). Source: Rajar,

U105 broadcasts to the whole of Northern Ireland in analogue and on all digital platforms. It is owned by UTV Media, which has expanded its media interests beyond Northern Ireland. It owns 17.8% of commercial radio licences in the Republic of Ireland, making it the largest single player in the Irish market and also has one of the biggest commercial radio portfolios in the UK, including 14 commercial radio stations and stakes in five of the UK's 14 digital radio bundles. In June 2005, the company bought The Wireless Group (TWG) and rebranded it UTV Radio. Although UTV reported a fall in profits in 2009, down 8% from the previous year (BBC News online, 23 March 2010), its commercial radio businesses still generate two-thirds of its total profits (McNally 2009).

The long term sustainability of the commercial radio sector in the UK looks uncertain but there is considerable potential for the community sector to survive and compete in the market yet still provide truly local content for local communities (Watkyn 2009, 50). There are fourteen community stations in Northern Ireland, including Radió Fáilte which broadcasts in the Irish language on FM to the West Belfast area and also online. Another six stations provide an Ulster Scots service but these operate on Restricted Service licenses (Ofcom 2008b). It is a promising picture but if the sector is to develop as a real, long-term alternative, it needs the kind of "supportive and imaginative regulatory environment" not currently on offer (Watkyn 2009, 50).

Online News and Journalism

While internet and broadband take-up in Northern Ireland is 61%, slightly lower than the UK average of 65% (Ofcom 2009), there is very little in the way of professional online journalism in Northern Ireland apart from the websites of the major newspapers and broadcasters. The weblog *Slugger O'Toole*, featuring lively comment and discussion on Northern Ireland politics, cannot be described as journalism *per se* but it serves as a healthy alternative to mainstream political journalism (cf. Fealty 2009). Founded by journalist Mick Fealty in 2003, it has since grown in size and political impact to a point where it is now monitored by 96% of Northern Ireland Assembly members and enjoys the support of Channel Four's iP Fund (Andrews 2009).

With an annual budget of £2m, BBC NI online reflects the success of the corporation's principal site and, of course, presents a daunting challenge

October 2009-March 2010. For a detailed market analysis of the sector, see Ofcom, 2009; for a political-economic analysis, see Watkyn (2009).

to the regional print media and their online ambitions. Among the newspapers, all three have sites that offer digital audio and video news content but it is still difficult to assess how successful these are relative to their print versions. The *News Letter* and *Belfast Telegraph* both offer free sites and, for all its troubles, the latter won the 2010 Newspaper Award (UK) for best online, digital service. It seems, though, that the *Irish News* alone sees its e-version as a serious business proposition and an extra revenue stream. In 2009, it revamped its previously free service and currently offers a sliding subscription service, ranging from £5 per week to £150 per year. To date, the new venture has attracted only 1215 subscriptions but the *Irish News* also sells its unique paywall technology to regional newspapers in Britain and Ireland. This is part of a package that includes server maintenance and video streaming for fees starting from £435 (Oliver 2010; Greenslade 2010).

Concluding Remarks

As in England, Scotland and Wales, the news media in Northern Ireland face a future of declining circulations, fragmented readerships and audiences, concentration of ownership and control, increasing competition, closures and industrial action as economic policy at the centre continues to bite. As indicated in the introduction to this chapter, it is possible to take a purely market or industry perspective and call these trends evolutionary; in other words, as part of a painful but necessary adaptation to harsh economic realities and to the age of digital with its much hyped promise of truly 21st century journalism—whatever that might be. This seems very reasonable if one wishes to see journalism in purely business terms. However, such a perspective neglects consideration of the professional and political implications of market upheaval, of what journalism is supposed to be and what it is for in a liberal democracy.

Given the worrying trends in the regional print media, it seems that local journalism and its traditional democratic roles will be safest in the public service broadcast sector. BBC NI offers forms and spaces that have otherwise disappeared from the regional media scene. Its mix on TV and radio of current affairs, investigative journalism and public debate would simply not survive in the purely market-driven broadcast model James Murdoch (2010) has in mind. Yet the BBC also has its regional media critics, including former *Belfast Telegraph* editor Ed Curran. Appearing in 2009 before the UK House of Commons Select Committee for Media, Culture and Sport, he described the corporation as "a bogeyman" whose expansion in the regions since the 1960s has been "detrimental to the overall regional media". The time had come for it to be restricted, particularly its regional online news service, otherwise it would lead to newspaper jobs losses and closures. "In a region like Northern Ireland" he said, "the BBC employs more journalists than all three daily newspapers in Belfast put together. It's almost impossible to compete against that".[7]

This sounds perfectly understandable coming from the former editor of a newspaper in trouble and it raises questions about regional media diversity and pluralism that deserve serious debate. But it is worth noting that the *Belfast Telegraph*, along with the *News Letter* and the *Irish News*, shed no tears for the future of regional journalism when the republican newspaper, the *Daily Ireland*, ceased publication in 2006 after only 18 months in publication. In fact, they voiced loud protest against the paper when it sought funding from non-departmental public body InvestNI after devolved government denied it the right to tender for public advertising (Tryhorn 2006). The administration did so, not as an anti-republican conspiracy but on a purely value-for-money basis; with a daily circulation of just under 10,000 copies, the *Daily Ireland* could not compete with the advertising rates of its local, daily rivals. Yet in 2005 the Office of First Minister and Deputy First Minister (OFMDFM) warned *all* the local dailies that none of their rates were best value compared to those of the *Daily Mirror* and that it would expect them to be more competitive in future (McLaughlin 2006, 64). With plummeting circulation and advertising revenues, the *Belfast Telegraph* and *News Letter* may be the next to be denied the lifeblood of government advertising, which accounts for an average annual budget of nearly £9 million but which is currently under review.[8]

As long as regional editors and journalists fatalistically buy into the rhetoric of the free market, they will miss the bigger picture here. What Rex Cathcart once described as that "contrary region" has emerged out of forty years of conflict to build a functioning civic society. An independent and democratically engaged journalism culture is indispensible to that task and while it has to survive in a capitalist market, there are viable alternatives—mixed models like those in Sweden and Germany (Curran 2010)—which offer subsidy and protection from the brute logic of profit and loss.

---

[7] Future for regional and local media. Commons Select Committee for Culture, Media and Sport: Examination of Witnesses, 7 July (Q120).
http://www.publications.parliament.uk/pa/cm200910/cmselect/cmcumeds/43/0907 0704.htm. Accessed May 2010.
[8] Deputy First Minister NI; NI Assembly Debates, 8 February 2010.
http://www. theyworkforyou.com/ni/?id=2010-02-08.7.14. Accessed May 2010.

Acknowledgements

Thanks to Alice Watkyn for her invaluable research and editorial assistance for this chapter; and to my colleagues, Stephen Baker and Colm Murphy, for their helpful comments and suggestions. The research was funded by the Centre for Media Research (CMR) at the University of Ulster, Coleraine.

Works Cited

Andrews, R. 2009. C4 invests in political blogger Slugger O'Toole. *Paidcontent: UK*, 24 November 2009. http://paidcontent.co.uk/article/419-c4-invests-in-political-blogger-slugger-otoole-draft/. Accessed April 2010.

Curran, J. 2010. Future of journalism. First published on 6 April 2010 at Taylor and Francis' early online publication system, iFirst. Forthcoming in *Journalism Studies*, 11: (4).

Dekavalla, M., B. McNair, R. Boyle and G. Meikle. 2009. Mapping Futures for News. Unpublished report, Institute of Advanced Studies, University of Strathclyde, 2010.

Fealty, M. 2009. "Slugger O'Toole": The new media as track two diplomacy. In *Public Diplomacy, Cultural Interventions and the Peace Process in Northern Ireland*, edited by J. Popiolkowski and N. Cull. 89-98. Los Angeles, CA: Figuera Press.

Franklin, B. 2006. Attacking the devil? Local journalists and local newspapers in the UK. In *Local Journalism and Local Media: Making the local news*, edited by B. Franklin. 3-15. London: Routledge.

Greenslade, R. 2010. Harsh lessons to learn from the Irish News paywall. Greenslade Blog, Guardian.co.uk, 28 May 2010. http://www.guardian.co.uk/media/greenslade/2010/may/28/paywalls-local-newspapers. Accessed June 2010.

McCaughren, S. 2010. Belfast Telegraph titles made just €3m in operating profits. The Sunday Business Post online, 28 March 2010. http://archives.tcm.ie/businesspost/2010/03/28/story48189.asp. Accessed May 2010.

McDonald, H. 2005. Belfast readers offered a Troubles-free experience, *The Observer*, 10 April 2005.

McLaughlin, G. 2006. Profits, Politics and Paramilitaries: The Local Media in Northern Ireland. In *Local Media, Local Journalism*, edited by B. Franklin. 60-69. London: Routledge.

McLaughlin, G. and S. Baker. 2010. *The Propaganda of Peace: The role of media and culture in the Northern Ireland peace process*. Bristol: Intellect Books.

McNair, B. 2006. News from a small country: the media in Scotland. In *Local Journalism and Local Media: Making the local news*, edited by B. Franklin, 37-48. London: Routledge.

McNally, P. 2009. UTV Media now makes two thirds of profits from radio. *PressGazette*, 12 March 2009.
http://www.pressgazette.co.uk/story.asp?sectioncode=1&storycode=43318. Accessed May 2010.

Murdoch, J. 2009. The Absence of Trust. McTaggart Lecture, Edinburgh International Television Festival, 28 August 2009.

Ofcom. 2008a. RTÉ Submission to Ofcom's Second Public Service Broadcasting Review, Phase Two: Preparing for the digital future, 4 December 2008.
http://www.ofcom.org.uk/consult/condocs/psb2_phase2/responses/rte.pdf. Accessed May 2010.

—. 2008b. Communications Markets 2008: Nations and Regions: Northern Ireland.
http://www.ofcom.org.uk/research/cm/cmrnr08/nireland/nireland.pdf. Accessed May 2010.

—. 2009. Local and regional media in the UK: nations and regions case studies: Annex 2, September 2009.
http://www.ofcom.org.uk/research/tv/reports/lrmuk/lrmannex2.pdf. Accessed May 2010.

Oliver, L. 2010. Irish News builds on paywall revenue by selling the design. Journalism.co.uk, 26 May 2010.
http://www.journalism.co.uk/2/articles/538852.php. Accessed June 2010.

Plunkett, J. 2008. NUJ attacks O'Reilly's regime. Guardian.co.uk, 8 May 2008.
http://www.guardian.co.uk/media/2008/may/08/independentnewsmedia.pressandpublishing. Accessed May 2010.

Sweney, M. 2010. Independent: Lebedev deal 'expected very shortly' as losses continue', Guardian.co.uk, 24 March 2010.
http://www.guardian.co.uk/media/2010/mar/24/independent-news-media-alexander-lebedev. Accessed April 2010.

Thomas, J. 2006. The regional and local media in Wales. In *Local Journalism and Local Media: Making the local news*, edited by B. Franklin. 49-59. London: Routledge.

Tryhorn, C. 2006. Daily Ireland to close. MediaGuardian, 7 September 2006/
http://www.guardian.co.uk/media/2006/sep/07/pressandpublishing2. Accessed May 2010.
Watkyn, A. 2009. Commercial local radio is dead. Long live… what? A political economic analysis of commercial local radio in the UK. MRes Dissertation. University of Ulster.

WHAT'S NEWS IN WALES?
WELSH-LANGUAGE JOURNALISM TODAY AND IN HISTORICAL CONTEXT

GLYN MON HUGHES

The Language Struggle

In the 1960s, swinging London was the capital of a new world as the dour atmosphere following World War II was fast being replaced by a fresh optimism, both economic and political. Things, however, were very different in *Y Fro Gymraeg*, those remaining parts of Wales where the Welsh language, and a whole way of life, were under threat. Census after census demonstrated that the decline in the use of Welsh in everyday life seemed unstoppable. At the beginning of the 19th century 80% of the Welsh population spoke the language. By the end of the century that had dropped to 50%. The 1911 census recorded around one million Welsh speakers but, by 1961, the percentage had shrunk to just 26%, declining by 1991 to 18.7% of the population—under half a million speakers.

That linguistic decline was punctuated by comments from politicians and academics who prophesied the death of a nation. Most famous and, arguably, most influential was a defiant message in Saunders Lewis's radio lecture of February 1962. In *Tynged yr Iaith*—"The Fate of the Welsh Language"—Lewis, a former president of Plaid Cymru, the Welsh nationalist party, said "restoring the Welsh language in Wales is nothing less than a revolution. It is only through revolutionary means that we can succeed" (Cymdeithas yr Iaith Gymraeg).

That was the call to arms for Welsh speakers and led to the formation of the radical and campaigning Welsh Language Society which, in turn, coincided with the outbreak of Wales-wide civil disobedience where hitherto law-abiding people began, amongst other things, refusing to fill in official forms unless they were in Welsh and embarking on a campaign of withholding TV licence payments until a Welsh-language channel was established.

Until then, Welsh risked becoming little more than a museum-piece "ghetto" language, the tongue of the dour non-conformity of Welsh chapels and somewhat introspective "Welsh societies", where people could chat over tea and *bara brith* (Welsh fruit loaf). Primary schools conducted lessons through the medium of Welsh but secondary education was mainly, even exclusively, carried out in English and the use of Welsh in further and higher education was sporadic. Save for chapels and cultural societies, Welsh was comparatively little used elsewhere. It was hardly the language of court or council where its use was scant, and, although broadcasters had seen Wales redefined by the BBC as a "national region" in 1937, Welsh programmes were scattered randomly round schedules, often filling "graveyard" slots when few, if any, people consumed the output. Indeed, much of the output of the Welsh Home Service, precursor of Radio 4 Wales, which, in turn, gave birth to the distinct Radio Wales and Radio Cymru services of the BBC, as well as TV programmes, was restricted to subjects deemed by executives in English boardrooms to be of interest to Welsh speakers. These included a fairly limited news service, although both BBC Wales and its independent competitor—firstly TWW, then Harlech which mutated into HTV (see below) —ran a half hour news magazine programme each weekday evening. But, in the 1960s and 1970s, *Heddiw* (BBC) and *Y Dydd* (HTV) were usually broadcast concurrently and off-peak, thus diluting an already meagre audience. TWW first won the franchise for Wales and the West in 1958, being succeeded by Harlech in 1968. Harlech and its successor HTV still hold the Wales and the West franchise. Programmes such as the soap opera *Coronation Street* (it was often claimed more than half the nation watched events in Weatherfield, the fictional setting of this highly popular serial), could not be shifted even to provide programmes in the indigenous language of the same nation.

The Welsh language, until the 1960s, had had a chequered history. The government of Wales, until the Laws in Wales Acts of 1536 and 1543, was somewhat fragmented. Following the conquest of the Princedom of Gwynedd in 1282-3 and the imposition of the new acts in the 16th century, Wales was governed by a piecemeal collection of princes and dukes who all had their own legal systems and customs. The increasing lawlessness of the Marcher lords who ruled the princedoms alongside the English border concerned Henry Tudor (descended from the great Welsh Tudor family) who, in 1485, seized the English throne. His son, Henry VIII, directed Thomas Cromwell to find a solution. Cromwell advised annexing Wales, incorporating it into England, and subjugating its legal systems, which was done under the above acts.

The effect of annexation on restricting the use of Welsh was profound. Those using Welsh would be banned from public office in Wales—"the people of the same dominion have and do daily use a speche nothing like ne consonant to the naturall mother tonge used within this Realme"; the intention of the English crown was "utterly to extirpe alle and singular sinister usages and customs" which could be found in Wales (Fast-Archive.com).

Henry created a new middle class which, seeing the side upon which their bread was buttered, abandoned Welsh. Besides, in such turbulent times, those defying the whim of the king could well have found heads separated from the rest of their bodies. The new Welsh subjects had equality with those over the border but, as Nationalist historian A.O.H. Jarman noted, that equality came at a price. Under the second of the Acts of Union, the Court of Great Sessions was set up to deal with major crimes in Wales. Of the 217 judges who sat on its benches in nearly 300 years of its existence, only 30 were Welshmen and, of that number, only a handful would have spoken Welsh (Jarman 1950, 97).

Henry VIII's acts were only fully withdrawn when the Welsh Language Act of 1993 found its way onto the statute book. But between the incorporation of Wales into England and the 1993 act, much was done to attempt the eradication of Welsh. Attacks on the language were legion, yet despite the assault from its powerful English neighbour, Welsh did not die out. While Henry VIII tried to extinguish Welsh, others—even contemporaries—worked against his efforts. Bishop William Morgan's translation of the Bible appeared in 1588, 23 years before the King James version in England. It was a publishing sensation and Welsh books appeared regularly from as early as 1546.

Part of this continuing success can be attributed to the fact the Welsh were highly literate, thanks to the "circulating schools" of Carmarthenshire preacher Griffith Jones (1683-1761) who had travelled all over teaching adults and children basic literacy in their mother tongue in as short a time as possible. By the end of the 18th century Wales was one of very few European countries with a literate majority, something noted by Catherine the Great of Russia who, in 1764, commissioned a report to look at Jones's educational activities.

By the end of the 19th century, Wales had developed two distinct cultural identities. There was the traditional culture, based on the Welsh language, but industrialisation—mainly in South Wales, but also in pockets of the North—had helped propel the British Empire to its pre-eminence and helped nurture a whole new Anglo-Welsh culture. This culture has remained in place, despite industrial decline, and embraces male-voice choirs, rugby union, brass bands and a literature characterised by the likes of Dylan Thomas—an English-language culture with a distinctly Welsh accent. "The dragon", as historian Gwyn A. Williams proclaimed in his 1985 HTV Wales series *When Was Wales?* "has two tongues".[1]

Yet it is still the language which defines Wales, even among non-Welsh speakers. The fact it could not be used in most public places led to those violent protests in the 1960s. Motorists became used to seeing roadsigns daubed in green paint and "Cymraeg!" ("Welsh!") signs stuck over English-only directions. People risked their lives to climb TV transmitter masts to support a Welsh TV channel in the 1970s, and Gwynfor Evans, the first nationalist from either Scotland or Wales to enter Westminster (he famously won the Carmarthen by-election in 1966), threatened to fast to the death if Margaret Thatcher's government did not implement the recommendations of the Annan Committee to use the available fourth TV channel frequency in the Principality for a Welsh-language service. The lady who famously proclaimed she was "not for turning" executed an uncharacteristic and little-publicised *volte-face* and did more than any other British politician to arrest the century-old decline in Welsh speakers by paving the way for the establishment of S4C, the fourth TV channel in Wales which shares much of the programming of Channel 4 but produces Welsh language broadcasts for consumption in Wales and, in recent years, nationally and internationally on digital channels. It eventually went on air in 1982.

The advent of S4C has contributed, with other measures, to a rise in the number of people now speaking Welsh. While the Tudors spawned an anglicised middle class which rejected Welsh, to use the language is now a somewhat middle-class thing to do. Arguably more people round the world speak Welsh than at any time in its history with estimates putting the figure at more than one million.

Journalism in Wales

The Welsh-language press was born out of radicalism. Historian Gwyn A. Williams suggested that "from the middle of the 19th century, most people lived their lives within the orbit of, or in reaction to, the chapels. Their literacy, their world outlook, increasingly their politics, were deeply affected by the morality of the chapels" (Williams 1985, 206).

---

[1] The dragon is a symbol of Wales and indeed appears on the Welsh flag.

Thomas Jones, who produced almanacs, referred to a Welsh news-sheet in his 1691 and 1692 editions and Lewis Morris produced a periodical *Tlysau yr Hen Oesoedd* at Holyhead in 1735. It lasted just one edition. But it was those ministers preaching fiery sermons who began to produce "pulpit publications". The first, *Seren Gomer*, appeared in Swansea in 1814 and circulated amongst workers and smallholders. It did not last long—barely one year—but the efforts of Baptist minister John Harris provided the catalyst for a regular flow of Welsh publications. *Cronicl yr Oes* appeared in Mold in 1836 and *Yr Amserau* in Liverpool in 1843 which, by 1848 had decamped to the Isle of Man to avoid taxes (it was taken over in 1859, merged with *Baner Cymru* and only ceased publication in 1992). E. Morgan Humphreys listed dozens of Welsh newspapers and magazines in his 1945 volume, *Y Wasg Gymraeg* (The Welsh Press). By the middle of the 19th century and building on the efforts of Griffith Jones during the previous century, the two-thirds of the Welsh nation which spoke the language were intensely politically aware, fully immersed in the ways of religion, literature and traditional culture, with radical clergymen setting the Welsh-language presses turning. They were, said Williams, the "dedicated clergymen, dedicated in particular to popular religious instruction, which gave the Welsh press a significant boost and was perhaps the major contribution to Welsh language literature" (ibid, 150). Indeed, denominational newspapers such as *Y Tyst*, published by the Independents, and the Presbyterian publication *Y Goleuad* are still extant, most published solely in Welsh.

In 1889 J.E. Vincent wrote in *The Times* that "the growth of journalism and of vernacular journalism in particular in the Principality has been little short of phenomenal. My impression, indeed, is that Wales supports more journals in proportion to its population than in any other part of the civilised world" (National Library of Wales).

Shortly before Vincent's comments—in 1885—there were 61 newspapers circulating around Wales, 13 in Welsh. By 1893, that rose to 95 newspapers, 15 in Welsh. The explosion of new titles paralleled developments in England where major titles were being founded—the *Daily Mail, Daily Express* and *Daily Mirror* between 1896 and 1903. Those English papers, though, were tame compared to Welsh papers. "A characteristic of Welsh newspapers of the 19th century is the gusto with which they attack their opponents—political, religious or otherwise—and the seeming boundlessness of their personal abuse" (Newsplan).

That was the apex of traditional Welsh newspaper publishing. Almost from the day Victoria died, the Welsh language press—or, to be more correct, traditional, paid-for, newspapers—began a gentle decline, almost into oblivion. The end of the 19th century was what Robert Smith described as a "golden age", predating the era when major publishing conglomerates would move into Wales and buy English-language titles to close them down, thus stamping out competition (Smith 2000, 215).

It is probably fair to say that the traditional Welsh language press is a virtual skeleton, barely breathing. *Y Cymro* (The Welshman), a weekly newspaper, was established in 1932 and its circulation peaked in the 1950s at around 25,000 a week but now sells under 3,000 copies. As established English daily newspapers struggle with circulation decline, what hope for a small publication tapping a very limited market? That said, *Y Cymro* was sold in 2004 to Tindle Newspapers—which also owns Radio Ceredigion—becoming part of the Cambrian News Group. It is supported with a grant from the Welsh Books Council, something provided annually since 1996. Sales are stable and the paper, unlike some UK national titles, is profitable.

It is not such a happy tale at the once highly-influential *Herald Gymraeg* and sister newspaper *Herald Môn*. They ceased publication as stand-alone papers in 2005 and, for around three years, *Yr Herald Gymraeg* was published as a free supplement to Trinity Mirror's *Daily Post*. Their last paid-for sales were around a mere 1,300, a catastrophic drop from the 30,000 weekly sales at their peak. However, even that concession fell by the wayside, to be replaced by a Welsh-language web version of the *Welsh Daily Post*, published every Wednesday. At the time of its first publication, editor Rob Irvine noted that the site provided a full service of news, videos and audio, as well as links, stressing the absence of external grant support.

Golwg, a weekly magazine, was established in 1988 and is a digest of news and current affairs. *Barn*, established in 1962, is published ten times a year and could be compared to the *Spectator* or the *New Statesman*. It receives an annual Welsh Books Council grant of around £80,000. *Golwg* is also supported by a similar grant from the WBC and the company supports two other grant-aided periodicals: *Lingo Newydd* and *Wcw*, both aimed at a younger readership.

There were plans for a Welsh language daily newspaper—*Y Byd*—which would, in effect, have been the first national daily newspaper in Wales. The two morning English language newspapers published in the Principality are not nationals in the true sense of the word. The *Western Mail* has scant circulation in the north while the *Daily Post* is an unashamedly North Walian publication, having bolted its long-time stable in Liverpool to take up residence in Llandudno Junction. However, *Y Byd*'s debut has been shelved indefinitely with no plans for publication, despite, at one point, hiring editorial staff for its planned base in

Machynlleth, Mid-Wales. A Welsh-language Sunday paper, *Y Sulyn*, launched on 12 October 1982 and published only 14 issues.

The Papurau Bro

It is, however, the Papurau Bro ("district" newspapers) which are a major success story in Welsh-language journalism. First launched in 1973, there is now a network of 59 publications in Wales, with two published outside her borders: in Liverpool and London respectively. They are hugely independent publications which are subsidised to a small degree by the Arts Council of Wales and the Welsh Books Council, and rely on a largely volunteer workforce with little or no training in journalism.

They often break newspaper conventions—the lead story, for example, will often be buried inside, there is a concentration on hyper-local stories, sometimes little more than gossip. Politics are barely broached and they shun controversy. They are edited by committee, the editor's role often rotating. Individual circulations are small—rarely more than 1,500—with distribution areas sometimes comprising a few scattered villages. In recent years, the BBC's Welsh language website has picked up stories running in the Papurau Bro, thus giving them additional exposure, yet most publications resist the idea of creating their own website.

As English-language newspaper ownership in Wales has become ever more concentrated in fewer hands, the Papurau Bro (along with Welsh magazines) remain true to their roots: "The diversity of ownership, which was lost in the newspaper press, has been maintained in the magazines and other periodicals" (Evans 2000, 275). Their combined circulation, throughout Wales, is something approaching 75,000. Anecdotal evidence suggests each publication is read by around four people, meaning these "newspapers" reach almost two thirds of the Welsh-speaking population of Wales.

However they have their critics. Lord Elis-Thomas, National Assembly Presiding Officer, writing in *Y Faner* in 1983, savaged the papers: "Reading the Papurau Bro raises a certain melancholy in one looking for signs of Welsh modernisation and the new political consciousness so necessary today" (Elis-Thomas 1983). He went on to criticise their conservatism, saying they wanted to keep things as they are in their respective areas "or, to be totally honest, keeping them as they were. The ideal of a conservative Welsh 'bro' is what governs the Papurau Bro" (ibid).

Journalism and the Public Sphere

The 2008 Institute of Welsh Affairs' report *Media in Wales: Serving Public Values*, revealed that most Welsh people—87%—consume journalism produced outside the country, mainly by London-based journalists. The circulation of the two morning papers produced in the country—the *Western Mail* and the *Daily Post* —is a small fraction of the Welsh circulation of London-based products. Those reading Welsh-language publications, a majority of the Welsh-speaking population, at least read something produced by Welsh-based journalists.

The same problem exists for broadcasting, where a daily torrent of English-language programming engulfs Wales and TV viewers close to the border are tuned to English transmitters. In the early days of radio, J.C. Griffiths-Jones, wireless correspondent of the *Western Mail*, wrote that "Wales is finding itself these days, and in this cultural renaissance we want the radio to play its part. The BBC should not have to be conscripted for this crusade; it should be in the joyous forefront of the battle, of its own free will" (Griffiths-Jones, 1931). But, as Robert Smith noted, radio-listening clubs of the time, as well as films imported from England or, more probably, Hollywood, all conducted their activities in English and, decades later, the BBC and HTV were heavily criticised for their reluctance to make Welsh-language programmes.

The reluctance of the BBC to produce Welsh programmes in the 1920s and 30s was defended by the Corporation saying there was insufficient interest or talent in the area (Smith 2000, 217). Maybe that, combined with an equal reluctance by TWW—which was awarded the ITV franchise for Wales and the West (for which read much of South Wales and Western England)—to make Welsh programmes led Granada Television to produce Welsh-language programmes from its base in Manchester in an attempt to serve the Welsh-speaking northern part of the country.

Attitudes did change slowly, with the BBC establishing a dedicated Welsh-language radio channel—BBC Radio Cymru—in 1977 which now broadcasts a wide range of programmes in Welsh, at least 20 hours a day. Around 12.5% of the output is devoted to news and current affairs (Davies and Morris 2008). Commercial broadcasters who, in the early days of non-BBC radio, offered a smattering of Welsh within their schedules as an aid to landing a licence, now see Welsh as a real selling point, with some stations in Welsh-speaking areas broadcasting more than half their content in Welsh. Heart Cymru broadcasts across Anglesey and Gwynedd with a number of daily bilingual programmes while half of Radio Ceredigion's output is in Welsh. Swansea Sound, one of the first wave of commercial stations in the UK, provides up to twelve hours of programming a week, while a range of stations in North Wales provide Welsh programming. To date, no community radio licence has been issued to a station which is predominantly devoted to Welsh-language broadcasting.

But it is S4C which has had a profound impact on Welsh-language journalism. When it started, the BBC was contracted to provide news services and HTV to provide current affairs. In addition, dozens of independent companies sprung up all over Wales making programmes which employed journalistic output. Today, S4C broadcasts around 15 hours of Welsh-language programmes per day. In 2006 that comprised 13.4% news, 16.9% general factual programmes and 5.8% current affairs (ibid).

The great growth area for Welsh language journalism is, without doubt, online. There is the weekly digest of news in Welsh provided by the *Daily Post* and there is *Y Cymro*. The *Cymro* is a subscription service, with one edition costing 50p. The dailypostcymraeg.co.uk site does not presently charge. Other sites include Golwg360, *Golwg*'s news site, a general portal called Cymry ar y We, a poetry discussion site called cynghanedd.com and the discussion forum maes-e. Radio Acen is an on-line radio station for Welsh learners. Wikipedia, Facebook and Amazon also provide Welsh language sites.

Prime amongst on-line providers is BBC Cymru'r Byd, an in-depth news site which was launched on St David's Day 2000.[2] Its impact is immense and, from a hoped-for target of 5,000 page visits a week at the outset, it was responding to 1,500,000 page requests a month within five years (Davies 2005). Grahame Davies, executive producer of BBC Wales's Welsh-language New Media Services, revealed other startling statistics. While the bulk of users live in Wales, some 25% live in the UK but outside Wales, with around 10% of users are outside the UK—mainly in North America. Notable, too, was the fact that a much younger user accesses the site, with 43% in the 15-34 age group, mainly seeking information on news and current affairs. Some 80% of users are estimated to be under 45. Further, in a 2008 report to the Welsh Language Board, Tony Bianchi noted that "other features of BBC Cymru'r Byd, particularly blogs, podcasts and games for children and parents, and links to YouTube, maes-e ... attracted users unfamiliar with reading Welsh" (Bianchi 2008, 39).

Those accessing all forms of Welsh-language journalism, therefore, consume something produced by journalists living in the country. However,

---

[2] Saint David is the patron saint of Wales.

as few Welsh residents consume English-language journalism generated in Wales, analysts fear a serious democratic deficit. Just as Wales becomes more democratically accountable to itself, over 80 per cent of the Welsh population is potentially ill-informed about her political destiny: "If we don't have a vibrant and vigorous set of journalists working in Wales, we are not going to have the kind of democracy people were voting for when they voted for the Assembly," said Martin Shipton of the NUJ in Wales (Shipton 2007).

Professor Bob Franklin of Cardiff University has noted that most UK national newspapers do not have Welsh correspondents: "English journalists are not well informed about the Welsh constitution. For example, people were reading about student top-up fees when they don't apply in Wales, and the same with health care stories" (Franklin 2007). So could it be the Welsh-language journalists who are helping Welsh speakers regain their democratic rights?

> While all newspapers sought to inform, educate and entertain their readers, Welsh-language titles were also, implicitly or explicitly, engaged in a cultural mission to preserve, improve and extend the Welsh language. This more specific linguistic and cultural dimension added urgency to their task and gave them an importance (including, no doubt, a self-importance) far beyond that which may be suggested by their circulation figures or their profit margins (Jones 2000, 175).

There is little doubt journalists have been at the forefront of defending the language and increasing its use in everyday life. Quite how writers of anti-Welsh pamphlets from the 17th century would see life today might well be another matter. *Wallography* from 1682 willed the speedy demise of Welsh:

> The native gibberish is usually prattled throughout the whole of Taphydom[3] except in their market towns, whose inhabitants being a little raised do begin to despise it. 'Tis usually cashiered out of gentlemen's houses ... so that (if the stars prove lucky) there may be some glimmering hopes that the British language[4] may be quite extinct and may be Englished out of Wales (Hughes 1924, 45).

---

[3] "Taphydom" refers to Wales and comes from the children's rhyme "Taffy was a Welshman, Taffy was a thief. Taffy came to my house and stole a side of beef". It is now not repeated because of the racist overtones.

[4] The British language refers to Welsh. It is thought that the forerunner of the modern Welsh language was spoken right through most of England and up to the Scottish borders prior to the Roman invasion which forced the Welsh back into Wales and the Scots over Hadrian's Wall into Alba.

Times have certainly changed.

Works Cited

Bianchi, T. 2008. *A Review of the Welsh Language Print Media*. Cardiff: Welsh Language Board.

Cymdeithas yr Iaith Gymraeg (Welsh Language Society). http://cymdeithas.org/dadlwytho/tynged.pdf (in translation: original text of Saunders Lewis' lecture *Tynged yr Iaith* broadcast by BBC Wales in 1962). Accessed 28 April 2010.

Davies, G. T. and N. Morris. 2008. *Media in Wales: Serving Public Values*. Cardiff: Institute of Welsh Affairs.

Davies, G. 2005. Beginnings: New Media and the Welsh Language. *North American Journal of Welsh Studies*, 5(1), 13-22.

Elis-Thomas, Dafydd. 1983. *Papurau Bro yn Codi Felan. Y Faner*, August 5.

Evans, D. G. 2000. *A History of Wales 1906-2000*. Cardiff: University of Wales Press.

Fast-Archive.com. http://www.fact-archive.com/encyclopedia/Act_of_Union_1536 Accessed 19 April 2010.

Franklin, B. 2007. What Price Welsh Media? *Big Issue Wales*. December 3.

Griffiths-Jones, J. C. 1931. Radio in Wales. *Western Mail*. December 1.

Hughes, W. J. 1924. *Wales and the Welsh in English Literature*. Wrexham: Hughes and Sons.

Humphreys, E. M. 1945. *Y Wasg Gymraeg*. Liverpool: Gwasg y Brython.

Jarman, A. O. H. 1950. Cymru'n Rhan o Loegr 1485-1800. In *Seiliau Hanesyddol Cenedlaetholdeb Cymru*, edited by Arthur Wade-Evans. 48-57. Cardiff: Plaid Cymru.

Jones, A. The Welsh Language and Journalism in *The Welsh Language and Its Social Domains 1801-1911*, edited by Geraint H Jenkins. 81-92. Cardiff: University of Wales Press, 2000

National Library of Wales. http://www.llgc.org.uk/index.php?id=524. Accessed 19 April 2010.

Newsplan Cymru. http://www.newsplanwales.info/s005.htm. Accessed 28 April 2010.

Shipton, M. 2007. What Price Welsh Media? *Big Issue Wales*. December 3.

Smith, R. 2000. Journalism and the Welsh Language. In *Let's Do Our Best for the Ancient Tongue*, edited by Geraint H. Jenkins and Mari A. Williams. 115-124. Cardiff: University of Wales Press.

Williams, G. A. 1985. *When was Wales?* Harmondsworth: Penguin.

"POSTCODE LOTTERY":
THE FUTURE OF CROSS-BORDER MEDIA
IN POST-DEVOLUTION WALES

SIMON GWYN ROBERTS

As political devolution evolves and matures in several countries across Europe, questions of civic and individual engagement with the process are becoming increasingly pertinent. These questions echo wider concerns about disengagement from national political systems, but in the context of devolution are often more clearly linked to the politics of identity. As a result, engagement with political devolution has particular relevance to areas historically marginalised by the dominant national narrative in the devolved entity. Further, devolution tends to strengthen and develop coherent narratives as the devolved nation takes the opportunity to define itself more clearly both politically and culturally. Areas marginalised by this process are often on the geographical periphery of the devolved entities and have a less coherent sense of identity. The consequent lack of engagement with devolved politics expresses itself most clearly in an unwillingness to vote, giving rise to a relatively new dynamic in terms of identity politics.

By definition, devolution as a potent political issue is confined to "plurinational" countries, where identity is contested, and which often have no history of federalism: the UK and Spain are perhaps the most obvious contemporary European examples. In both countries, the constructed and contested nature of their political status has been increasingly called into question over the past three or four decades, with political devolution the inevitable, but equally contested, political response. It is, generally, a response that has emerged after many years of claim, counter-claim and referenda. In the case of Wales, the 1997 devolution referendum was passed by the most slender of margins in the country as a whole, and rejected emphatically by certain constituencies, notably those adjacent to the English border. Yet the Assembly Government has gradually gained support in Wales as a whole, and its power has increased since 1997. Further, as Phillips (2005) argues, there can be no doubting the symbolic importance of the creation of the Assembly for initiating fundamental debates about the nature of nation, identity and culture in contemporary Wales.

In the Welsh (and British) context, devolution has been accompanied by a rapid reconfiguring of national identities and allegiances. Indeed, McCrone et al. (1998) argue that the British Isles is a good place to study the impact of what they call the "new identity politics" because there is something problematic and contested about British identity. Much recent work has been devoted to questioning conventional histories of the UK, in particular the way in which the centrality of English history has been prioritised at the expense of more "peripheral" historical narratives (Samuel 1998). The result has been an emphasis on the UK as a "Union of Multiple Identities" (Brockliss and Eastwood 1997). This process has been particularly marked post-devolution to the point that other British identities (Welsh, Scottish, English) have been "reconfigured" and are now strongly embedded in the public imagination, often at the expense of theoretically all-encompassing "Britishness".

Writing two decades before devolution, the Welsh historian G. A. Williams (1979, 192) predated the oft-cited work of Anderson (1983) when attempting to articulate the Welsh experience of identity definition: "Nations are not born, they are made. Nations do not grow like a tree, they are manufactured". Phillips (2005) points to the role that these new histories have in the creation, and recreation, of national identity. If national identity is a continuous process of making and remaking, invention and construction, singular narratives are clearly redundant. In this context, where multiple narratives compete for legitimacy as the nations of the UK attempt to assert themselves post-devolution, the news media have an obvious, defining role. They constitute the arena in which the processes of devolution are transmitted to the voting public.

The established tradition of cross-border media along the Anglo-Welsh border therefore offers an interesting case study. Newspapers reflect, and construct, a geographical and cultural reality: the Anglo-Welsh border is often urban in character and in some areas suburbs spill across what was (pre-devolution) merely an "administrative" boundary. Inevitably, these areas are characterised by a certain ambiguity of identity and, as a partial consequence, newspaper remits and readerships often transcend the border. However, the critical contemporary point about this traditional cross-border media remit is that it has inevitably become something of an anachronism, singularly failing to reflect the *zeitgeist*, the fundamental political realities post-devolution, in which exclusive English, Scottish and

Welsh identities have expanded at the expense of theoretically inclusive "Britishness".

The Margins of Devolution

Wales as a whole has long been characterised by a fragmented political and cultural geography. In the words of Dai Smith (1999, 71) "Wales is a singular noun but a plural experience". Numerous attempts have been made to encapsulate that fragmentation, the most frequently cited being Denis Balsom's "Three Wales Model" (1985). Balsom argued that Welsh voting patterns, alongside related issues of identity and language, could best be illustrated by dividing the county into three broad units. The "Bro Gymraeg" (literally "Welsh neighbourhood") represents the Welsh-speaking, culturally distinct areas of north-west and west Wales characterised by widespread support for Plaid Cymru, the nationalist party. "Welsh Wales" consists of the industrialised South Wales valleys and West Glamorgan (largely Labour-voting, primarily Welsh identifying, but English speaking), with "British Wales" forming the rest (Pembrokeshire, north-east Wales and other areas adjacent to the English border). In "British Wales", argued Balsom, voters' primary loyalty is to the British state, and residents prioritise their British identity ahead of their Welsh identity.

Flintshire, in the north-eastern corner of Wales, encapsulates "British Wales", particularly the urbanised and industrialised eastern fringe along the English border. The area is marginalised from the centres of Welsh political life by a combination of geographical location, in-migration, and culture: particularly if one accepts that the two dominant national narratives in post-devolution Wales echo Balsom's "Welsh Wales" and "Bro Cymraeg". Both narratives are coherent and "credible" in terms of identity markers and stereotypical Welsh characteristics, and both contrast sharply with the unusually nebulous cultural identity of Flintshire, which expresses itself politically in a marked reluctance to engage with the newly devolved Welsh political system.

Borders and Identity

The form and function of borders are central to the relationship between devolution and identity. The function of borders, in the European context, has changed in several directions, almost simultaneously, over the past decade. While the EU's external boundaries have become increasingly rigid, its internal boundaries have largely lost their significance as a consequence of the Schengen agreement. Yet simultaneously the process of political devolution has shaped domestic politics in several EU countries over the past 15 years. The result is that internal boundaries have become codified to an extent not seen for centuries.

Borders need not necessarily be political: they also have a symbolic significance. In this context, the anonymity of the Welsh-English border, particularly where that border is urban or suburban in character, is notable. Cross-border suburban sprawl renders the region intriguingly nebulous in terms of identity. For example, the border runs through ordinary suburban streets on the outskirts of Chester. It is largely unmarked, and has little social, cultural or historic significance. Despite this, it has been lent a real political significance, a kind of artificial reality, by devolution.

The ambiguity of Flintshire's position post-devolution therefore seems pertinent to the wider debate in Wales, but has received little academic attention. Williams (2005b) points to the fact that much contemporary writing on "postcolonialism" celebrates the fractured identity of those on the "edge" and gives a voice to those on the margins of the nation. In a Welsh context, he suggests, this might mean paying greater attention to the geographical borderland as well as the affective borderland. Eastern Flintshire also has to deal with the geographical reality of a highly urbanised, culturally coherent and distinct English region immediately adjacent to it.

Examining "problematic" national identities has featured prominently in both political and academic debates in recent years, partly because, as Kiely et al. (2000) point out, in contexts where national identity is not taken for granted the complex process of identity construction becomes more clearly apparent. The post-devolution image of Wales as a coherent national unit, the contemporary dominant national narrative, is contradicted by the heterogeneous reality in areas like eastern Flintshire. As Horsman and Marshall (1995) argue, there has always been a tension between the fixed, durable and inflexible requirements of national boundaries and the unstable, transient and flexible requirements of people. Bhabha (1992) goes further, positively embracing the ambivalent, fractured identity of the margins in his work on post-colonialism. And whereas traditional views of nationhood ignore this marginality, Williams (2005a) points out that post-colonial perspectives value it as an enabling rather than as a disabling condition. In that context, the critical point about cross-border media in this region is that they are often deliberately charged with representing the socio-cultural ambiguity that is typical of border areas.

Media Constructions

This ambiguity has a long history (Williams 1985, Smith et al. 1999), but has been put into sharper focus by the processes of devolution. As a result, there is a developing appetite among residents for discussing identity politics and related issues of civic engagement within the media. Equally, the media's role in framing and articulating often complex and diverse issues of identity politics is increasing in importance as devolution takes root. But since devolution, the mainstream media's role in providing a platform for the discussion of identity politics has been limited. Television receivers are often tuned to masts in north-west England or unable to pick up Welsh signals (Thomas et al. 2003), and there has never been a Welsh national newspaper industry. Further, evidence suggests that London-based UK newspapers are increasingly disinclined to cover devolved politics in the UK. This is not necessarily a problem in Scotland, which has always had its own newspaper industry, but is a problem in Wales, where there is no independent journalistic tradition (at least in English) and where most people buy London-based newspapers (Denver 2002). None of these provide Welsh editions, following the well-documented collapse of the *Welsh Mirror* in 2003. This is increasingly cited as a serious democratic deficit: legislative changes deriving from the Assembly Government are simply not conveyed, via the mainstream news media, to those they affect. These changes may (in the case of education and health, for instance) have a significant impact on Welsh residents, yet go largely unreported (Davies and Morris 2008).

Equally serious is the fact that the mainstream UK press has a tendency to ignore the fragmented cultural and social reality of Wales that is such a critical issue post-devolution. As Griffiths (1994) argues, British media representations of Wales remain constructed upon unchanging stereotypical and monolithic images. Further, the portrayal of Wales, and Scotland, has become increasingly reductive post-devolution. In interviews, Rosie et al (2004) found that London journalists felt able to express the view that since "the Scots" had their own parliament so too they had their "own news" and their own newspapers to carry it. The virtual absence of a Welsh national press is put into sharp focus by such sentiments. Barlow et al (2005) highlight concerns that the media fail to adequately represent the diversity of Wales, leading to a sense of cultural deficit. This sense of deficit is rarely related to intensively "anglicised" parts of Wales. Even when real issues are acknowledged, journalistic reliance on simplified linguistic conventions discourages the elaboration of meanings necessary for a full understanding of contexts ("postcode lottery", when referring to the Welsh abolition of prescription charges, for example) and has a tendency to obscure real debate (Conboy 2007, Richardson 2007).

A recent poll suggested that a small majority in Wales would now vote in any future referendum for the Assembly having full law-making powers (BBC 2009b), which makes the shortcomings of the news media still more notable politically. Yet the situation looks set to worsen, with the recent announcement that Trinity Mirror is seeking to amalgamate its Welsh operation with its newspapers in North-West England. This decision, in January 2009, led Blaenau Gwent MP Dai Davies to say that "Wales is becoming a media wasteland in which only the publicly subsidised BBC and S4C seem secure. This is very, very worrying for democracy" (BBC 2009a).

Most local newspapers in Flintshire have a "cross-border" remit and scope, in that they are tasked with appealing to, and selling to, residents on both sides of the Anglo-Welsh border. The specificity of the local press is notable in this context, and potentially provides a source of competitive advantage in a climate of declining circulations. This is not to say that celebrating the region's ambiguity is an ideological aim for these newspapers, merely that commercial realities have long dictated a blurring of the boundaries. Targeting a cross-border audience, though, is now fraught with a new form of journalistic difficulty as a result of the new cultural paradigm in which political changes have forced a reconfiguration of national identities from British to English and Welsh. If borders are, traditionally, places that facilitate the identification of difference and of congruence, then this border's new status raises interesting questions in terms of how the local press chooses to address its audience. On the Welsh side, residents find themselves subject to an increasing number of distinctive changes enacted by the Assembly government. While most of these changes have gone unnoticed by the British media some, like the removal of prescription charges in Wales, have been widely reported by the national UK press, as well as the local and regional press on both sides of the Anglo-Welsh border. They have contributed to a renewed sense of "difference", of distinction, and of significance of the border.

The Anglo-Welsh border has a long tradition of newspapers that bridge the divide: a tradition that inevitably appears somewhat anachronistic post-devolution. The *Shropshire Star* publishes six editions and straddles the border between mid Wales and Shropshire, while Flintshire is served by several daily and weekly local newspapers, all of which have "cross-border" remits. The *Chester Chronicle*, owned by the Trinity Mirror group, has six editions, three of which circulate in Flintshire, and all of which are written in Chester with a degree of common content. However,

The Leader (owned by NWN Media) is the most notable example of a newspaper tasked with appealing to a cross-border audience in the area. It has a total circulation of around 66,000 and produces three editions from its base in Mold, Flintshire. Two serve Wrexham and Flintshire, on the Welsh side of the border. One serves Chester, in England. In terms of circulation, few copies (1-2000) of the Chester (English) edition are sold, compared to around 18,000 copies in Flintshire and 33,000 in Wrexham (NS Database 2010). Editorial policy is unusual in that most of the content is shared between all the editions, with only the first three pages specific to the region. An analysis of the Chester edition carried in December 2009 suggested that an average local news split was 40% "English", 50% "Welsh", with the remaining 10% "cross border" in tone. This is partly a resource issue, in that the Chester edition is clearly a lesser priority as a result of the circulation statistics, but it is also partly a reflection of the long-standing tendency to regard this cross-border community as coherent enough to be addressed as a singular unit.

The analysis also pointed to clear evidence that *The Leader* is responding to the realities of devolution by revealing an increasing willingness to split the two titles along national political lines. The clearest evidence of this emerged on 9 December 2009, when the Welsh editions ran with a full front-page editorial headlined: "Make us a real nation, just like the Scots",an unprecedented direct appeal to increase the powers of the Welsh Assembly. Plaid Cymru councillor Marc Jones (2009) highlighted the significance of this headline in a newspaper aimed at a "British Welsh" audience traditionally regarded as sceptical about devolution: "Times really have changed when the paper that serves the border areas of Flintshire and Wrexham starts making noises like that". He went on to argue that the story represented a "symbolic bridging of the divide between North and South Wales, from a daily paper that has led the charge in emphasising the north-south divide in the past". On the same day, the Chester edition led with a story about community safety wardens, yet the editorial, now in its normal position on an inside page, remained the same: a direct, and overtly political, pro-devolution appeal for more Assembly powers.

The Leader chose to directly involve its audience in this appeal, in that it linked the story to a poll (about increasing Assembly powers) of its readers conducted by its publisher, NWN Media. An interesting move, in a journalistic climate where the public tend to be represented more as apolitical consumers than citizens (Lewis 2005). Indeed, Lewis et al. found that the great majority of references to public opinion in the UK national press—over 95%—are not based on any identifiable sources of evidence. This tendency to speculate about public opinion without supporting evidence has had the effect, in Flintshire's case, of obscuring debate on a topic of profound contemporary importance in terms of democratic engagement. If the news has a central role in informing citizens in any democracy, then the extent to which the public is portrayed as passive and disengaged is pertinent.

In this context, the poll illustrates a shift in this approach among the local press. The *Leader* column acknowledged the scepticism of the region towards devolution, answering its own rhetorical question ("why are we in the North East more sceptical of devolution?") with the following speculation: "Perhaps it's because we feel neglected by Cardiff lawmakers, or because we feel a more natural affinity with parts of the North West of England". It goes on to acknowledge that the question of increased powers for the Assembly becomes increasingly vexed in such a climate, a tacit concession that the tone of its headline essentially runs counter to majority public opinion among its target audience. It concludes by appealing to the new first Minister Carwyn Jones to "understand the rich tapestry of opinion across the region, unpick it and weave a consistent, articulate narrative about how he sees the future of the Assembly and its role in our lives".

Media Solutions?

The Parekh Report (2000), tasked with examining the future of "multi-ethnic Britain", sought to reinvent Britain as a community of communities. Flintshire residents' engagement with the post-devolution political paradigm is beginning to be articulated in the media, an acknowledgement of the competitive advantage derived from local newspapers' knowledge of their audience's preoccupations, values and characteristics. Indeed, one could argue that an acknowledgement of the inevitable ambiguity that characterises border communities is desirable post-devolution, and might lead to increased engagement with devolved Welsh politics. As previously stated, the area currently shows a marked reluctance to engage with devolved politics: only 25% of the Alyn and Deeside constituency voted in the 2003 Welsh Assembly elections, the lowest percentage in Wales, although this did increase to 35% in 2007, perhaps an early indication of increased engagement: a statistic exploited by *The Leader*. It is rather early to make assertions about trends, however, and indeed Wales's internal divisions remain a focus of concern and policy for the Assembly Government, as revealed by its Welsh Spatial Plan of 2003 which addresses the continuing disconnect between the Welsh Assembly government and the significant minority within Wales which remains opposed to the principle of devolution.

The Anglo-Welsh border has no tradition of emphasising its marginality or celebrating its ambiguity, in contrast to, for instance, Berwick-upon-Tweed, where Kiely et al.'s study (2000) of the residents of the town on the English-Scottish border found that people developed alternative identity rules of their own: "People ... turned out to be claiming, attributing, rejecting, accepting and side-stepping national identity, in ways that we had seldom or never previously encountered". Yet a comparable approach in Wales would be one possible solution to the post-devolution paradigm in terms of political identities and civic engagement, and would chime with Parekh's "community of communities" manifesto for the UK as a whole. It is worth pointing out that Williams (2004), however, argues that such "solutions" merely displace the problems of identity definition and collective exclusion onto a different level. In the Welsh context, Williams argues that none of these collectivities are viable foundations for a future politics of inclusion. Instead, he argues for a post-national Wales as a means of constructing a national identity embracing those who tend to be marginalised in the dominant national narrative: observing that the diversity of the country tends to be ignored as it attempts to define itself post-devolution.

The power to frame national identities by exaggerating the nationally specific (Conboy, 2006) encapsulates the media's potential role and influence post-devolution. For Lewis (2008), regional Spanish newspapers' changing role following devolution derived from sub-state nationalism which provided momentum for (in this case) bilingual journalism to emerge. This journalism, targeted on the newly devolved entities of Catalonia, Galicia and the Basque Country, played a crucial subsequent role in the construction of new national identities arising from a confluence of changing political, cultural and journalistic forces. In the context of the Anglo-Welsh border, such issues should perhaps be considered in the light of the statistics released by the Welsh Assembly Government which confirmed that Alyn and Deeside was the Welsh constituency where the lowest percentage of school pupils consider their national identity to be Welsh—20.5%—while 27.27% consider themselves English (Illingworth 2008). Given the decline in an all-encompassing "British" identity, an optimistic prognosis in terms of likely civic and political engagement in the context of Welsh devolution is difficult, hence perhaps the overtly politicised *Leader* front page previously highlighted.

As Williams (2005b) points out, a Wales that does not take proper account of the ambiguities and complexities which render the national project problematic will only generate a future embraced by a minority of its citizens. In Flintshire, these issues are compounded by a weak sense of local identity that has implications in terms of broader civic engagement on a local level: residents seem less willing to mobilise a form of "Berwickesque" localised identity as a means of dealing with the mixed identity markers many of them send out.

As commercial pressures on the media intensify, distinctively local media do find themselves in a potentially advantageous position in terms of their ability to address a target audience which faces highly specific cultural and political issues deriving from devolution. Their distinctiveness is allowing them to address the new paradigm by acknowledging the ambiguities of the region's identity, and then exploring its implications in the post-devolution political context.

Works Cited

Anderson, B. 1983. *Imagined communities*. London: Verso.

Baldwin, C. 2008. *Broadcasting Britishness? Identity, diversity and the role of the national media*. Ofcom/Oxford Said Business School conference report.

Balsom, D. 1985. The Three Wales Model. In *The national question again: Welsh political identity in the 1980s*, edited by J. Osmond. 1-17. Llandysul: Gomer.

Barlow, D. P. Mitchell and T. O'Malley. 2005. *The media in Wales: Voices of a small nation*. Cardiff: University of Wales Press.

BBC 2009a. *Group denies paper merger claims* (15 January 2009) http://news.bbc.co.uk/1/hi/wales/7829263.stm

—. 2009b. *Majority back law-making assembly* (26 February 2009) http://news.bbc.co.uk/1/hi/wales/wales_politics/7912263.stm

Bhaba, H. 1992. Postcolonial authority and postmodern guilt. In *Cultural Studies*, edited by L. Grossberg, C. Nelson and P. Treichler. 56-68. w York: Routledge.

Bohman, J. 2004. Expanding dialogue: The internet, the public sphere and prospects for transnational democracy. In *After Habermas: New perspectives on the public sphere*, edited by N. Crossley and J. M. Roberts. 131-156. Oxford: Blackwell.

Billig, M. 1995. *Banal nationalism*. London: Sage.

Brockliss, L. and D. Eastwood. 1997. *A Union of multiple identities. The British Isles 1750-1850*. Manchester: Manchester University Press.

Cohen, A. 1986. *Symbolising boundaries: Identity and diversity in British cultures*. Manchester: Manchester University Press.

Conboy, M. 2006. *Tabloid Britain: Constructing a community through language*. London: Routledge.

—. 2007. *The Language of the News*. London: Routledge

Davies, G. T. and N. Morris. 2008. *Media in Wales: Serving public values?* Cardiff: Institute of Welsh Affairs.

Denver, D. 2002. Voting in the 1997 Scottish and Welsh devolution referendums: Information, interests and opinions. *European journal of political research*, 41: 827-43.

Franklin, B. 1998. *Local journalism and local media: Making the local news*. London: Routledge.

Gill, F. 2005. Public and private: National identities in a Scottish Borders community. *Nations and Nationalism*, 11 (1): 83-97.

Gillespie, M. 2003. Transnational communications in diaspora communities. In *Critical reading: Media and audiences*, edited by V. Nightingale and K. Ross. 145-61. Maidenhead: Open University Press.

Griffiths, A. 1994. Ethnography and popular memory: Postmodern configurations of Welsh identities. *Continuum: The Australian Journal of Media and Culture*, 7 (2): 307-326.

Horsman, M. and A. Marshall. 1995. *After the nation-state: Citizens, tribalism and the new world disorder*. London: HarperCollins.

Illingworth, A. 2008. Children on Welsh border 'more English'. *Evening Leader*, 27 May.

Jones, M. 2009. *The North-South divide and how devolution bridged it*. http://waleshome.org/2010/01/the-north-south-divide-and-how-devolution-bridged-it/

Jones, R. W. and R. Scully. 2004. *Devolution in Wales: What does the public think?* Economic and Social Research Council Research Programme on Devolution and Constitutional Change, Briefing 7.

Jones, R. W. 2008. Devolution: the next step. *Planet: The Welsh Internationalist*, 188: 38-44.

Kiely, R., D. McCrone, F. Bechhofer and R. Stewart. 2000. Debateable land: National and local identity in a border town. *Sociological Research Online*, 5 (2), pars 1.1-6.2.
http://www.socresonline.org.uk/5/2/kiely. html

Lewis, J., S. Inthorn and K. Wahl-Jorgensen. 2005. *Citizens or consumers? What the media tell us about political participation*. Oxford: Oxford University Press.

Lewis, S. 2008. News, nationalism and the imagined community: The case of bilingual journalism in Spain. *Journalism Studies*, 9 (3): 409-429.

McCrone, D. R. Stewart, R. Kiely and F. Bechhofer. 1998. Who are we? Problematising national identity. *The Sociological Review*, 46 (4): 629-52.

McCrone, D. 1997. Unmasking Britannia: the rise and fall of British national identity. *Nations and Nationalism*, 3 (4): 579-96.

McNair, B. 2000. *Journalism and democracy: An evaluation of the political public sphere*. London: Routledge.

NS Database. 2010. Retrieved from: www.nsdatabase.co.uk

Parekh, B. 2000. *The future of multi-ethnic Britain*. London: Profile Books.

Phillips, R. 2005. Island stories and border crossings: School history and the discursive creation of national identity in Wales. In *Postcolonial Wales*, edited by J. Aaron and C. Williams. 39-54.Cardiff: University of Wales Press.

Philo, G. 2002. Television news and audience understanding of war, conflict and disaster. *Journalism Studies*, 3 (3): 173-86.

Richardson, J. 2007. *Analysing newspapers: an approach from critical discourse analysis*. London: Palgrave.

Rosie, M., J. MacInnes, P. Petersoo, S. Condor and J. Kennedy. 2004. Nation speaking unto nation? Newspapers and national identity in the devolved UK. *The Sociological Review*, 52 (4): 37-58.

Samuel, R. 1998. *Island Stories: Theatres of Memory*. London: Verso.

Smith, D. 1999. *Wales: A question for history*. Bridgend: Seren.

Thomas, J., J. Jewell and S. Cushion. 2003. *Media coverage of the 2003 Welsh Assembly elections*. Cardiff: Wales Media Forum.

Van Dijk, T. 1988. *News as discourse*. Hillsdale, NJ: Lawrence Erlbaum.

Williams, C. 2005a. Borders and identities in a globalising age. In *E-dentity: Borders and identities in the internet age*, edited by D. Cunliffe, R. Thompson and C. Williams. 3-9. Pontypridd: University of Glamorgan.

—. 2005b. Problematizing Wales. In *Postcolonial Wales*, edited by J. Aaron and C. Williams. 3-22.Cardiff: University of Wales Press.

Williams, G. A. 1979. When was Wales? In *Nationalism in Europe*, edited by S. Woolf. 192-205. London: Routledge.

—. 1985. *When was Wales? A History of the Welsh*. London: Penguin.

TO THE PERIPHERY OF THE PERIPHERY: THE REGIONAL PRESS, MICRO-NEWS AGENDAS AND LOCAL IDENTITY

ANDY PRICE

This study aims is to explore a particular dimension of the multi-layered concept of Centres and Peripheries through the evaluation of a regional newspaper website and its hyperlocal news strategy. It will also consider how such community participatory news may contribute to civil society and cultural identity in marginal urban areas. In particular, it considers how new overlapping public spheres may be emerging through a reconfiguration of ownership and control of this media and as a result how a more "emancipatory" (Enzensberger 1974, 95-128) media environment may be developing. The study examines the development of online micro-news agendas (in particular around localness) and the emerging geography of hyperlocal participatory news and takes a highly pragmatic view of this phenomenon, perhaps at odds with the more established critical approach.

The object of study is a local newspaper news website, *Gazettelive!*, in Middlesbrough, UK (www.Gazettelive!.co.uk). The data collected was inherently geographical and a new, novel web based system was developed with Dlab at Teesside University which accessed the collated data and displayed it spatially, thereby allowing the relative frequency and distribution of different activities of different post-code areas to be observed.

The media are commonly seen as a major contributor to the notion of spatial and cultural identity, for example through the idea of an "imagined community" (Anderson 1991). In *Reading Berlin* Fritzsche (1996) notes the role of the press in the creation of new urban identities in 19th Century Germany, as does Buchanan (2009, 62-84) with regard to American daily newspapers. Castells in *The Power of Identity* (2004) outlines the role of the internet and networked society in the formation of contemporary identity.

Morley in *Home Territories* (2000) identifies how national media both "bind" centres and peripheries together in national identity whilst simultaneously highlighting "otherness" at the margins—an otherness reflected in Said's examination of western constructions of the East in *Orientalism* (1995). When Said describes James Balfour MP addressing the Commons in 1910 on the problems of Egypt and the Egyptians' "difference", he could just as easily be articulating a view of the English regions and wider British Isles as understood through a Whig view of Englishness and history (Morley and Robins 2001)—a view that celebrated the superiority of the English, and their generosity in "sharing" their progress with those less fortunate than themselves.

The difference which Said describes may be paralleled by that which exists between the "ruling" class of southern England and the periphery, wherever it is found in the British cultural experience.

The idea of the media being a cultural influence within a "place" helpfully relates to Massey's (1994, 157-172) concept of "place" as a fluid or dynamic space with multiple cultural forces at work at any one time.

Participatory news and newspaper websites

Newspaper websites of the type central to this study have existed in Britain since 1997, when the national daily *The Daily Telegraph* launched its online edition. Most regional (or local) newspapers soon followed suit and the Newspaper Society (2010) reported that there are now over 1500 individual news websites produced by its members in Britain, a substantial network of local digital platforms and news environments.

Commentators such as Deuze et al. (2007), Allan (2006) and Bruns (2005) have very usefully begun to examine evidence of new forms of journalism and news production online in these websites. Whilst some of this innovation has come from commercial news producers, much has come through the growth of the "news" blogger (Bradshaw 2010, 97-106).

In this dynamic and constantly shifting environment it is difficult to categorise the different forms of online journalism/news production that are emerging. They are perhaps best understood as constituting a form of "Participatory Journalism" (Deuze et al. 2007) where two contrasting forces are at work. In this model there is seen to be a convergence taking place between top-down, commercially driven journalism and bottom-up public contributors. Deuze at al. (2007) and Bruns (2005) all point out that the "inherent logic" of the web and digital technology is forcing conventional news producers in this direction and that the creation of new, hybrid third spaces of participatory news is the result. From their study of national newspaper websites, Thurman and Hermida (2010, 49) identified nine different "generic formats" of user participation which are "used to encourage contributions from the public".

One of the specific developments in news production that has been driven by newspaper publishers in the UK has been hyperlocal or geo-tagged news. Slightly different strategies have been pursued in different locations, but in essence they all revolve around the spatial "tagging" of digital content (news, video, picture, etc) which is then published to hyperlocal web pages e.g. neighbourhood, postcode, or village. When published, this content is then often complemented by different forms of user participation, such as blogging or comments. So the publisher adds value to existing material via its local newsworthiness and benefits from free content provided by members of the public who are motivated enough to engage with it. As Deuze et al. (2009, 258) point out with regard to citizen news projects, the most successful are "distinctly hyperlocal". And as Jones (2010, 165) says of hyperlocal news in *Web Journalism*, "The local level is where much of the genuine experimentation in participatory media will take place. It is here that content producers are closest to their audiences".

Teesside and the *Evening Gazette*

In terms of marginality, national geography and the centre/periphery debate, Teesside is in the North East of England (250 miles from London). Within the North East region, Newcastle in the north is the cultural and economic centre, being home to the BBC and the commercial broadcaster ITV Tyne Tees, with Teesside on the southern periphery (bounded to the south by the North Yorkshire Moors national park). Within Teesside (population 500,000+) Middlesbrough is the major conurbation (along with towns such as Stockton-upon-Tees, Redcar and Hartlepool) and surrounding it are the estates, suburbs and villages that form the urban periphery of Teesside and the circulation area of the *Evening Gazette*. As a result a number of centre-periphery tensions play out; North/South, Regional/Sub-regional and local.

In Teesside the local daily evening newspaper is the aforementioned *Evening Gazette*, a Trinity Mirror Group publication (daily ABC circulation of 43,937) (ABC 2010). Through its website *Gazettelive!* it has been a leading exponent of web publishing in the regional press. It presently has 216,919 Unique Users and 2,325,681 Page Impressions per month (*Gazettelive!* 2010). Since it launched in 1997 it has won several national awards (e.g. Online Community Website of the Year 2007) as well as innovating in a number of ways: in particular the development of hyperlocal (participatory) online news through its twenty "Gazette Communities" postcode micro sites. In Britain, a postcode area (e.g. TS,

Teesside) generally covers a town or city: it is then subdivided into postcode districts (e.g. TS1, central Middlesbrough) which are then further subdivided into postcode units (e.g. TS1 3BA, Teesside University) which constitute a single large delivery point or a limited number of individual addresses.

This study examines the intermediate layer of this phenomenon: the twenty postcode "district" micro sites published on *Gazettelive!* which cover both the centre and periphery of Teesside.

Method

The data came directly from the website *www. Gazettelive!.co.uk*. Five sources were used: site visits, daily hyperlocal news published on community postcode micronews sites, the most popular stories in the community postcode micronews sites determined by the number of reader comments, the most popular "Forum" topics on the site judged by visits per community postcode micronews site, and postcode population data.

Information on what hyperlocal news was published on community sites was collected from the URL of each microsite daily over a four week period from 3 March 2009 to 18 April 2009 (no *Gazette* news was published on Sundays). Each postcode web page had the most popular stories ordered by the number of comments that readers had made in response to them; this data was also recorded. *Gazettelive!* also has a "Forums" section (separate from the community news sites). This data was also collected to evaluate the content for its relevance to hyperlocal community issues.

Website activity data (page impressions and unique users) had been published on each community site during the previous December. It was felt that the time period between the news sampling data and the site-visit data was close enough for it to be of use in an analysis of the behaviour of readers in each microsite. It was believed that these separate data sources (three of which—hyperlocal news, site visits and most popular comments—were spatially discrete) provided a rich basis from which to work.

Results

Site visits

The distribution of web activity in the microsites via the number of page impressions generated in the microsites was found not to be a homogenous distribution and some areas were more active than others. In fact the most interesting observation is that the urban centre (postcode districts TS1/TS2 and TS4) is almost the least active of all the postcode areas, while TS10 (Redcar) at the eastern periphery and TS17 (Thornaby, Ingleby Barwick) in the west are the most active. Overall a broad picture emerges of low to limited activity in the centre, greater activity in two peripheral nodes and stable, moderate activity elsewhere.

Microsite news

During the twenty-four day period from Monday 23 March 2009 to Saturday 19 April 2009, 1032 stories were published on the *Gazette* community microsites. Of these 743 (72%) were stories that had been published in the newspaper and had been "repurposed" for local community audiences, and 289 (28%) comprised original local content. Most—334 stories (207 were from the newspaper, 92 web only)—were published in Week 3 (6–10 April 2009), and the smallest number was published in Week 1 (23–28 March) with 196 stories (156 from the newspaper, 40 web only). There was an average of forty-three stories per day on the community web sites, of which thirty-one were from the newspaper and twelve were unique to the web. This amounted to an average of 2.15 stories per day per site. Of these, 1.55 had been published in the newspaper and 0.60 were unique web-only content.

There was a marked difference between the most active postcode area for the publishing of content—TS1/TS2, with 130 stories over the 24 days (5.41 per day)—and the least active—TS16, with 14 (0.57 per day) over the same period. The distribution centred on central Middlesbrough (TS1/TS2) and progressively reduced in frequency the further it travelled from this point and the more peripheral it became. It transpires that one important factor in the dominance of the centre (TS1/TS2) is the location of the head offices of organisations such as local authorities, police and health authorities, and their public relations activity, which is of significant importance to local journalism.

In terms of newspaper-only content, TS1/TS2 remained the most active with 107 stories in this period, with TS16 the least active with 9. In terms of non-*Gazette* (unique-Web) content TS17 was the most active with 29 stories (1.11 per day), TS8 the least with 2 (0.08 per day). Looking at the data for the gross distribution of postcode-based news, a number of areas appear significantly more active than others, in particular TS1/TS2, TS6, TS10 and TS12/TS13. Others are notably less active, including; TS16, TS8, TS21/TS22, TS9 and TS19.

Comments

Gazettelive! has been designed to allow readers to comment on each story published and show each microsite's ten most popular stories by the number of comments added. Whilst not strictly blogging, the addition of comments to existing stories is a form of user-generated content, and is perhaps an indication of the relative importance to readers. This information (comments on stories) also forms another metric of relative online activity by microsite areas. In addition, the "gross activity" (the number of comments) demonstrates some of the qualitative issues (news values) that interest the readers.

From an analysis of the subjects of these stories four main themes emerged: death, crime, children and general civic issues. In terms of the number of stories commented upon, civic issues were the most popular with seventy-seven individual stories (out of 200) or 39.5%. Death was the next most popular with fifty-one stories (26.2 %), crime the next with thirty-eight stories (19.5%) and finally children with twenty-nine individual stories (14.9%).

However, when the number of comments is analysed a different picture emerges. Death (particularly unexpected) was by far the most motivating topic with 48.9% (1653) of all comments being about this subject, civic issues were the next most popular with 29% (980), next was crime with 486 (14.4%) and last were stories related to children with 8% (272). Analysing the microsite data shows that stories about death in the top ten most popular commented on generated on average 32.4 comments per story, crime 12.8 comments, civic issues 12.7 and stories about children 9.4.

With regard to the most active microsites (TS10 and TS17), an interesting picture emerged. For both of these areas "civic" stories are the most common, with six stories for TS17 and five stories for TS10. Death is still very important to the readers in these areas with 54.4% of comments in the TS17 area and 34.1% of comments in TS10. TS10's most commented story involved a very lively local debate about the virtues or otherwise of a recently opened bandstand: 126 comments were generated.

However TS17's most commented on story was about the untimely death of a young father in an industrial accident, with 159 comments. What is notable about these contributions is the large number from people who personally knew the deceased or his family.

Forums

The "Forum" section of *Gazettelive!* is an "open" discussion area where discussion and threads are not geographically defined and it does not reflect the micro-local news environment of the community microsites. It offers the opportunity for discussion around "communities of interest" rather than geographical communities. However, this is another rich data source of user-generated content and it was decided to examine the "micro-localness" of threads to see if the issues being discussed reflected local community concerns. The "Forum" is sub-divided into a number of sections: of these "Have your say" was the most popular with 68.7% of all postings, followed by "Boro" (the colloquial name of the local professional football team, Middlesbrough FC) with 29.6%; none of the other sub-areas achieved more than 1% of all postings. The subjects of threads were not necessarily stories carried by either *Gazettelive!* or the microsites, often being "spontaneous" issues of importance, off the published "news agenda".

The data available on the Forums allowed the number of postings, the number of views of a story and the number of replies to be collated, with the number of "views" being the volume of "passive" readers of postings and the number of replies being the number of "active" participants in the "thread". At the time of the analysis the Forums had a total of 87,957 individual postings, with 57,935 in the "Have your say" section. It was decided to concentrate on looking for evidence of localness in this section in particular and to look at the most popular (top ten) threads.

Each thread was evaluated for its geographical "localness". For example, the most frequently viewed thread (with 9715 views) was about the suspension of a local councillor. It was clear that whilst not all the participants in the thread were from the immediate area that the councillor represented, many did have a personal (local) relationship with her. Of the remaining threads the majority (70% in total) were discussing issues of local civic interest. Thus, there appears to be an interesting "confluence" of discussions forming around "communities of interests" and discussions involving "spatial communities". Once again "localness" appears to be a strong driver for participation.

Correlations

A moderately weak positive correlation (Pearson's $r = 0.27$) exists between the population of a microsite area and the overall amount of hyperlocal news published. This rises to a moderately strong positive correlation ($r = 0.65$) if TS1/TS2 is removed. There is little difference in the correlation of *Gazette* only news ($r = 0.22$) and locally produced news ($r = 0.31$), although the effect of TS1/TS2 is more strongly felt here as it rises to a moderately strong positive correlation ($r = 0.66$) for *Gazette* only news when this area is removed. This supports the observation that news is being unevenly published across the microsites, with a dominant centre in down-town Middlesbrough with more weakly served peripheries.

A moderately strong positive correlation ($r = 0.46$-0.49) exists between the population of an area and the level of interaction with *Gazettelive!* microsites (Page Impressions and Unique Users). This remains about the same ($r = 0.50$-0.51) if TS1/TS2 is taken out. This suggests that there is an underlying propensity for people in the microsite areas to engage with the microsites.

There is also a moderately positive correlation ($r = 0.47$) between the population of an area and the volume of comments posted. However, a very strong positive correlation exists between the total of comments and the number of site visits to the microsites ($r = 0.76$ for Unique Users and $r = 0.80$ for Page Impressions). There appears to be a very strong relationship between traffic and the volume of comments.

Data for the amount of news published in each microsite was normalised by dividing the population of a postcode area by the amount of news published to examine the underlying structure of the relationship of population to activity. When this normalised data was related to site visits there was an almost neutral correlation ($r = 0.08$ for Unique Users and $r = 0.03$ for Page Impressions). In terms of the relationship between the normalised data and news published, the picture is different. For all the news published there was a positive correlation of 0.71, although this dropped to 0.31 if TS1/TS2 was excluded from analysis. For *Gazette*-only news a correlation of 0.75 was found (dropping to 0.28 without TS1/TS2) and 0.27 for "local" only news. Once again the effect of the down-town centre area is very significant in the microsite news environment.

Conclusion

This analysis of the *Gazettelive!* microsites shows that whilst the internet has no physical geographical boundaries, it appears that a local news organisation still has cultural constraints in news production and distribution. The overemphasis of news on the down-town, Central Middlesbrough area shows the on-going influence of institutional news providers and their structural support of a centre/periphery model and the existing institutional status quo, mirroring the national news structure and the existing spatial relationship of the metropolis and the regions.

It also shows that where the centre/periphery model begins to break down is where readers become active participants in the news production process. Engagement with stories via comments appears to lead to a significant increase of visitor activity for certain microsites. Whilst this appears to be related to a very narrow range of news values, the relative importance of the civic stories perhaps shows that, within this discursive space, elements of a local public sphere now exist. Certainly when this is related to the analysis of the Forums, strong evidence can be seen of the importance people attach to "local" civic matters and their propensity to exploit the online space provided. Whilst not every visitor to a microsite will necessarily be an active commentator, they will (if they follow a story thread) be exposed to a range of non-institutional voices from their local community debating and arguing issues related to their local lived experience. In the case of this study local "places" are experiencing "new" media influences which are both unique to them (and their community), perhaps running counter to the existing global, national, regional and metropolitan media ecology. Not only that, but these new media forces are at least to some extent "participatory" and represent a new form of engagement with a previously "separate" and "exclusive" hegemonic culture. This is perhaps an example of some sort of reconciliation of the dichotomy described by Dahlgren (2004, 33-55) between the market and the public sphere.

It could be argued that one of the unintended consequences of the regional news industry's hyperlocal strategy is a loosening of the traditional model of ownership and control and perhaps the development of a new form of Community Media. Unlike traditional Community Media which are set up in conflict with mainstream media (Howley 2010, 1-12), this permutation is to some degree allowing the exploitation of the corporate space provided for individual and community ends. And as Howley (2010, 4) says of Community Media:

> By providing local populations with access to the means of communication, community media offer a modest, but vitally important corrective to the unprecedented concentration of media ownership which undermines local cultural expression, privatises the channels of public

communication, and otherwise threatens the prospects for democratic self-government.

Howley (2010, 5) also makes the useful point that community media are often instrumental in "protecting cultural identify" and "challenge the ghettoisation of marginalised groups". He also outlines the relationship of place, identity and culture within this context, arguing that "the relationship between place and identity is intimately tied to cultural forms, practices and traditions".

Whist some critics may argue that this "appropriation" of corporate media by citizens is too little and too modest to allow "real" change to occur, it is nevertheless an opportunity for individuals to participate in a previously excluded experience which may well give them new and significant insights into their own and society's relationship with the media. This experience may then go some way to achieve the emancipatory effect foreseen by Enzensberger (1974) in his exploration of participatory media technology.

Acknowledgements

The author would like to acknowledge the support and help of Professor Paul Van Schaik, Julie Martin, Paul Steel (and Dlab, the Centre for Design in the Digital Economy, Teesside University) and Carol Dell-Price.

Works Cited

ABC. 2010. http://www.abc.org.uk/Data/ProductPage.aspx?tid=20932. Accessed 30 June 2010.

Allan, S. 2006. *Online News*. Maidenhead: Open University Press.

Anderson, B. 1991. *Imagined Communities: Reflections on the Origin and Spread of Nationalism*. London: Verso.

Bruns, A. 2005. *Gatewatching: Collaborative Online News Production*. New York: Peter Lang.

Buchanan, C. 2009. Sense of Place in the Daily Newspaper. *Aether*, 4: 62-84.

Castells, Manuel. 2004. *The Power of Identity*. Oxford: Blackwell.

Couldry, N. and A. McCarthy, eds. 2004. *Mediaspace: Place, Scale and Culture in a Media Age*. London: Routledge.

Dahlgren, P. 2004. The Public Sphere and the Net; Structure, Space and Communication. In *Mediated Politics*, edited by W. Bennet and R. Entman. 33-55. Cambridge: Cambridge University Press.

Deuze, M. 2009. The Future of Citizen Journalism. In *Citizen Journalism: Global Perspectives (Global Crises and the Media)*, edited by S. Allan and E. Thorsen. 255-264. Oxford: Peter Lang Publishing.

Deuze, M., A. Bruns and C. Neuberger. 2007. Preparing for an age of Particpatory News. *Journalism Practice*, 1(3): 322-338.

Enzensberger, H. M. 1974. *The Consciousness Industry*. New York: The Seabury Press.

Fraser, N. 1992, Rethinking the Public Sphere: A Contribution to the Critique of Actually Existing Democracy. In *Habermas and the Public Sphere*, edited by C. Calhoun. 109-142. Cambridge, MA: MIT Press.

Fritzsche, P. 1996. *Reading Berlin*. Cambridge, Mass: Harvard University Press.

Jones, J. 2010. Changing Aunties: A Case Study in Managing and Regulating User-Generated News Content at the BBC. In *Web Journalism: A New Form of Citizenship*, edited by S. Tunney and G. Monaghan. 150-167. Eastbourne: Sussex Academic Press.

Massey, D. 1994. *Space, Place and Gender*. Cambridge: Polity Press.

Morley, D. 2000. *Home Territories: Media, Mobility and Identity*. London: Routledge.

Morley, D. and K. Robins. 2001. *British Cultural Studies: Geography, Nationality, and Identity*. Oxford: Oxford University Press.

Newspaper Society. 2010. http://www.newspapersoc.org.uk/Default.aspx?page =1228. Accessed 20 April 2010.

Preston, P. 2008. According to local sources, this could be a real winner. *The Observer*, March 30. http://www.guardian.co.uk/media/2008/mar/30/pressandpublishing. television. Accessed 12 June 2008.

Russell, D. 2004. *Looking North: Northern England and the National Imagination*. Manchester: Manchester University press.

Thurman, N. and A. Hermida. 2010. Gotcha: How newsroom norms are shaping participatory journalism online. In *Web Journalism: A New Form of Citizenship*, edited by S. Tunney and G. Monaghan. 46-62. Eastbourne: Sussex Academic Press.

REGIONAL TELEVISION NEWS AND ITS AUDIENCES

SAMANTHA LAY AND DEIRDRE O'NEILL

A recent report from the House of Commons Select Committee for Culture, Media and Sport noted that 90% of adults consume some form of local media, with local newspapers and ITV regional news the most popular forms (2010). Yet Hewlett argues that local news in the UK is "always the poor relation" (2009, 41) and this is not just the case economically, but in terms of scholarship too. Comparatively little attention has been paid to local and regional news in the UK, but gradually this is beginning to be addressed (for examples see Aldridge 2003 and 2007; Franklin 2006; O'Neill and O'Connor 2008). Audiences for regional news are shrinking. According to a recent BBC Trust Annual Review (2008), audience figures for BBC regional news programming "continued to show signs of a very slow, steady decline" (2008, 24). This is attributed to changes in the needs and wants of the audience and in their lifestyles and the ways in which they access news (ibid).

If the BBC's regional news audiences have seen a slow and steady decline, then the audiences for ITV's programmes have nose-dived. This led to ITV proposing that the network's seventeen regional news services be reduced to just nine, with 430 estimated job losses and a demand for public funding. In March 2009 the BBC and ITV agreed in principle to share regional news facilities to save costs and salvage a regional ITV service. More recently, ITV plc told the Select Committee for Culture, Media and Sport (2010) that production of regional news is no longer viable, and that it will not be able to deliver these services to England and Wales beyond 2011. The Committee's report (2010) on regional news goes on to say:

> Ofcom and the Government have proposed that the solution to the withdrawal of ITV plc as a regional news provider is to launch independently funded news consortia that would supply the content for the regional news slots on Channel 3 and are described by Ofcom as 'the most suitable way to secure sustainable plurality in regional television news.' IFNC

participation would be open, but not be limited to, existing television news providers, newspaper groups or other newsgathering agencies who would bid for the Channel 3 news contract in each region. The winner would be decided by an independent panel.

With the ITV service in decline, and with limited research time, we decided to focus on the BBC's provision, with its continued commitment to public service broadcasting funded by the relatively stable licence fee. We aimed to examine the BBC's regional provision in more detail, comparing the services in the north and in the south, and examining what viewers and producers had to say about these services. The BBC service also has a larger audience share—a 49% weekly audience reach for *BBC Look North*, or 29% share for the 6.30 pm programme, compared with ITV rival *Calendar*'s share of 22%, in the year to March 2008; and a 44% weekly reach for *BBC South East Today* for the same period, and a 32% share for the 6.30 programme compared with ITV rival *Meridian*'s 24% share, according to the BBC Trust's Annual Review (2008).

We conducted content analyses of the regional television news programmes *BBC Look North* and *BBC South East Today* in order to understand their form and composition. We then sought to understand the value of regional television news programmes for their audiences. We devised a questionnaire for members of the viewing public and distributed it to respondents in both regions. We then sought to understand the circumstances and contexts of production, and conducted qualitative interviews with news producers at *Look North* and *South East Today*; we also interviewed individuals who had worked or were working in other regions.

Content analyses of regional television news

Content analyses of evening bulletins of two BBC regional news programmes—*BBC Look North* and *BBC South East Today*—were conducted at three points. Programmes were recorded and analysed for one working week per month over a three month period (between December 2008 and February 2009). For each news bulletin, we noted the categories and frequencies of items by primary topics and duration of coverage. Primary topics for us are *what the story was mainly about*. Table 1 shows the top five topics in each region during the period sampled.

Table 1 Five most featured topics by number of items for BBC Look North and BBC South East Today from December 2008 to February 2009 (expressed as percentage of total number of topics featured)

BBC Look North	BBC South East Today
1. Sport 20%	1. Crime 21%
2. Business and Economy 12.1%	2. Arts, Heritage and Leisure 11%
3. Arts, Heritage and Leisure 9.4%	3. Business 8.5%
4. Snow 8.8%	4. NHS/Health 8.5%
4. Jobs and Strikes 8.8%	4. Extraordinary People 8.5%

What topics do audiences want and expect to see?

Asking the audience: questionnaires

One hundred questionnaires were distributed in both regions. The questionnaire sought to obtain the views from a cross section of respondents in both rural and urban communities and respondents were selected from different socio-economic and ethnic backgrounds, and at different life-stages. Schools, colleges, community, faith-based, and special interest groups proved very useful to this end.

In total seventy-four questionnaires were returned and analysed. The questionnaires were designed to gather broad data on the place and value of regional television news to its audiences. Four areas will be discussed, drawing on the findings: the daily news diet, topics of importance, improving regional news and the importance of being local.

The daily news diet

The findings suggest that the respondents sought a varied news diet. Some 93 per cent accessed two or more platforms for news. The majority are daily viewers of television news (81 per cent), and 69 per cent watch television news between one and three times per day. The respondents accessed news across a range of platforms. Most popular among these was television, with some 85 per cent tuning in. Online sources were accessed by 37 per cent of respondents.

The primary source for news across the sample was television. Online sources were primary sources for news for 16 per cent of respondents, closely followed by 15 per cent for whom national radio was the primary source for news. Regional and local radio and newspapers were not as popular with respondents, with the former being accessed by six per cent as a primary source for news, and the latter some four per cent, respectively.

Topics of importance

The respondents were asked to select five topics of importance, and to then rank these in order of most important to least important (1 being most important). These topics were drawn from the findings of the content analyses of programmes. These can be seen in Table 2 below.

Table 2 Topics considered by viewing public to be most important for regional news to cover

Yorkshire	South East
1. Crime 43%	1. Crime 33%
2. Politics & Local Gov. 18%	2. Ordinary People 17%
3. Business & Local Economy 12.5%	2. NHS and Social Care 17%
4. Employment 7%	3. Business & Local Economy 8%
5. Sport 5%	3. Politics and Local Gov. 8%

In both regions, crime stories are considered to be the most important stories for regional television news to cover, by some considerable margin, as the percentages show. There are other similarities. In both regions, business and the local economy, and politics and local government are considered to be important topics for regional news to cover. But there are differences, too. In Yorkshire, people regard employment and sport as important, whereas in the South East the NHS and social care, and stories focusing on ordinary local people doing extraordinary things are key concerns.

Improving regional news

Many respondents recorded ways in which their regional television news could be improved. Most of these suggestions were topic-based, ranging from environmental concerns and vandalism to youth issues and the activities of local charities. Respondents talked about the standards of journalism and the quality of the presentation, not just in terms of BBC regional news, but also taking into account ITV regional news. Most respondents watched regional television news at some point in their week. Not one respondent suggested that it should not exist.

The importance of being local

Respondents in Yorkshire and the South East suggested that they would like regional television news to be more local. One respondent suggested that regional television news might extend to covering different localities every evening. In the South East, a respondent wrote about the dilution of the local at ITV. He wrote, 'Since the *Meridian* news has changed, it covers Devon, Cornwall, etc. I preferred it when it was more local, the south east area' (male company director, 58, Hastings).

Asking the Audience: Focus Groups

The focus groups were conducted in May and June 2009, initially in four locations in West Yorkshire and two locations in the South East. Local book groups and church groups and groups of neighbours were contacted for participants. Each group contained between five and seven participants. The researchers aimed to include participants from a range of demographic groupings (in terms of gender, occupation, life-stage and ethnic background). Respondents included people who worked in IT, nursing, teaching, painting and decorating, farming, retail, charities, town planning or were students or were retired. Ages ranged from 20 to 80. What follows are some of the key themes and discourses that emerged during the focus groups.

Appointment viewing or on in the background?

Our focus groups reflected the view that the days of regional television news being "appointment viewing" (Aldridge 2007, 14) are over. Of the six focus groups, only one group watched regional news regularly. This group was largely comprised of senior citizens who not only watched *BBC Look North* fairly regularly, they also watched the ITV rival show, *Calendar*.

Many of the participants in our groups in the North and the South watched regional news programmes *if they were on*. This phrase cropped up time and again and in most instances was further clarified by stating that they might *catch* the regional television news because it follows on after the national news. Clearly, national news is still appointment viewing in most cases, even if regional television news is not. All participants agreed unanimously that regional news should be provided, even if it was not necessarily for them. Those who did watch, both north and south, cited the weather and transport information as the services they most needed. There was also a sense of real pride in their regions and those in the South East would like to see their regional programme show viewers' photographs of their region; interestingly, this is a regular feature of *BBC Look North*.

Politics, current affairs and interactivity

Many of our focus groups were interested in politics and current affairs. There seemed to be a tangible desire to hold those in power to account with more direct public participation. Four of the focus groups articulated the view that there should be new formats and new ways of engaging audiences in topical issues of the day. Ideas included more public involvement and debates at local level. One female in the ethnic minority group (postgraduate student, 24) said: "I'd rather see ordinary people ask the questions than journalists because I think they'd ask the questions I want answering".

This chimes with earlier research by Hargreaves and Thomas (cited in Aldridge 2007, 15) which found that a lack of relevant local knowledge and debate "could help explain why so many people find so much [in] politics meaningless or difficult to engage with because they are not able to judge its effects in their own communities". As our focus groups show, this is *not* the same as saying there is no appetite for this type of political information, context and debate.

Local programmes for local people

Other studies of regional news and their audiences have found that audiences most often complain that regional news is not local enough (see Sancho 2002; Hargreaves and Thomas 2002; Aldridge 2007). This finding is supported by our study. For instance, in Yorkshire many felt it was "ridiculous" that the news was trying to cover such a large area. And in the South East a female nurse in her fifties stated: "I want to hear about what's happening in Kent. Some of the news [on regional TV] comes from too far afield, so I find myself tuning out". Those in more rural locations disliked the concentration on big population centres and felt that the peripheries were too often ignored.

Identity and attachment to a locality

An interesting point about regional news, attachment and identity arose in some focus groups. In Brighton one woman (graduate, 22) who had moved there from Sheffield said she missed *Look North*, despite thinking it was a bit trivial. One (male, former chef, 22) said the regional news that people grew up with was a bit like the "family pet".

In a group consisting of ethnic minority members, two women (sisters of 24 and 28) had moved to Leeds from Leicester just a few years before and still watched ITV Central news, which they could get on satellite, to find out what was going on at "home". Another woman in this group (41) watched news from Tyne Tees where she was originally from.

This raises two points: regional news can help foster regional identity and, with the aid of new technologies, can provide a vital link for people whose regional identity goes beyond their immediate location. And of course this can work the other way: those new to an area can find regional programmes useful for orientating and embedding themselves in that area.

Interviews with regional news producers

Interviews were conducted with journalists, editors and producers of regional news in Yorkshire and the South East. In addition, interviews were conducted with journalists and producers who had worked in regional news in the past. Some asked to remain anonymous. In total, six interviews have been conducted. First we asked the interviewees about the main challenges of producing regional television news. Secondly, we discussed with them the findings of our content analyses, notably the findings on crime coverage. Thirdly, we asked them to assess the impact of new technologies on their working lives. And finally, we asked them to consider the future of regional television news. Interestingly, all the BBC journalists interviewed were keen to see competition, and thus plurality, in the provision of regional TV news.

Main challenges

Four clear challenges emerged from these discussions: region size and diversity, the BBC network, attracting and maintaining audiences, and finding original stories. The issue of original stories is of course universal to journalists everywhere and is not included here due to space restrictions.

Region

All interviewees cited *region* as one of the main challenges for them in regional television news production. The greatest challenge for *BBC South East* correspondent Ian Palmer was "First and foremost, region. If a big story breaks our big problem is how to cover it differently [from national news]"

Tim Smith, editor of *BBC Look North*, pointed to the size and diversity of Yorkshire as a major challenge. *Look North*'s region is diverse and includes cities that are very different from each other as well as large rural areas. However, he did emphasise that he was "lucky because Yorkshire has a strong regional identity, it's a strong brand".

A regional news producer in the North of England suggested that the size of BBC regions was a major challenge because "they are huge, I mean, vast"

For this interviewee the difficulties thus created for producers were about where to send resources like film crews, and how to respond to developing or breaking news if one's resources were committed at the other end of the county (ibid). He was also perturbed by the same local/regional tension as articulated by Smith and said public criticism that regional news programmes were not local enough "drives me nuts" (ibid).

Network

The BBC network presented challenges but also opportunities for regional television newsmakers. For Palmer, if a national story broke out of the regions, he was required to give his contacts and pictures to the BBC network. He admitted that sometimes this would leave the journalist with a problem of what to cover in the regional news programme, particularly since national news precedes regional news on BBC1. And while this was "sometimes a bit galling" on a personal/professional level, he essentially agreed with Tim Smith from *Look North* who said, "The [national] network will take them, but they are serving the public, one BBC". And Smith contends that prioritising the national network is one way of ensuring that the regions are well represented on national news, as a response to one of the most common criticisms from the public. And this can benefit regional news correspondents by giving them national network exposure.

Audience

For the regional television news producer in the North of England "the over-arching challenge is the audience ... maintaining our audience" (ibid). For Tim Smith the audience is the key to everything they do at *Look North*. But serving an area of five million potential viewers scattered across rural and urban communities does present major challenges in balancing coverage of towns and cities as well as rural communities.

The 6.30 pm regional news programmes on BBC are, according to Smith, the most watched news programmes on British television. Drawing on BARB figures, Smith contends that it regularly beats both the 6 pm and 10 pm national news bulletins in terms of audience figures (ibid). It could be argued that the popularity of the 6.30 pm regional news programmes on BBC1 is largely a consequence of the time the programme is on and that it follows the national 6 pm news. As Smith argues, "this is the time people are coming home from work, cooking dinner, or washing up" (ibid) and TV producers need to grab their attention. As a consequence, they deploy a number of strategies, including sending out studio-based presenters to cover stories so as to give the audience "the shock of seeing they have legs and move around" (ibid).

Topics of importance: covering crime

Crime emerged as the topic of most importance for the people we surveyed in Yorkshire and the South East. The topic most covered on *BBC South East* during the period sampled was crime. And yet Ian Palmer was surprised by these findings as it was "not a crime-heavy region". However, the concern with crime may have been an effect of the sample surveyed.

BBC Look North did not have crime as a most featured topic during the period sampled. This is interesting as Tim Smith has made a conscious editorial decision to ensure crime stories are not overly featured. Smith was very aware of the effects news has on a community's view of itself. He is not keen on crime stories as they can distort the real threat of crime; this "scares the audience" (ibid).

Technologies: video journalism and the re-configuring of regional journalism

In terms of producing regional news, the training and deployment of video journalists has been the key development. It is an issue that divides professionals: supporters of video journalism see it as a more intimate, less intrusive way of interviewing, as a method that gives the video journalist greater autonomy and flexibility. Critics regard its onward march across the regions as potentially dangerous for individual journalists working alone, and as a way of cutting costs by cutting staff, but the majority of those interviewed for this research took a pragmatic approach. For example, the regional television news producer in the north of England could see benefits and pitfalls: "In certain situations, like fly on the wall, it is better". He enjoyed the challenge of being able to shoot and edit his own packages and added, "It's great—I can cut my own headlines". While video journalism was a "revolutionary change", it was "obviously driven by economics".

Tim Smith argued for "a mixed economy" of traditional crew plus reporter and video journalists. While video journalism might not be appropriate, and perhaps even dangerous, in some situations, there was a place for it in regional television news. Smith suggested that there were three reasons why video journalism is a useful addition to the newsgathering process: it was a "good tool for original stories, a good way of building relationships with people—particularly health stories—and there are more cameras on the road" (ibid).

The future of regional television news

Given the current economic climate and much uncertainty over the future of ITV and the proposed top-slicing of the licence fee to finance non-BBC news, some of the interviewees were quite pessimistic about the future of regional news. For Ian Palmer, the continuing decline of regional and local newspapers and the funding proposals for ITV meant that regional television news was "at a crossroads" and the future looked "dire in its current form" (ibid), but he felt the network will ensure some BBC news presence in the South East region (and beyond). For Palmer, times have changed, and he could "inevitably" see a time when BBC regional television news did not exist, but added "The only caveat I would add to that would be that the network can't be everywhere" (ibid). But for Palmer, any future for regional television news ultimately … depends on the audience" (ibid).

The regional television news producer in the north of England felt he would still be delivering regional television news at an appointed hour for the foreseeable future. In the long term, he felt that there would be more video journalism, and over time interactivity would evolve and develop so that "technology takes us closer to people" (ibid).

Tim Smith also saw a future for regional television news because "MPs in the regions value regional news, it is popular" (ibid). For Smith the future is technologically driven and he predicted "more platforms, more 24/7, more interactivity" (ibid). But it may also depend on the future of ITV. As Smith argued, "If they do 15 minute programmes, we might have to; for example, controllers want audiences" (ibid). So it seems that the future of news might depend not only on what broadcasters can afford, but also on their interpretation of what audiences want.

Conclusion

Examining and cross-referencing between four separate data forms has been illuminating. Key issues have emerged and these are now discussed.

The "problem" of the local

Previous studies have found that audiences often feel regional news is not local enough. This finding is supported in our research. People want to see their communities and places they know. News producers are sensitive to this need—even if it does "drive [them] nuts". This is a problem for regional television news producers, and one that the BBC had plans to address.

Finding (and keeping) the audience

The issue of finding and keeping the audience is crucial. Changing the time of broadcasts or un-coupling them from the national news programmes could prove fatal. The interviewees all seemed to view audiences as their number one priority, although they were also aware that it was becoming harder to reach them. Through a range of strategies the BBC regional news teams attempt to grab audiences and to get BBC news out to the many publics the Corporation serves, faster than the competition. But are audiences aware of these efforts, and if they are, is the strategy working?

Our research suggests that the majority of people watch regional television news at some point in their week, if not regularly. Even if they do not, they know it is there. For some it is a connection to their home towns, for others it is like an old family pet that you find you miss only when it is gone. Only a few disliked regional television news, and no-one suggested that it should not be in the television schedules. But our research contradicts Aldridge's assertion (2007) that regional television news is appointment viewing.

Giving the people what they want

We found that in terms of what topics people believed to be most important and most interesting for regional television news to cover, *BBC Look North* and *BBC South East* are quite successful. However, it could be argued that *South East Today* reflected the needs of our participants more effectively.

As shown, audiences in the South East thought crime was the most important topic, and crime was the most featured topic on *BBC South East Today* during the period sampled.

For *Look North*'s audience crime stories were also thought to be the most important topic. Tim Smith, though, has taken an editorial decision to avoid too many crime stories for wider social and ethical reasons. Clearly, for Smith the BBC has a role in shaping the public consciousness and this outweighs the urge to only give the public what they apparently want.

Political tech-onomics and the future of regional television news

Political tech-onomics is a useful way for us to convey what is at stake in the changing media environment in the UK. Media power is shifting. All newsmakers interviewed felt that technological developments would play a major role in shaping news delivery in the regions in the future. Technologies were seen as liberating by some, but even the most ardent supporter of video journalism felt that it was a trend driven by economics.

The BBC has little choice but to attempt to be at the forefront of technological innovation in the UK. To survive in the new media landscape, the BBC must innovate and at the same time continue to justify the licence fee to parliament, and to its publics, national and regional.

The situation became even tougher for the BBC with the publication of Lord Carter's report *Digital Britain* in 2009 which proposed the top-slicing of the BBC licence fee to help ailing ITV in the regions, though this was not later included in Digital Economy Act. However, former Labour culture secretary, Ben Bradshaw, remained committed to top-slicing (Plunkett 2010). In the run-up to the May 2010 general election, all the main political parties gave a commitment to an independent and strong BBC. But the Conservative (at the time shadow) culture secretary Jeremy Hunt categorically stated that he would abolish the BBC Trust (Hewlett 2010) and that the BBC would be made more accountable. Hewlett (2010) feared that this, combined with unrestricted National Audit Office access overseen by the Parliamentary Accounts Committee, "would be an open and certainly irresistible invitation to politicians to interfere with the BBC" and could undermine the BBC's independence. Other media commentators were concerned that the BBC was "caving in to a Tory media policy dictated by Rupert Murdoch" (Freedland 2010), who sees the BBC as a major competitor with an unfair market advantage.

At the time of writing, a Conservative-Liberal Democrat coalition has just been formed and it remains to be seen if these concerns translate into reality and what the impact will be on BBC regional news and regional TV news in general. As Tom Thomson and Sue Wallace point out in their chapters, it would seem that as far as the IFNCs are concerned, they have died at birth with the change of government. It is now therefore extremely important to redirect the focus of the debate towards audiences rather than allow those with vested political or commercial interests to attack the BBC's funding, or to undermine further its capacity to provide a sound, independent regional service. A public debate about the future of regional television news is needed and it is hoped that our research might contribute to such a debate.

Works Cited

Aldridge, M. 2003. The Ties that Divide: Regional Press Campaigns, Communities and Populism. *Media, Culture and Society*, 25 (4): 491-509.

—. 2007. *Understanding the Local Media*. Maidenhead: Open University Press.

BBC Trust. 2008, *Annual Review*.
http://www.bbc.co.uk/england/ace/bbcannual_review_2008.pdf.
Accessed 8 July 2009.

Carter, Lord S. 2009. *Digital Britain*.
http://www.culture.gov.uk/what_we_do/broadcasting/5631.aspx/.
Accessed 8 July 2009.

Convergence Think Tank. 2007. *Seminars and Workshops Reports*.
http://www.culture.gov.uk/Convergence/seminars.html. Accessed 8 July 2009.

Franklin, B. 2006. *Local Journalism and Local Media: Making the Local News*. London: Routledge.

Freedland, J. 2010. The BBC is caving in to a Tory media policy dictated by Rupert Murdoch. *The Guardian Comment is Free* (2 March 2010) http://www.guardian.co.uk/commentisfree/2010/mar/02/rupert-murdoch-tory-media-policy. Accessed 12 May 2010.

Hargreaves, I. and T. James. 2002. *New News, Old News*. London: Broadcasting Standards Commission/Independent Television Commission.
http://www.ofcom.org.uk/static/archive/bsc/pdfs/research/news .pdf

Hewlett, S. 2010. Manifesto support for the BBC... for now *The Guardian* (19 April 2010).
http://www.guardian.co.uk/media/organgrinder/2010/apr/19/steve-hewlett-manifestos-bbc. Accessed 12 May 2010.

——. 2009. For TV News, the News Isn't All Bad. *British Journalism Review*, 20: 41-46. http://bjr.sagepub.com. Accessed 8 July 2009.

House of Commons Select Committee for Culture, Media and Sport Report. 2010. *The Future for Local and Regional Media* (6 April 2010). http://www.publications.parliament.uk/pa/cm200910/cmselect/cmcum eds/43/4306.htm. Accessed 11 May 2010.

Lay, S. 2008. Unpublished conference paper: Journalism and Media Convergence: a report on the work of the government's Convergence Think Tank, *Association of Journalism Educators Annual Conference*, University of Sheffield, 12 September 2008.

O'Neill, D. and C. O'Connor. 2008. The Passive Journalist: How sources dominate the local news. *Journalism Practice*, 2(3): 487-500.

Plunkett, J. 2010. Ben Bradshaw confirms BBC top-slicing plan. *The Guardian* (29 April 2010) http://www.guardian.co.uk/media/regional-tv-news-consortiums. Accessed 11 May 2010.

Sancho, J. 2002. Pride of Place: What Viewers Want from Regional Television, July 2002, London: Broadcasting Standards Commission/ Independent Television Commission. http://www.ofcom.org.uk/static/archive/bsc/pdfs/research/pride.pdf

PAYING THE PRICE?
SUSTAINING REGIONAL TELEVISION
NEWS IN BRITAIN

SUE WALLACE

Terrestrial television news has been a powerful focus for developing regional identities in the UK. Independent Television (ITV) was established in 1955 as an alternative broadcaster to the British Broadcasting Corporation (BBC). ITV was intended as a counter to what the Beveridge Report in 1951 had criticised as the London-centred metropolitan structure of the BBC; consequently it was organised as a federation of fifteen regional enterprises, each producing programming (Johnson and Turnock 2005). As well as maintaining individual regional output, at certain times these enterprises also contributed to the pool of network programmes for shared national schedules. The BBC's English Regions later similarly devolved news programming. ITV was to have an alternative system of funding through advertising (rather than the licence fee which pays for the BBC). However anxieties over the implications of commercial provision led it to be regulated with the Public Service Broadcasting (PSB) requirement to inform and educate as well as entertain, and that included producing regional news. Tensions, then, have been inherent in the structure of ITV since its inception, in particular between commercial demands and PSB commitments, as well as between national and regional imperatives, creating what has been characterised by Harrison in relation to the national news service Independent Television News (ITN) as having a "hybrid nature" (2005, 120). Those tensions have increasingly brought pressures to bear on the management of ITV until by the end of the first decade of the 21st century its PSB commitments are being erased.

The earlier years of ITV broadcasting alongside the BBC have been labelled an era of "comfortable duopoly" (Peacock 1986). However technological developments in production and delivery systems such as digitisation, cable and satellite broadcasting have enabled the launch of a multitude of television channels in the UK. These have been encouraged politically through the spread of neo-liberalism—with the belief that market forces provide more choice for consumers—and an emphasis on light-touch regulation. The Broadcasting Act of 1990 brought far-reaching consequences for the ITV companies by instituting an auction of existing franchises, one consequence of which was increasing financial pressure on successful companies which had offered high bids. Later regulatory change made possible the formation of larger alliances in the ITV network, culminating in the amalgamation of all but a handful into one company in 2004, ITV plc.[1] However this proved not to be a sufficient bulwark against increased competition and financial pressures. With fragmentation of audiences, and advertising migrating to the internet, ITV began sounding warnings that it would need to retreat from the provision of regional news.

The UK broadcasting and telecoms regulator, Ofcom, had become increasingly sympathetic to such warnings. In 2007 it reported that whilst no form of television news in the UK currently paid its way, the economics were particularly stark for news programming for the nations of Wales, Scotland and Northern Ireland, and the English regions, and constituted the biggest challenge for commercial broadcasters:

> The combined cost to ITV of producing simultaneous programmes for 15 regions (or 27 including sub-regions) is very high compared to the low advertising revenue—although, of course, the provision of specific PSB programmes was never expected to be profitable in isolation (Ofcom 2007, 8).[2]

The conclusion was that it would require regulatory intervention if the long-term presence of regional news was to be assured on commercial PSB. Two months later, ITV's executive chairman Michael Grade announced plans to reduce its regional newsrooms from seventeen to nine by merging some services, with the aim of saving between £35-40million a year, subject to regulatory approval (BBC 2007b).

The theme was taken up in September 2008 by Ofcom when it published its second consultation into the future of Public Service Broadcasting. That document suggested that £145-235 million of replacement

---

[1] With the merger of Carlton and Granada, ITV plc owned the eleven regional licences in England and Wales. The two Scottish licences, Scottish Television and Grampian, are owned by the STV Group, while UTV owns the service in Northern Ireland, and Channel Television the licence in the Channel Islands. For a fuller description of the development of ITV, see Johnson and Turnock (2005).

[2] At the BBC the nations and regions services, mostly concentrated on news and current affairs programming, took a sizeable proportion of the licence fee—£884 million in 2006-7 (BBC 2009a)—more than a quarter of the corporation's total income for 2007 of £3,211.8 million (BBC 2007a).

public funding would be needed by 2012 if public service programmes on Channels 4 and 5, as well as ITV regional programming, were to continue. However as far as ITV specifically was concerned, Ofcom proposed to accept the organisation's plans to reduce its news output in England and the Scottish Borders from seventeen separate main programmes to nine. Although Ofcom's consultation lasted into December, on 30 September ITV announced plans to cut more than 400 jobs in regional news services (ITN 2008). The following month, Michael Grade noted: "Ofcom clearly recognises that the model is—in its own word—'broken'. In the very near future the various channel 3 [ITV] licences will start to go negative, the cost of their obligations exceeding their benefits" (Broadcastnow 2008). Stating that ITV would prefer to remain a licensed PSB, if justified economically, he suggested that news in the nations and regions might be provided longer term by a publicly funded third party, but broadcast on ITV to maximise the potential audience. This would be, according to one commentator "a win-win for the commercial network—it loses a loss-making commitment, keeps the fiction alive of regional roots, and doesn't have to make further redundancies" (Brown 2008).

ITV regional news

In January 2009 Ofcom published its Second Public Service Broadcasting Review, and announced approval of the changes previously proposed to restructure ITV's regional news in England and the Scottish Borders (Ofcom 2009a). By then the changes were well underway in ITV newsrooms. One case study, ITV West, serves to illustrate events. Cost cutting had been acknowledged as the motivation for ITV's reorganisation of its news services. The aim was to remove some £40 million from the regional news budget. The process of reducing its number of newsrooms down to nine necessitated the amalgamation of some regions, including ITV West with ITV West Country, which brought protests from local viewers.[3] The latter's Plymouth base was to be closed and the ITV West newsroom in Bristol would serve the new, larger region, which would stretch some 200 miles from Land's End to Tewkesbury, and include a population estimated at nearly 3.7 million (ukfree.tv 2009).

More than eighty jobs were to go, and the main evening news programme would consist of fifteen minute opt-outs for the West and the West Country sub-regions, with fifteen minutes of shared programming.

---

[3] A similar amalgamation of Border TV with Tyne Tees also aroused widespread opposition. Under the proposals only the London, Granada and Wales regional services would be unaffected.

Here and elsewhere, the conundrum of how to gather news across a much larger region with fewer staff was addressed by ITV through a greater emphasis on videojournalism: what were initially called "camera-enabled reporters" would operate as solo newsgatherers, while specialist camera operators were retained to film with correspondents.

Videojournalism has been examined by the present author in a longitudinal study of terrestrial regional television. The study began in the late 1990s with a focus on the then relatively novel practice of one journalist working as both reporter and camera operator combined. Journalists, managers and technical staff were interviewed at two BBC regional centres (Bristol in 1997 and Southampton in 1999), and in 1998 at HTV West, the ITV regional company based in Bristol. Ten years later there was a return to Bristol, to what was then ITV West, followed up by more interviews in 2009, plus follow-up interviews that same year at BBC West and BBC South.

Data collected at the three sites in the 1990s highlighted tensions over definitions of quality television journalism, compounded by anxieties about potential job losses if one person could do the work previously undertaken by at least two (reporter and camera operator). Journalists and their fellow newsworkers, concerned to maintain their professional status, often feared that videojournalism would bring a reduction in the quality of output, particularly under management pressure to increase productivity (Wallace 2009). Nevertheless some videojournalists and managers also held the view that solo newsgathering could improve quality in innovative ways, such as enabling more intimate access to interviewees.

Research was resumed in the ITV West newsroom in November 2008, when staff were in the process of applying for the new jobs in the reorganisation yet to receive final sanction from Ofcom. Those interviewed were often not only hyper-sensitive to the critical condition of the parent company, but also reflective about the nature of commercial regional television news. There were once again concerns about the impact of videojournalism on quality of output, with interviewees who were more experienced in solo newsgathering expressing more doubts about what it could achieve, than those who were novices. Nevertheless, many considered that videojournalism offered advantages in flexibility of response, one reporter with their own camera generally being able to reach a news event more quickly than a team. One journalist pointed out the importance of making the new strategy work to cover the whole region:

> I think [regional news] is the lifeblood. I know so many people in the community who know about things because they've seen it on the telly. And we act as a voice for the people, and if we aren't going to reach those

people, aren't going to listen to them, we're nothing ... If you don't give a community a voice then the community won't thrive (Interview November 2008).

The importance of viewers being able to receive television news from and about their own region was stressed by another ITV West journalist:

The world has become so big that people can focus on global issues to such an extent that what happens in your own backyard almost becomes secondary. I think it's important people know and understand their communities and I think we play an important role in doing that in local decision-making processes and that side to life really (Interview November 2008).

BBC regional news

Historically, ITV had enjoyed better viewing figures for its regional news than the BBC. In 1994 viewing figures for ITV regional news programmes averaged at about 45% of the audience share, compared to the BBC regional news figure of around 34% (Ofcom 2004). The balance had changed, however, particularly after the ITV regional evening news programmes had been rescheduled from 6.30 pm on weekdays to 6 pm, where they were in competition with the BBC national news programme. Hargreaves and Thomas reported in 2002 that ITV early evening news was "now less favourably scheduled in terms of inheritance and competition ... The familiar pattern now is for the BBC regional television news programme to have overtaken its ITV equivalent" (2002, 32). In 2006 BBC nations and regions news programmes at 6.30 pm were reported to have attracted audiences shares of 28-29%, peaking at around 6 million across the UK, compared to ITV regional news audience share averaging at 19-20%, peaking at 4 million (Ofcom 2007).While ITV languished, the BBC strengthened its regional services, following some criticism from the BBC Trust. In 2008 it began a major reorganisation of its nations and regions, including promotion for the controllers of Scotland, Wales and Northern Ireland. The 3,000 staff working in the English regions were also reorganised, to become part of the BBC's News division, the stated aim being to strengthen journalism rather than to make savings (Douglas 2008).

As the clouds gathered over the funding of commercial PSB, including regional news, the BBC looked to be in an increasingly superior position. The idea of top-slicing the licence fee to support a body that would use the money to subsidise public service content from broadcasters other than the

BBC had already been floated. A specific proposal was to use the £130 million per annum said to be surplus in the BBC's funding after the switchover to digital television by 2012 (Ofcom 2008). Top-slicing proposals had been countered by the chairman of the BBC Trust who argued that the success of the existing PSB system had been in its enabling of competition for audiences rather than for funding. Sir Michael Lyons (2008) called for a fully informed debate before far-reaching decisions were made. Later that year the BBC publicised proposals for an alternative strategy—partnerships with commercial public service broadcasters (Sweeney 2008).

In March 2009 a Memorandum of Understanding was signed by the BBC and ITV which it was claimed could over the next decade help deliver cost savings for regional news on ITV. The stated aim was to secure a long term future for regional news on the main commercial channel through moves such as co-location of regional news centres and bureaux, sharing technical facilities and resources, and pooling some of the video pictures gathered by BBC crews for use in ITV regions. An ITV estimate was that it could save them £1.5m in 2011, rising to around £7m p.a. by 2016 (BBC 2009b). But that aroused concern about the erosion of competition between the two news providers, with a corresponding impact on plurality of services. Such concerns were shared by both ITV and BBC news staff interviewed for the videojournalism research project in 2009: they were anxious to protect editorial independence. Nor did the scheme offer a complete answer to the problems of the commercial broadcaster: according to ITV, the current cost of its regional news services in England, the Borders and Wales was around £55m p.a. excluding news provision for the Channel 3 licences in Scotland, Ulster and the Channel Islands (BBC 2009b).

Videojournalism in action

Further evidence of the need for support for ITV came in March 2009, when in the midst of recession the company announced its annual results for 2008. The headline news was a loss of £2.7 billion after a major write-down of assets. When that was discounted, the company made a profit, but that had dropped by 41% on 2007,[4] and the prediction was that advertising revenue would fall 17% in the first three months of 2009. Six hundred jobs were to be cut in ITV general programming businesses in London and

---

[4] ITV's Group Finance Director, Ian Griffiths, later confirmed pre-tax profit for 2008 as £112 million (ITV plc 2010).

Leeds: a studio in Leeds was to close and popular series such as *Heartbeat* were cancelled (BBC News 2009).

To maintain its regional news service, ITV was now putting its videojournalism model into practice. In Bristol, the merger of ITV West and ITV West Country had resulted in the combined news staff being reduced by approximately half, while evening news programme output was 75% of that previously broadcast. The latter half of the programme was pan-regional, but the first half consisted of two versions, one for the West and the other for the West Country, as had been mooted earlier. There were nine reporters (or videojournalists) to cover the area with about half a dozen correspondents who worked with camera crew. Most district offices had been axed. The consequence was that the reporters were travelling great distances to film and then to find a suitable place to feed their material back to the newsroom from their laptops via the internet. Staff were said to be so stretched that an original plan to use the solo newsgatherers simply to record elements such as interviews, to be amalgamated later into a report, had to be abandoned. Videojournalists were producing complete packages themselves. Nevertheless interviews with ITV news staff in Bristol in July 2009 found a common conviction that ITV output was superior to that produced by videojournalists working for the BBC. Explanations offered included that ITV videojournalists were provided with better training and equipment. There was a sense of pride in what was being accomplished, and a conviction that the price of survival was not a reduction in quality.

However, in another region, a BBC journalist considered that the changes at ITV meant that its regional news programmes had lost their previously very good local focus, as exemplified by composite pieces being made to be used across a number of areas to extract maximum benefit from newsgathering efforts:

> The story's been shot with the idea of its being used by two or three different regions. So they're re-versioning. You see a version going out in London, you see a version going out in Southampton and a version goes out ... for the South East. They're still doing some good newsgathering, there's still an element of competition there, but it's certainly not at the level it was (Interview 2009).

One conviction which continued to be shared by both BBC and ITV journalists was that there should be plurality of news provision. Competition was seen to be essential to maintain a proper public service. One journalist at ITV West put it like this:

I just passionately believe that there should be two providers of regional news because I think quality will drop if there isn't. Quality will drop on the BBC side ... they'll be in a position where they don't need to invest so much and I think that'll be a real shame ... I think healthy competition improves the quality of service, i.e. the level of regional news that's provided and the standard to which it's provided (Interview 2009)

The Way Ahead?

Plurality of provision of regional news is important to audiences as well, according to research conducted by Ofcom (2009b). Both the regulator and the then Labour government were concerned to devise competition for BBC services. Partnership agreements to share resources and facilities with the BBC were not considered to provide enough benefit to overcome ITV's financial difficulties in funding regional news. The proposed solution now was independently funded news consortia (IFNCs), which might include newspaper groups, radio as well as television companies and other interested parties, to provide on Channel 3 (ITV) "a choice of high quality news alongside the BBC" (Ofcom 2009a). The Digital Economy Bill granted Ofcom the power to establish IFNCs from 2013. Before that, three IFNCs were to be chosen for pilot schemes in regional news provision in Wales, Scotland and the Tyne Tees/Borders region in England. The aim, according to the chair of the selection panel, Richard Hooper, was for:

quality news reporting with a mix of local, regional and national (in the case of Wales and Scotland) audiences firmly in mind; genuine innovation, not just business as usual; strong multiplatform applications working together across the web, local newspapers, local radio and television where appropriate, utilising each different medium's special characteristics; and finally, a revenue generation model that aspires to longer term sustainability (Department for Culture, Media and Sport 2009).

The plan was for the pilot schemes to jointly receive £47 million in government funding over two years. The three preferred bidders for the pilot schemes were announced on 25th March 2010 (Department for Culture, Media and Sport 2010a), each consortium a mix of newspaper and television interests. However, circumstances were changing. The opposition Conservative party was against the government's plans for IFNCs, and a general election was looming. Under pressure to hasten the progress of legislation before the election on May 6th, the Digital Economy Act (2010), which received Royal Assent on 8th April, had been amended to remove the clause enabling the national rollout of IFNCs. It also proved impossible to sign the contracts for the pilot schemes before the election.

Meanwhile, fortunes were improving for ITV. As Adam Crozier took up the role of chief executive in April 2010, alongside the new chairman, Archie Norman (a former Conservative MP), the company was enjoying increased advertising revenues, with the promise of a further surge expected during the World Cup later in the year. As to the future of its regional news, the company said it would take no further steps until the outcome of the general election was known, and the position on future funding clear (Sweeney 2010). Its journalists in Bristol had hoped that their efforts in the new regional news model would earn backing for commercial regional news to be retained, as one journalist explained:

> I think what we've done is we've demonstrated that [with] such a small team and with a lot of hard work we're still able to put out a quality service, and I think that only ... stands us in good stead both with ITV to show the powers that be that what we're doing is achievable, and frankly amazing [given] the numbers we have, and that also hopefully demonstrates to any future management structure within the regions that this is how it can be done, this is how it should be done and hopefully secure a future for regional news (Interview 2009).

The Conservatives had stated that they would scrap IFNCs if elected. The Liberal Democrats, on the other hand, were supporters of the idea. Following the coming to power in May 2010 of David Cameron as prime minister, leading a coalition Conservative-Liberal Democrat government, deregulation was on the agenda. As Tom Thomson reports in his earlier chapter, the new culture secretary, Conservative Jeremy Hunt, called off the plans for IFNCs; the minister said they risked "turning a whole generation of media companies into subsidy junkies" (Department for Culture, Media and Sport 2010b). The BBC's surplus funds for digital switchover would instead be used for the spread of superfast broadband. Mr Hunt also announced relaxation of local cross-media ownership rules. The new emphasis in media provision was on local television stations (in contrast to the existing larger regional concerns) which might be owned by local newspapers, along with local radio stations. Where might funds come from? The culture secretary cited potential sources of revenue as advertising, sponsorship, product placement, sub-letting of spare capacity, or carriage fees. However observers, such as the media research firm Enders Analysis (2010) were sceptical that local media companies would prove to be commercially viable.

At the end of September, the culture secretary received an interim report from a small steering group he had set up to assess the necessary financial conditions to sustain local television in the UK. The group's leader, Nicholas Shott (2010), the Head of UK Investment Banking at Lazard, advised that local television was unlikely to be commercially viable in sparsely populated areas, and while more success was possible in urban areas, it would still be challenging to gain funding mainly through advertising. Suggestions for additional revenue included selling locally generated news content to other broadcasters, and the collective sponsorship of the local TV sector by a large corporate concern. The group also emphasised the need for a minimum quality threshold for news content. Its final report was expected at the end of the year.

Jeremy Hunt acknowledged the interim report in a speech to the Royal Television Society detailing the government's commitment to decentralise broadcasting and increase localisation (Department for Culture, Media and Sport 2010c). He outlined a vision for a network of local, cross-platform multimedia TV services which would broadcast for as little as an hour a day, be free to affiliate with each other to bring down costs, and be able to offer nationwide deals to advertisers. He remained convinced that Britain could sustain local TV, as did other European countries and the United States, and stressed that such a network would be important to hold local government to account. To this end, Mr Hunt confirmed that the government would shortly remove all remaining local cross-media ownership rules.

One answer to the difficulties of financing local TV came in the funding settlement for the BBC agreed by the government in advance of the Comprehensive Spending Review in October 2010. As well as freezing the licence fee at £145.50 for the following six years, it imposed new obligations on the Corporation, such as assuming responsibility for funding the World Service, BBC Monitoring and S4C from the licence fee, as well as providing up to £150 million per annum for improved broadband services. Also among the new obligations was the requirement for the BBC to play an active role in supporting new local television services through a partnership fund providing capital costs of up to a total of £25 million in 2013/14 for up to 20 local TV services. Additionally, the BBC was committed to paying after that date up to £5 million annually for local TV content to be broadcast on BBC services (Department for Culture, Media and Sport 2010d).

This top-slicing of the licence fee has been embarked on despite criticisms that such a practice would damage the BBC's independence, criticisms which had come from both the BBC Trust chairman and its director general when it was proposed under the Labour government the previous year (Holmwood 2009). At that time Jeremy Hunt, then shadow culture secretary, had argued that any surplus money in BBC funding should first be considered for returning to licence fee payers. Now, as secretary of state, he wrote that the government would respect the BBC's editorial and operational independence, and that "the requirement on the BBC to take on important new funding obligations and efficiencies provides the value to licence fee payers necessary in the current economic climate" (Department for Culture, Media and Sport 2010d, 1). The new licence fee settlement obliged the BBC to make savings of £560million, requiring 4% of efficiency savings in each year covered. However at a time when the government was imposing £81 billion of cuts from public sector budgets by 2015, the director general Mark Thompson said "Anyone who believed that the BBC could have achieved a licence fee settlement at any stage, and under any government, which would have called for lower efficiency targets than other public bodies were facing, is deluding themselves". He argued that the settlement would strengthen BBC independence (Thompson 2010). On the specific question of local television, the BBC commented that its next task would be to develop detailed plans for the future. While some observers considered that the surprise deal on the licence fee had prevented the Corporation from facing more savage financial measures, others viewed the addition of extra obligations and the breakneck speed with which they were imposed/negotiated over a 48 hour period as involving the sacrifice of the long-established principles that the Corporation operates at arm's length from government and that changes in its remit should involve extended discussion and public debate.

For ITV, one question still remaining was whether to continue as a public service broadcaster in the light of the culture secretary's earlier proposals, including the stated intention to redefine PSB to emphasise local content. In terms of government intervention, Jeremy Hunt had indicated the principal means would be legislation to clarify which public service broadcasters should be listed on the front page of electronic programme guides and their online equivalents. The clear intention seemed to be to give competitive advantage to those broadcasters which invested in content of social or cultural benefit.

Against this backdrop, with a better than expected financial performance in annual results for ITV plc (2010), the company advertised a 12-month news traineeship scheme at the end of October. It was said to be aimed at those with a real interest in regional news, and offer the chance for those selected to publish their stories "on our flagship 6 pm regional news programmes or our online services" (Media Guardian 2010). Nevertheless, with the focus in public policy fixed firmly on local television, the question remained as to what price was worth paying to sustain regional television news.

Works Cited

BBC. 2007a. BBC Annual Report and Accounts 2006/7. The BBC executive's review and assessment.
http://www.bbc.co.uk/annualreport/2007/pdfs/bbcexec_eng.pdf.
Accessed 19 May 2010.
—. 2007b. ITV to merge regional newsrooms. Wednesday 12 September 2007.
http://news.bbc.co.uk/1/hi/business/6991206.stm. Accessed 14 August 2008.
—. 2009a. Annual Report and Accounts 2008/9
http://www.bbc.co.uk/annualreport/exec/financial/index.shtml.
Accessed 19 May 2010.
—. 2009b. ITV and BBC work together on future of news in the English regions and Wales.
www.bbc.co.uk/pressoffice/pressreleases/stories/2009/03_march/12/news.shtml. Accessed 15 December 2009.
BBC News. 2009. Troubled ITV cuts jobs and costs.
http://news.bbc.co.uk/1/hi/business/7922770.stm. Accessed 5 March 2009.
BBC News Politics. 2010. Culture Secretary Jeremy Hunt backs local TV stations. 28 September 2010.
http://www.bbc.co.uk/news/uk-politics-11424065 Accessed 30/9/10.
Broadcasting Act. 1990.
www.opsi.gov.uk/acts/act1990/Ukpga_19900042_en_2. htm. Accessed 28 April 2010.
Broadcastnow. 2008. Speech: Michael Grade, 8 October 2008.
www.broadcastnow.co.uk/news/2008/10/speech_michael_grade_8_october_08. Accessed 5 March 2009.
Brown, Maggie. 2008. ITV regional news cuts, ITN and the gathering thunderstorm.
www.guardian.co.uk/media/organgrinder/2008/oct/09/itv.ofcom.
Accessed 18 November 2008.
Department for Culture, Media and Sport. 2009. Successful bidders announced for next stage of IFNC pilot process

http://www.culture.gov.uk/reference_library/media_releases/6569.aspx
Accessed 23 February 2009.
—. 2010a. Preferred bidders announced for Independently Funded News
Consortia pilots.
http://www.culture.gov.uk/reference_library/media_releases/6782.aspx
Accessed 28 April 2010.
—. 2010b. Media keynote speech 8 June 2010.
http://www.culture.gov.uk/news/ministers_speeches/7132.aspx.
Accessed 6 July 2010.
—. 2010c. A vision of local media 28 September 2010.
http://www.culture.gov.uk/news/news_stories/7450.aspx
Accessed 5/10/10.
Digital Economy Act 2010.
http://www.opsi.gov.uk/acts/acts2010/pdf/ukpga_20100024_en.pdf.
Accessed 28 April 2010.
Douglas, Torin. 2008. What price for regional TV news? 9 October 2008.
http://news.bbc.co.uk/1/hi/entertainment/7660067.stm.
Accessed 2 March 2010.
Enders Analysis. 2010. IFNCs and the politics of local news provision
[2010-22]
http://www.endersanalysis.com/publications.aspx?q=ITV. Accessed 6
July 2010.
Hargreaves, I. and J. Thomas. 2002. *New News, Old News*. London: ITC.
Harrison, J. 2005. From Newsreels To a Theatre Of News: The Growth
and Development of Independent Television News. In *ITV Cultures:
Independent Television over Fifty Years*, edited by A. Johnson and R.
Turnock. 120-139. Maidenhead: Open University Press.
Holmwood, Leigh. 2009. BBC's Mark Thompson attacks plans to 'top-
slice' licence fee.
http://www.guardian.co.uk/media/2009/jun/24/bbc-mark-thompson-
top-slice Accessed 26/10/10.
ITN. 2008. ITV announces job cuts. 30 September 2008.
http://itn.co.uk/news/73eca4bc9c080b484dd98f4aefc64d6f.html.
Accessed 2 October 2008.
ITVplc 2010 Full Year Results 2009
http://www.thomson-webcast.net/uk/dispatching/?event_id=
ae0aac0c72d7a7acf5fb454e6724ccfc&portal_id=6d1c366a24337d6f27
2a69b7d311649a. Accessed 6 July 2010.
Johnson, A. and R. Turnock. 2005. From Start-Up to Consolidation:
Institutions, Regions and Regulation over the History of ITV. In *ITV*

Cultures: Independent Television over Fifty Years, edited by A. Johnson and R. Turnock. 15-35. Maidenhead: Open University Press.

Lyons, M. 2008. Putting audiences at the heart of the PSB Review. 17 January 2008.
www.bbc.co.uk/bbctrust/news/speeches/ml_ippr.html. Accessed 24/4/08.

Ofcom. 2004. Ofcom Review of Public Service Broadcasting. Cultural Identity.
http://www.ofcom.org.uk/consult/condocs/psb/psb/volume2/social_val ues/cultural_identity/culture_communities. Accessed 19 May 2010.

—. 2004b. Review of Public Service Television Broadcast. Phase 3 – Competition for Quality.
http://www.ofcom.org.uk/consult/condocs/psb3/ Accessed 28 April 2010.

—. 2007. New News, Future News.
http://www.ofcom.org.uk/research/tv/reports/newnews/newnews.pdf. Accessed 18 February 2010.

—. 2008. Ofcom publishes its second consultation into the future of Public Service Broadcasting.
http://www.ofcom.org.uk/media/news/2008/09/psb_england.pdf. Accessed 18 February 2010.

—. 2009a. Ofcom's Second Public Service Broadcasting Review: Putting Viewers First.
http://www.ofcom.org.uk/consult/condocs/psb2_phase2/statement/. Accessed 23 February 2010.

—. 2009b. Sustainable independent and impartial news in the Nations, locally and in the regions Ofcom's public response to the DCMS. http://www. ofcom.org.uk/consult/ofcomresponses/dcms.pdf. Accessed 28 April 2010.

Peacock, A. 1986. *Report of the Committee on Financing the BBC*. London: HMSO.

Shott, N. 2010. Local Television in the UK.
http://www.Culture.gov.uk/images/publications/NShott_interimFindin gsLocalTV_240910.pdf. Accessed 5/10/10.

Sweeney, Mark. 2008. BBC plans tie-in with ITV for regional newsgathering. 11 December 2008.
www.guardian.co.uk/media/2008/dec/11/bbc-itv-partnerships-psb-regional-news. Accessed 17 December 2008.

—. 2010. Digital economy bill: government forced to drop key clauses. 7 April 2010.

http://www.guardian.co.uk/technology/2010/apr/07/digital-economy-bill. Accessed 28 April 2010.

Thompson, M. 2010. Opinion. "It strengthens BBC independence." Media Guardian. Monday 25/10/10 p. 1-2.

Ukfree.tv 2009. ITV Regional News to change. www.ukfree.tv/fullstory.php?storyid=1107051293. Accessed 19 February 2009.

Wallace, S. 2009. Watchdog or witness? The emerging forms and practices of videojournalism. *Journalism. Theory, Practice and Criticism.*10 (5): 684-701.

KNOWING ME, KNOWING YOU: WHITE BUT NOT QUITE RIGHT

MARC STANTON

Television news in western democracies is expected to be fair, honest and balanced. It is expected to be non-partisan and to allow viewers to decide their own personal interpretation of events. It has always been the claim of the major British broadcasters ever since the days of John Reith, the BBC's first Director General, that they comply with these standards. However that claim has been called into doubt, with the work of Greg Philo and his colleagues of the Glasgow Media Group—*Bad News* (1975) and *More Bad News* (1980), to be followed by *Really Bad News* (1982)—being among the best-known critiques of news values.

The first people to undertake serious study of news about Non-Developed Countries (NDCs) were Norwegian scholars Johan Galtung and Mari Ruge with their (1965) investigation into print news stories on international topics. Although ethnocentric bias had always been suspected—indeed Lord Beaverbrook famously once stated that, in news terms, "one dead Englishman is worth ten dead Frenchman, a hundred Egyptians and a thousand dead Chinese"—there had been no real empirical evidence to support these suspicions prior to Galtung and Ruge's work, and their examination of the presentation of NDCs, from the perspective of "peace" and the creation of a more equitable society, did much to fill this gap. The impact of their research is still being felt forty-five years later. Subsequent contributions to the field include Oliver Boyd-Barret's seminal work *The International News Agencies* (1980) which takes its place alongside analyses of different societies' representations of NDCs such as Said's *Orientalism* (1978), *The World, the Text and the Critics* (1983) and Bhabha's *The Location of Culture* (1994).

This chapter investigates whether claims to objectivity stand up to scrutiny with particular reference to reports about developing nations. A study was conducted from 10 October 2006 to 13 March 2007, during which period, in order to avoid the problem of "feast or famine", a month's worth of programmes was recorded: all the programmes on the

Monday of the first week were recorded, all the programmes on the Tuesday of the next week, and so on. This meant that if there was a sudden rush of stories about one particular event, it would not skew the entire study. The content—1262 stories—was analyzed in different ways.

Table One: stories categorised using Galtung and Ruge's classifications

	G3	G4	G5	G6	G7	G8	G9	G10	G11	G12
Classification applies	1257	1104	14	1054	360	948	243	286	470	683
Classification does not apply	5	158	1248	208	902	314	1019	976	792	579

First of all, the famous Galtung and Ruge news relevancy criteria were employed (the first two criteria—Frequency and Threshold—have not been included in Table One as it was felt that *all* stories complied with these). The categories and classifications are outlined and exemplified from the broadcasts studied below; stories do of course usually meet more than one of the criteria.

G1: Frequency. An item whose timeframe corresponds closely with that of the news cycle (for example a murder) is much more likely to be included than one which exceeds it (for example the building of a dam): in other words the news cycle tends to favour events over processes. At the same time, the infrequency or strangeness of an event makes it more likely to be included in the news. Repetition of such coverage, however, may have the unfortunate consequence of suggesting that the country where such bizarre events are happening is incapable of dealing with them successfully.

G2: Threshold. The "bigger" the event—for example the more gruesome the murder—the more likely it is to cross the "news threshold". In the case of non-developed countries this can have as a consequence the generation of predominantly negative news since it often only the most shocking events which cross the threshold.

G3: Unambiguity. The less ambiguous the event the more likely its inclusion. One thousand two hundred and fifty-seven of the stories transmitted were considered to be unambiguous, and the clarity of the situation judged obvious. The five stories that were deemed ambiguous were "and finally" stories which were intended to be humorous and capable of more than one interpretation.

G4: Meaningfulness. 1104 of the stories were considered to be in this category. The closer the cultural proximity of the event to the viewer, the more likely would be its inclusion—and comprehension by the audience. 158 stories were not considered to have cultural proximity to the viewer. The danger for developing nations is that these stories could be used to reinforce any previous opinion the viewer might hold (Viola 2003) that the world is a strange place and that the viewer's culture and civilisation are superior.

G5: Consonance. The greater the possibility of the event being predictable, the greater its possible inclusion. Only fourteen of the stories were considered to have consonance. This seems to be a relatively low number, given that much of the news, such as State visits and occasions, is pre-selected. The larger number of 1248 stories were about unexpected events which were of a newsworthy nature. Further research that needs to be done on this category would involve examining the amount of time spent on pre-planned events and occasions.

G6: Unexpectedness. The more unexpected and sudden the event the greater its chance of inclusion. For example Bernays (cited in Whitacker et al. 2004) claimed that *"News* is an outstanding deviation from the norm, *something* that doesn't ordinarily happen". This category is the concomitant of the previous category and the data supports the original presumption, with 1054 stories being unexpected and 208 stories being expected, such as the state opening of Parliament or the Queen's Birthday. The suicide bombing, the plane or train crash, it is these events which create the interest in news that continues to be its reason for existence. In other cultures and societies where autocratic governments maintain a greater level of control over the media, there is not the same interest in news or, where there is, it is rarely believed and is considered to be propaganda. It is the ability of news organisations to cover unexpected events despite the constraints imposed by various gatekeepers that provides their lifeblood.

G7: Continuity. The continuation of an event increases the possibility of its on-going coverage, since the reporters are already on the ground and so the cost of coverage is reduced considerably. Also, less background explanation is needed, leading to greater comprehension by the viewer. The value of exclusivity can also be increased as there is a wish to deny new entrants. Most news stories however are not continuations due to the progressive nature of the news. Because of the cost considerations though, they are popular amongst editors. In the sample studied 360 stories were considered to be continuations with 902 stories being completely new and not broadcast before.

G8: Composition. Serendipity may enable a story to be covered simply because it "fits" into the "balance" of the news programme. A lighter piece of news may be needed to balance several "heavy" news items. 948 stories were considered to fit this category.

G9: Reference to Elite Nations. Out of all the broadcasts, 243 stories were solely about elite nations, the other 1019 were about national issues or other news areas. Although the number of stories about elite nations is numerically smaller than the number about other subjects, the influence elite nations have on the news is disproportionate. Elite nations are considered to be more newsworthy than developing nations. It may be argued that more newsworthy events happen in developed nations. However, to accurately report the events of the world needs a balanced presentation. Failure to give proper weight to non-developed nations may create the impression in the mind of the viewer that whenever something happens in non developed nations, it will always be bad (Glasgow Media Group 1975, 1980, 1982). This also has the result that when news events do occur in these countries, they have to be more violent or spectacular than the last event to be considered as newsworthy. The impression then develops that, for example, wars are always happening in Africa, that Asia is an area of natural disasters, South America is an arena of revolution and the Middle East is completely corrupt.

G10: Reference to Elite People. In a similar way to the previous category, 286 stories were about elite people, with 976 not involving elite people. Again, although the numerical difference shows the majority of stories were about non-elite people, the number concentrating on elite people is disproportionate. This is because elite people are considered to be more important and newsworthy than non-elite people (Glasgow Media Group 1975, 1980, 1982, Kocher 1986, Spurr 1993). Clearly this does not mean that news events only happen to them. Murders and rapes rarely occur to elite people and so news stories which cover these types of events will have to include non-elite people.

G11: Reference to People. Reference to actual people rather then just events will increase the value of a story. 470 Stories involved actual people whereas 792 did not actually involve people but were about events.

G12: Negative References. Negative references can often avoid the requirement of corroboration: the manifest fact that something has exploded or a person has died often seems to require no explanation or examination, as a result of which such stores are easier to "prove" than positive ones. This is evidenced by the fact that 683 stories were considered to be negative, with a minority of stories, 579, being positive. Natural disasters and events are clearly negative. They require no corroboration, they have happened and the evidence is available for all to see. Of the stories that were examined, those from developing nations were almost invariably negative, with only two stories being positive. Even neutral stories were found to have a "sting in the tail". A story about a success in a non-developed country such as the building of a dam or increase in literacy rates will often include a caveat that there had been a cost in the form of, for example, environmental damage, with the concomitant effect on human life or need for support from the West.

Table Two: transmitted stories by broadcaster

	Total	Percent	Cumulative Percent
BBC	728	57.7	57.7
ITN	534	42.3	100.0
Total	1262	100.0	

Table Two categorises the stories by broadcaster. The total number transmitted during the study period was 1262. Of these, 728 were transmitted by the BBC and 534 by ITN. This is as expected, since the BBC news programmes are longer due to the absence of adverts

Table Three: transmitted stories by bulletin

	Number of stories	Percent	Cumulative Percent
BBC 1pm	259	20.5	20.5
BBC 6pm	258	20.4	40.9
BBC 10pm	213	16.9	57.8
ITN 1pm	165	13.1	70.9
ITN 6:30pm	182	14.4	85.3
ITN 10pm	185	14.7	100
Total	1262	100.0	

Table Three provides a breakdown of the number of stories carried by each news programme differentiated by time of transmission. For the reason given above the number of stories carried by the BBC is greater than the number carried by ITN. There is however an interesting difference in the numbers of stories covered by each station at different times of the day. The number covered by the BBC is relatively similar for the lunchtime and early evening news. The number of stories though reduces from 258 to 213 for the late evening news. This means that the stories which are covered are dealt with in more depth than in previous transmissions. ITN's coverage is completely different. The number of stories increases throughout the day. This means that the actual time devoted to each item is reduced. An alternative interpretation would be that as the number of stories available to the news editors increases through the day, there are more stories which need presenting. This interpretation would suggest that the BBC is exercising a greater gate-keeping function in their selection of news stories for transmission.

Table Four—Breakdown of stories by geographical Category

	Number of stories	Percent	Valid Percent	Cumulative Percent
National	845	66.9	66.9	66.9
National/International	10	0.8	0.8	67.7
National/Non-Developed	70	5.6	5.6	73.3
National/Developed	8	0.6	0.6	73.9
International	101	8.0	8.0	81.9
Developed	58	4.6	4.6	86.5
Non-Developed	170	13.5	13.5	100.0
Total	1262	100.0	100.0	

This table breaks down the stories from both broadcasters into geographical categories.

- National: stories about Britain.
- National/International: stories about Britain and its relationship with international events.
- National/Non-Developed: stories about Britain that included an element about non-developed countries, such as illegal immigration.
- National/Developed: stories about Britain and other developed countries such as those in the EU or other developed countries.
- International: stories about international events.
- Developed: stories about developed countries.
- Non-Developed: stories about non-developed countries.

The table clearly demonstrates that the largest number of stories broadcast by the terrestrial broadcasters in the UK were national stories. Out of a total of 1262, 845 of them were stories about Britain itself. It would be expected from any broadcaster that the highest number of stories would be about their own country. What is surprising is that the next largest number of stories is about non-developed countries. 170 stories during the period of study were about non-developed areas of the world. This would tend to support the arguments of both the BBC and ITN that they pay a lot of attention to these areas and are not ignoring them. The next largest category of stories is those concerning international events: 101, 8% of the total coverage. This reflects well against the figure of 70 or 5.6% of all stories that were about National/Non-Developed topics, in other words stories which originated in Britain but contained an element about non-developed areas of the world: these could include, for example, illegal asylum seekers. Developed areas of the world, such as the EU countries and other such countries, accounted for only 58 or 4.6% of the stories, with the National/International category accounting for 10 stories during the entire period. The only score lower than this was for those stories about National/Developed areas of the world which had a total of 8.

Table Five—Categories of stories about non-developed countries

	Number of stories	Percent of total	NDC Percent	Cumulative Percent
Neutral	12	1.0	5.6	5.6
War-Positive	15	1.2	7.0	12.6
Non-war-Positive	2	0.2	0.9	13.6
War-Negative	80	6.3	37.4	50.9
Non-War-Negative	105	8.3	48.1	100.0
Total	214	17.0	100.0	
Other	1048	83.0		
Total	1262	100.0		

This table presents the breakdown of stories which are concerned with NDCs in any context. Of the total of 1262 carried by the broadcasters, 214 were in the categories Non-Developed or National/Non-Developed. There is however an obvious conflict between the figures in Tables 4 and 5: the number of stories in Table 4 of Non-Developed (170) and the number for National/Non-Developed (70) gives a total of 240. This compares to the total in Table 5 of 214 stories. The reason for this anomaly is that 26 of the stories were about National events which had a component of news about a non-developed country but were neither positive nor negative and so were removed from the analysis. They were factual stories that required no balance or presentation of both sides. Examples included the inflation rate in China rising to 3% or 2347 illegal immigrants being removed from the UK.

Of the Non-Developed stories, each was identified as to whether it fell into the categories of neutral, war-positive, non-war-positive, war-negative or non-war-negative.

Of 1262 items, it can be seen that 214, 17% of all stories broadcast, had an element about NDCs. Only twelve of the stories, 1%, were considered by the author to be neutral. This was less than the fifteen (1.2%) which were about war situations and presented in a positive manner. Considering that at the time of the study Britain was involved in wars in two different locations, Iraq and Afghanistan, it seems a remarkably small number of positive stories. A far higher number of stories, 80 (6.3%), were negative stories about a war situation. This would tend to indicate that the broadcasters were either reflecting the opinions of the audience, in that both conflicts were unpopular, or that both conflicts were going badly.

The remaining stories were about non-war situations. The highest number of stories in the entire study were about non-war countries, but were presented in a negative light. This negative portrayal might well suggest to the viewer that these countries were always having problems and had to be constantly watched (Davidson 1994). The expectation arising from this is that the next time there is a story about the country in question, it is likely to be even worse than the previous story (Hulme 1986). The lowest number of stories in any single category during the entire study period was two (0.2%). From a total of 1262 stories, only 0.2% were about non-developed countries portrayed in a positive manner. This may well fit with a general Western view that good things very rarely happen in these countries and when they do, they are not really very important, more likely to be of a humorous nature; indeed they will possibly be used as part of an "and finally" section of the programme (Spurr 1993).

Table Six: Comparison of stories with National interest

	Neutral	War-Positive	Non-War-Positive	War-Negative	Non-War-Negative	Total
Nat/Non-Dev						
BBC		6		10	14	30
ITN		5		8	6	19
Total		11		18	20	49
Non-Dev						
BBC	7	3	0	38	52	100
ITN	5	1	2	24	33	65
Total	12	4	2	62	85	165

This table presents further breakdown and analysis of story content by identifying those stories which have elements within them which are related to a national story as well as being about NDCs. These stories are then categorised by broadcast station and whether they are presented as neutral, war-positive, non-war-positive, or non-war-negative. Of the neutral stories, neither broadcaster carried any stories about Britain that had a component of interest about non-developed countries. The only neutral stories which were shown were about NDCs themselves. Of the two broadcasters, the BBC carried slightly more stories than ITN but such a small difference is statistically insignificant. For war-positive stories, the number of stories carried by both broadcasters was virtually identical. This could be because both stations carried stories about the same events, positive stories about the armed conflict involving British forces. This might suggest that broadcasters are keen to be seen to support "our boys" (Kocher 1986). The figures for coverage of war-positive stories about NDCs on their own were roughly half as many. The BBC, however, carried three times as many positive war stories about these countries as did ITN.

When examining the figures for NDCs which were not at war, the previous figure of only two stories now appears even more striking, in that the stories were carried by both ITN and the BBC. Neither the BBC nor ITN carried any positive stories about non-developed countries which were not at war during the entire period of study. This combined with the much larger number of stories about NDCs which were at war (38 BBC, 24 ITN) would support the argument that the BBC continues to present these countries in a negative light (Young 1995). It would also bear out

Said's (1978) theory of the "Other"—foreigners are not the same as "us" and cannot and never could be. This would also be substantiated by the increased number of stories that the BBC carried (38) as opposed to the number of stories that ITN carried (24). Both stations would have had access to the same stories, but the BBC gatekeepers considered and presented far more of these stories to the public than ITN. ITN's gatekeepers either did not wish to present these stories or considered that they were not newsworthy. This situation is continued in the negative presentation of NDCs which were not at war. There was a considerable increase in the overall number of these stories (52 BBC, 33 ITN). The fact that the BBC news broadcasts are longer than the ITN ones cannot account completely for the difference in numbers. This difference is also evident when the figures for the National/Non-Developed non-war category are examined. There are fourteen stories from the BBC and only six from ITN. This would raise questions about whether the BBC and ITN have different approaches to news values and that is analysed in the following graph.

Figure One: Categorisation of stories utilising Galtung and Ruge's criteria

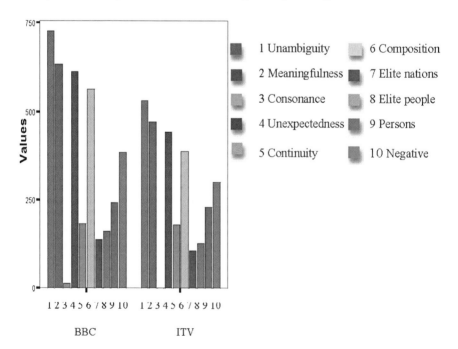

This graph uses the Galtung and Ruge categories. The table clearly shows that, although the number of stories per category varies, the actual proportions of the categories appear to be identical. This suggests that both stations adhere to similar news values.

Table Seven: Numerical analysis utilising Galtung and Ruge's categories

	Nat	Nat/Int	Nat Non-Dev	Nat/Dev	Int	Dev	Non-Dev
Unambiguity	842	10	70	8	101	57	169
Meaningfulness	836	10	61	8	100	57	32
Consonance	10		1				3
Unexpectedness	689	8	65	8	79	50	155
Continuity	258	2	15	1	15	3	66
Composition	664	6	46		76	42	114
Elite Nations	127	5	35		34	25	17
Elite People	201		15		49	12	9
Persons	333	4	27	8	28	19	51
Negativity	414	2	53	6	37	18	153

Table Seven presents in numerical form the news categories of Galtung and Ruge with regard to National, National/International, National/Non-Developed countries, National/Developed countries, International, and Developed countries. Examination of the National/Non-Developed and Non-Developed sections of this table shows that the great majority of the stories had a component of unexpectedness. The impression could thus be given that only events such as natural calamities and disasters occur in these countries, events that were beyond the control of the people in these countries; or perhaps too that when citizens of such countries come to Britain, they could be component factors in situations which would require solutions to be found by British society (Ashcroft 1995). Very few of these stories, 10% in the case of non-developed countries and 20% in the case of National/Non-Developed countries, involved elite people, but the vast majority of all stories were presented in a negative manner.

Table Eight: Breakdown of stories about National/Non-Developed Countries

	Neutral	War Positive	Non War Positive	War Negative	Non war Negative
Unambiguity	12	15	2	80	104
Meaningfulness	2	14	1	25	36
Consonance	2				1
Unexpectedness	10	15	2	69	100
Continuity	2	2	1	33	36
Composition	5	13	1	45	83
Elite Nations	3	12	2	22	9
Elite People		12		7	2
Persons	4	1		19	45
Negative		14	1	73	95

This table utilises, as does Table Seven, the news values of Galtung and Ruge but for items that contain storylines about National/Non-Developed Countries, International/Non-Developed and Non-Developed Countries, and indicates whether they have been presented with a neutral, war-positive, non-war-positive, war-negative or non-war-negative attitude.

News coverage of a non-developed country usually fulfils the unambiguous category and will reinforce the impression that when stories about these countries are presented, there is no doubt that they deserve to be in the news (Ferro 1997). In comparison, only three of the stories fulfilled the category of consonance and were not follow-ups to any previous story. 196 of the stories were unexpected, suggesting perhaps that nothing is planned in these countries and that therefore there is no control over events. Out of 214 stories, only 48 of them had any involvement with elite nations, implying perhaps a lack of importance for viewers in elite countries. In addition, only 21 of the stories contained any reference to elite people, whilst 183 stories contained a negative connation.

This negative presentation of non-developed nations, whether in a war zone or not, leads to the perpetuation of an impression of these areas as always being at war, or always having to be saved by the West (Koebner 1961). When not at war, these countries are seen as being failures and, by implication perhaps, ungrateful for the aid which has been given by the West in the past. This may well confirm the feeling of superiority amongst the viewing public in the West—Said's "Orientalism" again manifesting itself. The perpetual presentation by the West of negativity within these countries reinforces the assumption that developing countries are undemocratic, corrupt and strife ridden. The broadcasters whose work is examined in this study purport to be truthful and non-judgemental but in fact the evidence indicates that they are anything but.

Works Cited

Ashcroft, B., G. Griffiths and H. Tiffin. 1995. *The Post-Colonial Studies Reader.* London: Routledge.

Bhabha, H. K. 1994. *The Location of Culture.* London: Routledge.

Boyd-Barrett, O. 1980. *The International News Agencies.* London: Constable

Davidson, B. 1994. *The Search for Africa, History, Culture, and Politics.* New York: Random House.

Ferro, M. 1997. *Colonialisation: A Global History.* London and New York: Routledge.

Galtung, J. and M. Ruge. 1973. Structuring and selecting news. In *The manufacture of news: Deviance, Social Problems and the Mass Media*, edited by S. Cohen and J. Young. 4th Edn. 52-63. London: Constable.

Glasgow Media Group. 1975. *Bad News.* London: Routledge.

—. 1980. *More Bad News.* London: Routledge.

—. 1982. *Really Bad News.* London: Routledge.

Hulme, P. 1986. *Colonial Encounters: Europe and the Native Caribbean 1492-1797.* London: Methuen.

Kocher, R. 1986. Bloodhounds or Missionaries: Role Definitions of German and British journalists. *European Journal of Communications*, 1 (1): 43-64.

Koebner, R. 1961. *Empire*, Cambridge: Cambridge University Press.

Said. E. 1978. *Orientalism: Western Conceptions of the Orient.* London: Penguin.

—. 1983. *The World, the Text and the Critic.* Cambridge MA: Harvard University Press.

Spurr, D. 1993. *The Rhetoric of Empire: Colonial Discourse in Journalism, Travel Writing and Imperial Administration.* Durham and London: Duke University Press.

Viola, M. 2003 *Interpreting TV News.* Created April 2002. www.aber.ac. uk/media/Students/mlv9802.html. Accessed 12 December 2005.

Whitacker, W., R. Ramsey, J. E. Smith and D. Ronald. 2004. *Media writing: Print, Broadcast, and Public Relations.* N.J: Lawrence Erlbaum Associates.

Young, R. J. C. 1995. *Colonial Desire: Hybridity in Theory, Culture and Race.* London: Routledge.

LOCAL JOURNALISM IN A PERIPHERAL AREA: NEWSPAPERS IN THE SCOTTISH HIGHLANDS

MIKE CORMACK

Metropolitan news media usually dominate media in peripheral areas. This is true both in terms of the popularity of the media themselves (such as television, radio and newspapers) and in terms of their content (indeed "news" often just means national news from metropolitan media). Which immediately suggests, however, that non-metropolitan media can have an important role in peripheral areas in providing some of the networks of communication which metropolitan media do not provide. Given that peripheral areas are, by definition, weaker economically and politically, does regionality function as an element which can strengthen peripheral areas by linking local news media together, or is journalism in peripheral areas rather to be characterised as a patchwork of unrelated reporting dominated by metropolitan media? Closely linked to this is the question of whether local media play any role in maintaining regional—as opposed to merely local—identities, and thus help related peripheral areas to develop their common interests and to defend themselves against the power of the metropolis.

Raising this issue immediately demands some clarification of the idea of regionality. "Region" is taken here to be a subdivision within a state (rather than, for example, in its use in international politics and economics as a term for groupings of states into world regions). Raymond Williams has made clear the complexity of the term, noting both its relational quality (a region of what?) and its implication of subordination to the metropolitan centres of power (Williams 1988, 264-6). In the context of the United Kingdom, regions fall somewhere between the metropolitan and the local. These latter notions are relatively straightforward. Between them, however, the concept of the region is much vaguer, particularly with the United Kingdom's national subdivisions in Scotland, Wales and Northern Ireland (all of which are liable to be treated by broadcasters, for example, as if they were regions on a par with the regional subdivisions of England). Notions of the local and the regional will, of course, vary in different countries, according to the size of the country and the distribution of its population. Despite these complications, the region is taken here to be a geographically and historically distinct area within a larger jurisdiction, but one which contains many significant smaller local communities. Furthermore, regions are here treated not just as geographical entities but also as historical ones. Both aspects are necessary for the formation of a publicly-recognised region within a country.

In the United Kingdom, the Scottish Highlands and Islands perhaps constitute *the* classic peripheral region. Although the region is often defined (at least partially) in terms of a geological feature (the Highland Boundary Fault, stretching from Helensburgh on the Firth of Clyde across to Stonehaven on the north-east coast), this conceals some uncertainty, particularly north of the line where the boundary turns back, and excludes the north-east of Scotland. Some districts at times feature as parts of the Highlands and at times not, most notably Caithness (especially north-east of the Wick–Thurso line). In some areas the boundary is rather vague, for example, in Morayshire. And of course the Northern Isles of Orkney and Shetland are very distinct from the Highlands and the Western Isles—both geographically and culturally. In whatever way the boundary is drawn, the Highlands and Islands includes about half of the landmass of Scotland, but a bit less than 10% of the population (given the uncertainty of the precise boundary and the lack of match between local government areas and the traditional Highland boundaries, it would be both difficult and misleading to be more precise). The concern in this chapter is with the mainland area and the Western Isles, since in these areas there has been more cultural cohesion than elsewhere.

The Highlands and Islands form a very distinct area—geographically, historically and culturally—with the Gaelic language as the particular marker of difference. Gaelic was the main signifier of cultural distinction throughout this area in the past, but the language has been retreating steadily to the west over the last two hundred years (within Scotland as a whole there were just 58,652 Gaelic speakers recorded by the 2001 Census, with many scattered throughout the country—only 31,950 of them lived within the Highlands and Western Isles). In modern times the region has been divided (1) by local government areas (the current Highland Council area does not include the Eastern, Southern or South-western Highlands, and the southern Hebrides are also all in a different local government area) (2) by lines of communication (major roads and railways link the region to the lowland cities rather than join up different parts of the region) and (3) by media (particularly newspapers, radio and television). Inverness with a population of around 51,000 (much larger

than other Highland towns such as Fort William with 9,900, Oban with
8,100, and Stornoway with 8,000) is the main media centre with the
presence of BBC Highland, the BBC's Radio nan Gaidheal, Moray Firth
Radio (part of Bauer's Big City Network) which broadcasts round the
Moray Firth from Caithness to Aberdeenshire, two local papers and a
freesheet (although all three, along with their nearest out-of-town
competitors, are owned by the same company). Local media elsewhere in
the region are either small-scale commercial or community radio stations,
or small-scale local and community newspapers.

Newspapers in the Highlands

The history of local newspapers within the Highlands goes back to the
establishment of the *Inverness Journal* in 1807, followed ten years later by
the *Inverness Courier*, explicitly set up as a rival to the earlier paper.
These early Highland papers were much more explicitly regional than their
successors. Eveline Barron (whose family had owned the *Courier* since
1888 and, following her uncle and grand-uncle, was herself editor from
1965 to 1988) quotes from the original prospectus for the *Inverness
Courier* which refers to "The Inverness Courier and General Advertiser for
the Counties of Inverness, Ross, Moray, Nairn, Cromarty, Sutherland and
Caithness" (Barron 1975, 294). In the 1820s, the *Inverness Journal* was
carrying advertisements from right across the Highlands, from Caithness
to Argyll. After 1850, a big expansion took place with most significant
centres of population getting their own paper. Although some of these
newspapers did not last long, it is worth noting how widespread they were
throughout the region, and that by the later 1870s several small Highland
towns had more than one title—Wick, Campbeltown, Oban and Dunoon,
in addition to Inverness.

The economic context in which these newspapers appeared was
transformed in the second half of the nineteenth century by the
development of railways. By 1880 lines not only linked Inverness and
Oban with the lowland cities, but also reached as far as Wick in the north
and Strome Ferry on the west coast (Thomas and Turnock 1989, 311–7).
The railways made the Highlands more accessible for visitors, and also
made the lowlands more accessible for Highlanders, greatly increasing the
region's interaction with other areas. They also helped to bolster the
position of the developing towns, particularly Inverness, Oban, Fort
William, Dingwall and Wick. And of course they made the transporting of
newspapers around the region much easier. In effect the railways were one
of the causes of the region's loss of a strong identity, since communication

lines emphasised the external links. Newspapers did exactly the same, with typical content mixing local news (from the newspaper's immediate circulation area) with Scottish and UK news, and even international news.

Also important at this time was the removal of various inhibiting taxes on newspapers—the advertisement tax was removed in 1851, stamp duty (a tax on each copy printed) in 1855, and the tax on paper in 1861 (Hutchison 2008, 58). The punitive effects of such taxes can be seen in Barron's comment that in 1817, when the *Inverness Courier* started, paper duty was 3d (just over one penny in modern terms) per pound of weight, stamp duty was 4d (almost 2p) on every copy and there was a tax of 3s 6d (17.5 p) on each advertisement (Barron 1975, 295).[1] Advertisements were particularly important to local newspapers, not only because they were a direct source of income, but also indirectly as they increased the newspaper's attractiveness and interest for its readers.

The story of the development of the local press in the Highlands in the twentieth century is very similar to the development of the local press elsewhere in the United Kingdom. Although media competition was strong—mass-circulation daily national newspapers became a reality at the start of the century, and radio began in the 1920s—local newspapers remained popular in the first decades of the twentieth century. Referring to the United Kingdom as a whole, Curran and Seaton write that "the national daily press with a predominantly middle-class public had a circulation of only 5.4 million in 1920, while the weekly local press (which was particularly strong in rural areas) had a 6.8 million circulation" (2003, 34). However they also note that the period 1890–1920 saw "a rapid growth of newspaper chains which incorporated national as well as regional papers" (2003, 39). The media had become big business. With national and international news appearing daily, the only news role left for weekly local newspapers was that of supplier of local news.

In the latter part of the twentieth century the market for local newspapers in the United Kingdom underwent several transformations. The establishment of commercial television in the later 1950s, the many mergers and closures in the 1960s, and the rise of commercial local radio from the 1970s onwards all had an impact on the viability of local titles. And there have been further encroachments on traditional local newspapers, particularly from freesheets (since the 1980s) and the internet (since the 1990s). Local newspapers do still flourish, although they are

---

[1] Prior to decimalisation in 1971 the units of British currency were pounds, shillings and pence, the respective abbreviations being £, s and d. Post-decimalisation "3s 6d" (three shillings and six pence") translated into seventeen and a half "new" pence (abbreviated to p).

currently experiencing the decline in readership and advertising revenue which is seen elsewhere in the industry. Few local newspapers now remain under independent ownership. By 2010, of the higher circulating titles in the Highlands and Islands, only the *Oban Times,* the *West Highland Free Press,* the *Shetland Times* and *The Orcadian* were not parts of larger chains. As David Hutchison notes, in both Scotland and England "Very few local newspapers are now owned by a company based in the area concerned" (2008, 65). However, the fact that the Inverness-based company Scottish Provincial Press (SPP) owns twelve paid-for and three free newspapers mainly around the Moray Firth from Wick to Banff makes that part of the Highlands at least untypical of current trends.

Four Highland Newspapers

To examine the role of regionality in Highland newspapers, four of the best-known local newspapers in the region were examined over a four-month period (January–April 2009). The papers chosen were the *Inverness Courier*, the *Oban Times*, the *Stornoway Gazette* and the *West Highland Free Press*. They cover the main parts of the Highlands and Islands—the central Moray Firth area around the largest community in the Highlands (Inverness), the main towns in Argyll in the south-western Highlands (Oban and Fort William), the largest community in the Western Isles (Stornoway), and the concentration of population living in the Wester Ross and Isle of Skye areas.

The Inverness Courier

Founded in 1817 (and now the oldest surviving newspaper in the Highlands), the *Inverness Courier* circulates principally in the city and its immediate surrounds (east as far as Nairn, south as far as Fort Augustus, and out to Beauly in the west). It appears twice each week and is also available free online. As noted above, it is now owned by SPP which has its production centre in Dingwall in Easter Ross. Audited circulation figures for the period July–December 2008 gave 12,278 as the average sales of the Tuesday edition and 16,924 as the average for that of Friday. The *Courier* is a broadsheet paper with a traditionally-printed masthead in Gothic lettering. Its local "rivals" are the tabloid *Highland News* and the freesheet *Inverness Herald*. All three are owned by SPP.

The Oban Times

Although centred on the towns of Oban and Fort William, the *Oban Times* circulates throughout Argyll (north as far as Spean Bridge, east as far as Tyndrum) and the southern Hebrides (from Barra and South Uist over to Skye and including all the islands south of these). It was established in 1866, at a time when many new newspapers were beginning in the Highlands. It is a weekly, with separate Oban and Fort William editions (it is the latter which has been examined, since Fort William is the larger of the two towns). It is owned by the Wyvex Group, a company which also publishes a number of magazines, mostly on fishing, and which is based in Oban and Edinburgh. Average sales in July–December 2008 were 16,961; the paper is free online.

The Stornoway Gazette

The *Stornoway Gazette* began in 1917 as the first weekly newspaper to be printed in the Outer Hebrides, and circulates principally on Lewis and Harris. It is the newspaper which is closest to the stronger Gaelic-speaking areas, although it has little Gaelic content. It is now owned by the Scottish-based Johnston Press, one of the largest chains of local newspapers in the United Kingdom. Average sales in July–December 2008 were 11,801. It is free online.

The West Highland Free Press

The *West Highland Free Press* was established on the Isle of Skye in 1972, not only as a newspaper catering for an area which did not have its own paper, but also as a politically radical publication. It is currently produced in Broadford on Skye. It circulates throughout the Isle of Skye, Wester Ross, Lochalsh, and also in Uist in the Outer Hebrides. It is independently owned by the West Highland Publishing Company and is a weekly tabloid, with average sales of 8,613 (July–December 2008). The full paper is available online only by subscription.

There is a certain amount of competition between these papers, especially between the *Stornoway Gazette* and the *West Highland Free Press* in Uist, but also between the *Oban Times* and the *West Highland Free Press* in South Skye and on the mainland south of Mallaig (before the 1970s the *Oban Times* was the most popular local newspaper on Skye). It is worth noting that three of these papers (the *Oban Times*, the

Stornoway Gazette and the *West Highland Free Press*) are very different from most British local papers because of their very wide and mixed distribution areas (including islands). These areas share problems, or particular outlooks on problems—housing, transport, energy, education, crofting, health—which might seem to benefit from a regional view. And they also share areas of controversy—Gaelic, religion, absentee property-owners. The *Inverness Courier* for its part, circulates in a more conventional geographical community, but one which is the hub of the region and the base of many organisations which serve the region as a whole (or at least, major parts of it).

The content

Examination of the content however makes it very clear that regionality simply does not figure in these newspapers. There is no regional angle on stories with such potential. During the period studied most of the front pages had a story with regional potential, such as some aspect of transport (which includes island ferries, the state of the main roads, public transport by both road and rail, and the price of fuel). But there was little reference to the Highlands as a significant regional entity of any kind. Indeed, apart from two exceptions to be noted below, there were no regional stories as such, although there were some references to the Highland region in the *Inverness Courier* but only because many headquarters—of organisations such as the Highland Council, Highland Health Board and Highlands & Islands Enterprise—are in the city. Even editorials in the papers did not refer to the region as a whole.

One minor exception to this pattern is sport, especially shinty (a traditional Highland game related to hockey) which, as a Highlands-only sport, and with teams coming from a large area from Ross-shire down to Argyll and across to Strathspey, has a clear regional dimension. But even here the treatment varies between major coverage in the *West Highland Free Press,* adequate coverage in the *Oban Times*, a little in the *Inverness Courier* and none at all in the *Stornoway Gazette* (shinty not being played in the Western Isles). As would be expected from any sports reporting, all the shinty coverage concentrates on the local teams in the different newspaper areas.

A more important exception to the rule is Gaelic which often treated as a regional story. General developments in Gaelic were reported, as well as controversies (for example over Gaelic medium education and bilingual road signs). But of course this topic has a national resonance to it as well, so it is only ambiguously a regional identifier (such matters were just as likely to be reported in the national Scottish newspapers *The Herald*, published in Glasgow, and *The Scotsman,* published in Edinburgh). And the relevant reports were almost always written in English, making Gaelic a topic, not a medium of communication in itself. Regular Gaelic columns do appear in these newspapers—two each week in the *West Highland Free Press*, one in the Friday edition of the *Inverness Courier*, one in the *Oban Times* (with English summary) and irregularly in the *Stornoway Gazette* (the one in question, oddly enough, reported on cultural activities in Edinburgh). Beyond that, there was very little use of Gaelic. Comparison with previous studies (Cormack 1995; Cormack 2004) shows that little has changed in this respect over recent years.

Clearly then the papers do not support any kind of regional identity or even regional interest, beyond Gaelic. The impression they give is that there is the local context, and then the national context, with nothing in between. In terms of the public sphere, they are part of a local one, and only when letters to the editor appear on broader issues (such as Gaelic or religion) do they expand on that. In effect the papers actually work against any regional Highland identity by the simple method of ignoring it.

There is, therefore, no real sense in which the region is considered as a whole in these newspapers. The papers are partly reacting to broadcasting, letting it provide the bigger picture, but yet the regional element hardly appears even there. There is very little English-language Highland news on BBC's Radio Scotland opt-out for the Highlands—just three bulletins of 6 minutes each and one of ten minutes each day. Regular Gaelic news appears on the BBC's Gaelic radio station, Radio nan Gaidheal, and on the Gaelic digital television channel, BBC Alba, but in both cases the news programmes are acting as general news providers, referring to international and UK-wide events as well as more local news.

Other "regional" newspapers

It might be argued that the only true regional newspaper in recent times was *An Gàidheal Ùr*. This was an all-Gaelic monthly title (and so clearly can not really be considered as a "news" paper), distributed free, being financed partly by subsidy and partly by advertising. It began in 1998 but ended in March 2009, due to the withdrawal of its subsidy from Bòrd na Gàidhlig (the official organisation which funds Gaelic development). Despite the desirability of a Gaelic newspaper (see Cormack 2003 for further discussion), it had a number of problems. Some were to do with distribution (it sometimes went out as a supplement in other papers) and some were to do with content (its inability to be a true newspaper keeping up-to-date with current news stories). However, the same comment on Gaelic content applies here as was noted earlier—Gaelic is not *just* a regional issue and *An Gàidheal Ùr* was of interest to Gaelic readers outside the region. Its prime aim was to support the language, not to serve the Highlands and Islands as such.

One other candidate for regional news provider is the *Press and Journal*. This is a daily newspaper, based in Aberdeen but circulating throughout the north of Scotland, and now owned by the Dundee media company D. C. Thomson. On its website, the *Press and Journal* claims to sell across the northern half of Scotland "from Arbroath in the east to Oban in the west". Of its seven editions, one is for Inverness itself and one for the rest of the Highlands and Islands. However it is essentially the newspaper of the north-east lowlands and the Moray Firth area. That said, its average daily sales for July–December 2008 were 15,026 in the Highlands and Islands, excluding Inverness, with another 6,830 in that city. This makes it a significant part of the Highlands' media mix, although the paper has always had a strong north-east identity. Its main drawback in the present context is that it does not cover, and does not sell significantly in, all parts of the Highlands. It is essentially a northern Highlands edition of a northeast lowlands newspaper.

Conclusion

It will be clear from the analysis presented here that local journalism in the Highlands focuses very closely on relatively narrowly-defined areas, and that regional issues fall between these and the larger national (Scottish and UK-wide) concerns of metropolitan news media, whether based in the cities of Scotland or in England. Local journalism is defined in opposition to national journalism, with regional journalism ignored. In fact the economics of local journalism actively militate against any sense of regional identity. It is cheaper and easier to cover a smaller area. The result is that an inherent weakness of local journalism—its lack of a larger context, what some would see as its parochialism—is magnified since it does not play into broader regional concerns. The situation in the Highlands and Islands shows this up very clearly since there has been historically a clearly defined regional identity. Rather than being a criticism of the papers themselves (which are just functioning like other local titles) this points more to lost opportunities. It also demonstrates one of the ways in which the media have had an impact on this peripheral area. Like the transport system, they have helped to ensure that the major economic and political links in the area run from the main communities to the outside urban areas (Glasgow, Edinburgh, Aberdeen, and, of course, London), rather than across the region.

All of this leads on to the question of how the media could structure a sense of locality/regionality, a sense of how different areas are inter-related. But in this respect contemporary Highland newspapers are simply reflecting a trend which was established when the media first began to penetrate that part of Scotland in the early nineteenth century.

Works Cited

Barron, E. 1975. The Printed Word. In *The Hub of the Highlands*. 291–305. Inverness: Inverness Field Club.

Cormack, M. 1995. The Use of Gaelic in Scottish Newspapers. *Journal of Multilingual and Multicultural Development*, 16 (4): 269–80.

—. 2003. The Case for a Gaelic Weekly Newspaper. In *Towards Our Goals: Broadcasting, the Press, the Performing Arts and the Economy: Minority Languages in Northern Ireland, the Republic of Ireland and Scotland (Belfast Studies in Language, Culture and Politics,* 10), edited by J. M. Kirk and D. P. O Baoill. 95–9. Belfast: Queens University Press.

—. 2004. Gaelic in the Media. *Scottish Affairs*, 46: 23–43.

—. 2008. Gaelic, the Media and Scotland. In *The Media in Scotland*, edited by N. Blain and D. Hutchison. 213–26. Edinburgh: Edinburgh University Press.

Curran, J. and J. Seaton. 2003. *Power Without Responsibility: The Press, Broadcasting and New Media in Britain*. 6th ed. London: Routledge.

Hutchison, D. 2008. The History of the Press. In *The Media in Scotland*, edited by N. Blain and D. Hutchison. 55–70. Edinburgh: Edinburgh University Press.

Thomas, J. and D. Turnock, 1989. *A Regional History of the Railways of Great Britain, vol. XV: The North of Scotland*. London: David & Charles.

Williams, R. 1988. *Keywords: A Vocabulary of Culture and Society*. Rev. ed. London: Fontana

Website

The Press and Journal: www.pressandjournal.co.uk/AboutUs.pdf

EÒRPA—
TAKING EUROPE FROM THE PERIPHERY
TO THE CORE?

DOUGLAS CHALMERS

The value of Gaelic lies precisely in the fact that it is not the language of commerce and technology; it is not the language of the mass media. It is the language into which one can retire from the hurly burly of an over-busy world. It offers an escape from canned, pre-packaged entertainment, from the superficiality of instant news and instant comment ... It is a folk language, in which people still make their own songs and write their own poetry ... Gaelic has no material value whatsoever and thank God for it. It is not the language of the rat race. That is its supreme value. An Commun Gaidhealach has its priorities right when it puts the emphasis on culture, music religion and education rather than debasing Gaelic by trying to make it an ordinary workhorse for business and administrative purposes.
—James Shaw Grant, former editor of the *Stornoway Gazette*, in a speech to the Stornoway Mod in 1972 (quoted in Hutchinson 2005, 99).

Although no Gaelic speaker himself, James Shaw Grant was by no means an enemy of Gaelic language and culture. Far from it, he had defended it during the thirty years of his stewardship of the *Stornoway Gazette*, and as a playwright had ensured some of his own plays were translated into Gaelic. However, his attitude towards Gaelic was, in its impact if not intention, very symptomatic of a modernising approach that served to help create a "potentially fatal dichotomy" in the way the language was seen by policy makers for many years, not least in the media itself, Gaelic being regarded as acceptable in the "church and home" but not in the world of business (MacInnes 2008, 117).

By 2001, a report of the Task Force on the Public Funding of Gaelic (The MacPherson Report) for the Scottish Executive was giving a sobering estimation of the perilous state of Gaelic in Scotland: "Gaelic is a critically ill patient on life support ... the prognosis is bleak" (Scottish Executive 2001). From a registered peak of 231,594 "habitual speakers" noted in the

1881 census, the figure had dropped to just under sixty thousand by 2001,[1] with the Western Isles of Scotland—the traditional "Gaelic heartland"— registering a loss of nineteen percent of its Gaelic speakers between 1991 and 2001 through depopulation and the problems of an ageing community (Chalmers 2006, 241). Many historical reasons have been cited for this relentless loss, including the effect of the Highland Clearances throughout the eighteenth and nineteenth century when landlords "cleared" their lands of (mostly Gaelic-speaking) people, replacing them with more profitable sheep,[2] the impact of the 1872 Education Act which banned the use of Gaelic in the teaching of primary school children, and, more recently, decades of neglect, both benign and deliberate, often in the guise of support for "modernisation" and progress (Chalmers 2009, 142).

In the second half of the 18th Century the Gaelic language had been linked in the eyes of the British establishment with "irredeemable poverty, social backwardness and political faction", "backward" and "fanatical" being typical currency to describe much of Scotland in the lexicon of "orthodox opinion" of the time (Beveridge 1989, 9). This was to last until a transformation in the early 1800s when writers such as Sir Walter Scott[3] sought to re-present and "re-invent" the Gaels no longer as savage highlanders (which had been the stereotype used since the failed uprising of 1745-46 when many of the Scottish clans had fought on the losing side in a battle to oppose the Hanoverian royal family in favour of the Stuart royal line), but instead as heroic and noble fighters who could serve the British Empire as the backbone of Britain's growing imperial army. Together with this successful re-invention of Scotland (and rehabilitation of tartan, as well as an emasculated "clan" system), a sanitised and "safe" version of Gaelic culture was also encouraged through the establishment of organisations such as An Comunn Gaidhealach (The Highland Association). Established in 1891 with Queen Victoria as its patron, for the first hundred years of its existence An Comunn Gaidhealach

---

[1] Although the 1881 Census referred to speakers "using the language daily" and later census reports referred to a "knowledge of the language" the direction of change is clear.

[2] "As a result of the Clearances … throughout the interior of the Gaelic mainland of the Highlands the first half of the 19th century witnessed the forced migration of virtually its entire population. In terms of the Gaelic speech community this could be regarded as the removal of its heartland" (MacKinnon 1991, 62).

[3] This was seen in the publication of his novel *Waverley* in 1814 which romanticised the events of 1745-46, and culminated in his stage-managed visit of a tartan-clad King George IV to Edinburgh in 1822, where the "Clans" were paraded in front of the King who for the occasion adopted the persona of a "Jacobite Clan Chief".

(mentioned in the opening quotation of this article) saw the role of Gaelic very much in the way that James Shaw Grant presented it—"conservation not innovation", with its main remit being to organise a yearly formal "Mòd" or festival of Scottish Gaelic song, art and culture. However, the lack of success of this approach led to a critical review in 1994 which stated that it had led An Comunn (and by implication its approach to Gaelic culture) into a "miasma at both strategic, and operational levels" (Compass 2002, 6).

The attitude of "conservation not innovation" (Dhòmhnallach 2006, 14) has now been rejected by many of those active in the development of Gaelic arts and culture. It has also been rejected within much of modern Gaelic broadcasting and has been replaced by an outlook situating "creativity and innovation" at the centre of its approach, an approach which it can be argued now questions some key modernist assumptions through its recasting of the concepts of "core and periphery" within Europe. This claim will be tested below with regard to the Gaelic current affairs programme *Eòrpa*.

This change in attitude may be as a result of a new perspective following from the years of dispersion and attrition mentioned above, a perspective which is now re-examining exactly where the traditional "Gàidhealtachd" or Gaelic heartland is (Glazer 2006).[4] As Oliver has also recently pointed out (2006, 157), today Gaelic is no longer restricted to the hearth within the croft. Gaelic is:

> 'in' the modern world and is 'in' the cities of Scotland, and being negotiated by modern civil society. It is increasingly 'unbounded' and being incorporated and perpetuated in ways that reflect the broader and instrumental context of Society.

This chapter argues that Gaelic broadcasting, and particularly Gaelic current affairs broadcasting represent a good example of this change being put into practice, and helping provide some of the best of the BBC's Public Service Broadcasting into the bargain.

Presenting Current Affairs from a Gaelic Viewpoint

Although the first Gaelic (radio) programme had appeared on the BBC as far back as 1923, and the first television broadcast in 1952, even as recently as the 1970s there were only ten hours of Gaelic television per year (in a good year) on BBC Scotland and some Saturday morning

---

[4] In a manner similar to how Walsh (2009, 76) re-examined the Irish Gaeltacht.

children's broadcasts on the advertising-funded ITV network. Public pressure, including demonstrations outside the offices of BBC Scotland in the 1970s, had led to an increase in the then very low level of Gaelic broadcasting by the BBC (MacKinnon 1991, 132) but it was only with the Broadcasting White Paper of 1978 that any substantial moves began towards serious consideration of minority language broadcasts in the UK. The White Paper stated that "Broadcasting has an important role to play in the preservation of Gaelic and Welsh as living tongues and in sustaining the distinctive cultures based upon them..." (Home Office 1978, 22).

Four years later, in 1982, the launch of Sianel Pedwar Cymru, S4C, (available from 2010 in digital form only) first saw Welsh language television begin to play a serious part in the media landscape in Wales although some broadcasting in Welsh had taken place from the early 1950s and with its launch in 1974, the Welsh language soap opera *Pobol y Cwm (People of the Valley)* still lays claim to be the longest running BBC TV soap opera on air (although now transmitted by S4C). Scottish Gaelic speakers, however, had to wait almost a further ten years until any substantial investment into Gaelic Medium Television was to take place. This followed the creation of the Comataidh Telebhisein Gàidhlig (CTG), the Gaelic Television Committee, subsequent to a decision of the Conservative government in 1990, which made available £9.5 million in funding—significantly less than the support given to its Welsh counterpart, but greater that the amount expected by supporters at the time (Moffat 1995).

As late as 1989, a System Three poll had indicated that only one per cent of Gaels thought that television served them well, while 80 per cent thought that TV used Gaelic "not very well" or "not at all well" (Hutchinson 2005, 191). In the words of Malcolm MacLean, head of the Gaelic arts agency Pròiseact nan Ealan, "until 1991 Scotland had no real Gaelic Television to speak of" (2000, 115).

The Gaelic-language current affairs programme *Eòrpa* (the Gaelic word for "Europe") was one of a tranche of initiatives made possible by CTG funding in 1993. It appeared together with the Gaelic soap opera *Machair* and the learners' programme *Speaking Our Language. Machair* was to run for 151 episodes until 1998, and its repeats can currently still be seen on the new publicly financed digital Gaelic channel, BBC Alba, which began transmissions in 2008, as can repeats of *Speaking Our Language.* Originally aimed not only at island Gaelic communities, but at the larger community of Gaelic sympathisers, the intention from the outset was that the programmes should be "attractive to the non Gaelic speaking majority" (Cormack 1994, 4).

Although not originally envisaged as a long running series, *Eòrpa*, which was originally transmitted on BBC2 Scotland before transferring to BBC Alba,[5] has over the last seventeen years established itself as a Scottish Gaelic flagship programme in terms of quality, winning Scottish Baftas[6] and being held up as an example of creative, quality output[7] by the Scottish Broadcasting Commission and others.[8]

Exact viewing figures are difficult to calculate, since the BARB[9] system used by the BBC to track viewer numbers is inappropriate for Gaelic broadcasting—having a viewing panel of only 500 in Scotland with no panel members located in the Scottish Islands (the traditional Gaelic "heartland") and no information available as to whether any panel member can speak Gaelic (BBC/MG Alba 2009). Instead, estimated viewing figures for the Gaelic channel for the Scottish population as a whole are collected from the polling organisation System Three's monthly "omnibus" survey of Scottish trends (1000 individuals Scotland wide). This is supplemented by weekly data from a panel of 300 Gaelic viewers throughout Scotland, which is collated and analysed by the Leirsinn research organisation based in the Gaelic college Sabhal Mòr Ostaig in Skye.

The latest combined figures released from the BBC (October 09) would suggest that overall the Gaelic channel BBC Alba is viewed by 220,000 individuals for at least 15 minutes per week (5% of the Scottish Population),[10] with Gaelic-speaking audiences watching it for an average of three hours plus per week. In terms of figures relating directly to *Eòrpa* (as part of the current affairs strand of BBC Alba) no exact viewing numbers are available, but it can be estimated that perhaps 22,000 viewers might watch each programme throughout Scotland, based on the twelve percent of Scottish adults watching Alba who watch its "current affairs"

---

[5] Although it continues to be shown on the BBC2 terrestrial channel each week following transmission on Alba.

[6] The British Academy of Film and Television Arts, who award yearly prizes for different category of film and television output.

[7] "It was intriguing to note that without fail at every one of our public events BBC2 Scotland's *Eòrpa* programme was raised, unsolicited, and by non-Gaelic speakers, as an example of a positive, well-respected programme". Blair Jenkins, Chair of the Scottish Broadcasting Commission (*The Herald* 2008, on-line). The Commission was established in 2007 by the SNP government to suggest ways in which broadcasting in and from Scotland might be enhanced.

[8] "Perhaps more surprising is how such a small community has been able to sustain programmes of quality such as Eòrpa" (Cormack 2008, 221).

[9] Broadcasters' Audience Research Board.

[10] Which can be judged as impressive against a baseline of approximately 60,000 fluent Gaelic speakers in Scotland—under two per cent of the population.

strand (BBC/MG Alba 2009, 54). Within the fluent Scottish adult Gaelic community encompassed in these figures the percentage watching "news and current affairs" is higher at one in five. To this estimated figure of 22,000 must, of course, be added those who watch the repeat on the terrestrial channel BBC2. Unfortunately no robust estimates of this were available at the time of writing although viewing figures on the same channel for current affairs in English varied between 39,000 for the *Holyrood Live* show, and 26,000 for *Scottish Questions*.[11] It could be argued that these might cater for similar audiences, however this is speculation given absence of any real evidence.

As a weekly magazine-type current affairs programme, *Eòrpa* "is one that looks at Europe from a non-metropolitan, minority perspective, thus making it different from its English language rivals" (Cormack 2008, 221). Although discussions of current affairs through Gaelic had been seen intermittently on TV previously, they had been "just a conversation really—a number of topics each week" (Hutchinson 2005, 69) without any particular focus, and certainly not that of Europe.

In 2009, access to data from the BBC Gaelic unit (now working within the much expanded BBC Alba service[12]) allowed the beginning of an on-going analysis of the first fourteen years of output of the *Eòrpa* programme, with the aim of ascertaining whether it might be possible to discern elements of a "Gaelic world view" of European affairs and, through this, of the Gaelic world itself. Datasheets of the first 330 programmes were analysed and the almost 900 topics within this examined to see how the "geography" of Europe was constituted in the minds of the producers. Similarly, an analysis of the topics allowed a view of the programme's editorial judgements as to what would be of interest to a mainly Gaelic constituency (although importantly, all *Eòrpa* programmes have been subtitled in English allowing mediated access for the UK's majority English-language community).

In terms of geography, where the transmission location could be ascertained, this was noted, firstly with regard to the British Isles, venues being categorised where possible into Scotland, England, Wales and the Island of Ireland. Where individual towns or cities seemed to play an important part in the topic, these were also noted, as was whether or not the transmissions were situated within mainland Scotland or the Western Isles (or Northern Isles etc). Specific locations in the Highlands and

---

[11] BBC Scotland Audience Report, November 2009.

[12] The channel is run in partnership with funders MG Alba (formerly the CTG), which transmits Gaelic material for approximately seven hours per day, available on satellite, but not yet on digital terrestrial.

Islands were also identified where possible. This is shown below in Table 1 below.

In a similar manner, Table 2 seeks to allocate transmission locations to areas outwith the British Isles, categorised as "Western European", "Former Eastern European" and "Other" geographical areas. Finally Table 3 outlines topics dealt with in the first fourteen series of the programme, with an attempt being made to allocate meaningful "subject tags" to each topic—with some topics being given more than one tag depending on how wide ranging the programme could be ascertained to be.

According to Crisell (2006), the unspoken principles that help determine which stories are included in news and current affairs programmes, include "a focus on tangible audience concerns; stories that can be presented in a clear, simple unambiguous way; stories that are out of the ordinary, and calamities, disasters and tragedies" (Crisell 2006, 49). He also states that although the reporter must be objective and self-effacing, "any report is a kind of editorialising—it is always to some extent subjective and value-loaded" (ibid, 50). It is based on a *sense of values*— the perspective coloured by what is deemed to be important, or interesting, or morally appropriate. Similarly, of course, Grierson had famously defined documentary as "the creative treatment of actuality" (1979, 11).

The preliminary observations below on which European current affairs merit an appearance within *Eòrpa* may begin to offer some tentative views on where a "Gaelic world view" within the media may exist, thus allowing discussion of a possible Gaelic "sense of values", research that it is intended to build on following interviews with current and previous *Eòrpa* production teams.

Making sense of the information—a cautionary note

As with any media text, there are clearly problems in trying to analyse output of *Eòrpa* in terms of why certain subjects were chosen and others not. Although the programme has been running for seventeen series to date (data for the first 14 of which has been obtained), transmission does not take place 52 weeks of the year—output of a typical season being twenty six weeks over the autumn to late spring schedule. This essentially leaves six months of the year when major events can take place within Europe, but can never feature on the radar of the programme unless in retrospect.

Since the programme's inaugural transmission in 1993, there have understandably been different production teams in charge with a series of different editors—all of whom can be expected to play some role in the dynamics of production, including topic choice. Clearly finance will be expected to play a part in the decisions regarding which topics can be affordably covered in a successful manner: as mentioned above, public funding for Gaelic broadcasting has always fallen far short of what is available even for its Welsh language counterpart. This also has other implications as to best use of resources. For instance, if a team is sent to one European location to cover a particular topic, unless this is for an extended programme, the norm would be to aim to cover other topics from that location (each half hour transmission has typically three topics within it)—with varying degrees of "top-line" importance in terms of current affairs[13] although, like the final item on many news programmes, one of the three items might be chosen on the basis of "stories that are out of the ordinary".[14]

According to staff in the BBC, until the launch of BBC Alba, as well as having been the only real current affairs programme in Gaelic for the previous fifteen years, given the absence for periods of Gaelic news bulletins, *Eòrpa* was also expected by the Gaelic community to play something of a dual role in terms of adding to "news" delivery (a role historically undertaken by Radio nan Gàidheal, with some intermittent additions on Television).[15] This is now something that is done in depth by the thirty minutes daily evening news programme *An Là* (Today) and its weekend summary *Seachd Là* (Seven days), only now allowing *Eòrpa*, in the view of the current production team, to take a more investigative approach to issues.

In terms of comparators with UK English-language current affairs programmes, a member of the BBC Alba staff suggested that it might be the case that BBC1's *Newsnight* is the best comparator for *Eòrpa*, albeit it has a world focus and is on nightly weekdays, whereas *Eòrpa* has a European remit and is normally on weekly for thirty minutes (when running). This is perhaps not too accurate, given the lack of "live" interviews on *Eòrpa* and their prevalence in *Newsnight*, however the lack of easy comparison with English medium broadcasts nevertheless illustrates a certain gap in English-language programming.

Finally, since constraints of time would prevent any individual from viewing the whole fourteen years of transmission, the identification of

---

[13] A point made to me during discussions with past and present staff.
[14] Such as the intriguing topic of "Spiders" catalogued in Table 3.
[15] Television News "bulletins" over this period had been extremely under-resourced, the main one being the five minute lunchtime "Telefios" bulletins concentrating on Highland news and Gaelic interest news stories from elsewhere. A two minute version of this was also repeated in the evening on the Independent TV Stations Grampian and STV. These were broadcast from 1993-2000

trends in location and topics etc. has been made from the programme data supplied by BBC Alba. As these are working documents, some of the data on them is less detailed than on other. In some cases the essential data may be restricted to location and topic title, in others more information is given. This inevitably leads to interpretation at several levels in terms of the issues raised by the programmes, based on my own experience of viewing *Eòrpa* over the years, discussions with the production team where possible, and in-depth viewing of programmes specifically requested from the very helpful production team. Given these caveats, some tentative insights can be drawn from the almost 900 topics dealt with below in Tables 1-3.

Table 1 The British Isles as covered in Eòrpa Series 1–14

Scotland Non-Highlands/Islands			
Scotland (no specific location highlighted)	255		
Edinburgh	3		
Glasgow	5		
Blairgowrie	1		
Scotland-Highlands and Islands			
Highlands un-specified	10	**Western Isles/Skye**	
Campbeltown	1	Western Isles	13
Helmsdale	1	Lewis	3
Lochaber	1	Stornoway	4
Moidart	1	Harris	10
Oban	1	Uists	8
Plockton	1	Benbecula	1
Sutherland	1	Eriskay	1
Wester Ross	1	Vatersay	1
Small Isles		**Northern Isles**	
Arran	1	Orkney	1
Gigha	2	Shetland	1
Islay	2	Unst	2
Lismore	1		
Mingulay	1		
Mull	1		
Taransay	1		
Tiree	1		

England	
England unspecified	4
Felixstowe	1
London	2

Wales	
Wales unspecified	6
Cardiff	1

Ireland	
Ireland (no specific location highlighted)	41
Dublin	2
Ulster	10
Belfast	2

Table 2: Non-British Isles as covered in Eòrpa Series 1–14

Western Europe	
Austria	9
Adriatic Sea	1
Belgium	23
Brussels	16
Cyprus	7
Denmark	23
Copenhagen	1
Faroe Islands	4
Finland	12
Helsinki	1
Sami areas	1
France	48
Brittany	8
Corsica	6
Strasbourg	1
Germany	48
Berlin	2
Frankfurt	1
Greece	14
Crete	1
Greenland	3
Holland	24
Amsterdam	1
Rotterdam	1

Former Eastern Europe	
Former USSR	
Russia	40
Chechnya	1
Moscow	1
Belarus	3
Crimea	2
Estonia	4
Georgia	1
Latvia	2
Lithuania	4
Moldova	2
Ukraine	9
Former Yugoslavia	
Yugoslavia	22
Bosnia/Herzegovina	11
Croatia	1
Kosovo	9
Macedonia	2
Montenegro	3
Serbia	9
Belgrade	3
Slovenia	4

Iceland	15	**Sovereign States**	
Reykjavik	1	**Albania**	6
Italy	34	**Bulgaria**	9
Capri	1	**Hungary**	20
Naples	3	Budapest	1
Sardinia	2	Poland	18
Sicily	3	**Romania**	11
Luxembourg	1	**Former Czechoslovakia**	
Malta	1	**Czech Republic**	8
Monaco	1	**Slovakia**	3
Norway	29		
Bergen	1	**Non-Europe**	
Oslo	1	**Argentina**	1
Portugal	15	**Canada**	1
Azores	2	**Quebec**	1
San Marino	1	**Chile**	1
Spain	53	**Iraq**	1
Basque Country	9	**Morocco**	1
Bilbao	1	**Sri Lanka (Tamils)**	1
Catalonia	4	**Thailand**	1
Galicia	1		
Madrid	1	**Unknown location**	21
Sweden	11		
Switzerland	6		
Turkey	13		
Vatican	1		

Table 3 – Topics as covered in Eòrpa Series 1-14

Environment Issues		**Social Issues**	
Technology	3	**Legal**	
Environment	69	Law	53
Islands	56	Corruption	5
Energy	20	Gambling	1
Transport	33	Drugs	16
		Alcohol	16
General developmental/ Economy/Europe		Prisons	3
Europe	139	Community wellbeing	7
Single Currency	4	Crime	13
EU Issues/ Structure	33		
Economics	149	**Family**	
Local Economy	192	Age	20

Agriculture	37	**Family**	49
Forestry	7	Divorce	2
Fishing	41	Adoption	5
Tourism	37	IVF	3
Crofting	20	Sex Education	2
Land	52	Orphans	5
Cities	20		
Rural	73		
Political Issues		**Social**	
Racism	43	Disability	4
Fascism	29	Health	67
Immigration	73	Education	23
Refugees	67	Sport	22
Roma	2	Xmas	3
Nationalism	107	Holidays	2
Devolution	64	Housing	9
Disasters etc	9	Social Services	34
Cold War	54	Civics	11
Collapse of Eastern	63	Euthanasia	3
Europe			
Right-Left politics	123		
Inequalities	49	**Gendered**	
Women	22	Domestic Abuse	5
Military	20	Abortion	9
War	34	Rape	3
Terrorism	12	Homosexuality	3
		AIDS	2
Cultural Issues		Prostitution/trafficking	9
Culture	119		
Music	212	**Religion**	
Poetry	6	Religion in general	48
Language	76	Islam	13
Gaelic language	46		
Festivals	8	**Other**	
Minority Communities	162	Spiders	1
Media/TV	5		
Film	1		
Heritage	16		
Customs	44		
Communications	98		

The British Isles in Europe from a Gaelic perspective

Table 1 above seeks to identify the number of programmes with transmissions located within the British Isles. The first issue perhaps worthy of comment is the lack of coverage of England, or matters "English"—only seven geographical locations in total appearing over fourteen seasons. With approximately fifty-two million of a population compared to three million for Wales and approximately six million for the Island of Ireland geographical "hits" are very limited—the same as those for Wales (at seven locations in total) and less than one tenth of those for Ireland (at fifty-five).

Discussions with programme staff however suggest that there is less to this than meets the eye in terms of values or views of what constitutes Europe. It appears that the paucity of hits in this instance is linked to the status of the majority UK language, English. One of the strengths of *Eòrpa* has undoubtedly been the insistence by the producers that interviews take place in the mother tongue of the speaker. According to programme staff, this has allowed direct contact with Prime Ministers, high officials and others whose grasp of English could be less than perfect—and who might not be prepared to tackle complex issues on screen in a language they did not feel they truly mastered, but would be willing to do so in their mother tongue. This is then translated into Gaelic voiceover for the programme, accompanied by English subtitles—allowing many programmes to be in effect trilingual. A specific difficulty arises however, when the interviewees in the programme speak only in English—in which, of course, all Gaels are fluent. Psychologically, the producers claim, it is difficult for the hearer to focus in on a Gaelic voiceover, given that English is being spoken in the background. Hence, it is rare that a programme is produced with the English language at the heart of it in terms of core speakers.

Perhaps more of a question for future analysis would be why a discrepancy seems to exist between coverage of Welsh and Irish location based issues. It is true that Gaelic and Irish come from a common Goidelic root in terms of Celtic languages, unlike Welsh which has a Brythonic base, meaning there is no mutual comprehension between Welsh and Gaelic or Gaeilge (Irish) while there is some inter-comprehension, depending on dialect, between Gaelic and Gaeilge. However in terms of minority language environments within the British Isles, Wales might intuitively be expected to have more to offer in terms of bilingualism, for instance, or its longer experience of operating with a Language Act—the major Welsh Language Act being instituted in 1993 compared to the Gaelic Language Act in 2005.

In terms of dispersion throughout the rest of Scotland, as might be expected, there is less coverage of areas where Gaelic has not historically been strong—the Northern Isles and Caithness for instance. However it would be wrong to say that the Gaelic heartlands, such as the Western Isles, alone dominate, with a fair coverage also existing of the small isles and parts of the Gaelic mainland. That said, of course, the level of detail within the programme schedules did not always allow specific identification of all locations, and that remains an area for further detailed discussion with the programme staff.

The European continent as viewed by the Gael

Table 2 aims to identify European (and other) locations featured in the programmes. The approach adopted to date has been to allocate locations where possible to states, split first of all into "Western Europe", "Former Eastern Europe" and "Other" locations. Where major cities or regions are also identifiable attention has been drawn to those.

In Crisell's suggestions of principles that might help determine a topic's inclusion in a current affairs programme, a key theme suggested was "a focus on tangible audience concerns". Intuitively, in terms of non-British Isles locations, it could be surmised that possible areas of interest/concerns could flow from the following themes:

- Scotland's historical links with France (the "Auld Alliance") and Scotland's European orientation during the Scottish Enlightenment.[16]
- Scotland's historical trading links with the Baltic states.
- Gaeldom's past links with Nordic countries.
- Cultural links with areas of high cultural diversity (Spain; areas of minority language use in France etc).
- Areas where community dispersion has taken place (given the significance of the Clearances in Gaelic history): Central Europe and former Eastern Europe might be expected to feature here.
- Areas where common lifestyle issues come to the fore—rurality; land use; religion etc.
- Matters dealing with EU law/governance as it affects the Gàidhealtachd, which might be expected to draw upon the countries (France and Belgium) where the EU Parliament meets.

---

[16] As documented amongst others by Camic (1983), Daiches (1996), Davie (1999), Herman (2003) and Broadie (2007).

Perusal of Table 2 in relation to Western Europe shows firstly that the Nordic group of countries is the geographical area most heavily covered, with 93 appearances—ranging from Norway at 29, Denmark at 23, down to Greenland at 3. Following this, unsurprisingly perhaps, Spain features next at 53—the trilogy of issues of language, culture and community within the Basque country, Catalonia and Galicia and their relationships with the Spanish state offering what one *Eòrpa* staff member suggested were many clear "parallels" worth investigation. France and Germany appear next in the rankings with 48 locations each. Some tentative points have been suggested above in relation to France. The equal ranking of Germany may be more difficult to explain. However, a study of the subject topics in Table 3 might suggest that the prominence of issues of racism, fascism, discrimination, unequal communities and fluid concepts of "nationality" may be something which has pushed Germany up the appearance table. These issues may conceivably fit with Crisell's view of tangible concerns to a mainly Gaelic viewership as interpreted by the production team. Italy features next at 34 appearances—a subject which merits further examination, but is perhaps linked to rurality and the rural economy in general.

Within the "Former Eastern Europe" much of the focus, understandably, has been on the turmoil of that part of the continent over the last 20 years, with the former Soviet Union featuring heavily—principally Russia, but importantly many of the "independent republics" also feature over this period—some such as the Ukraine a substantial number of times. Again, the turmoil in the Balkans/Former Yugoslavia could be expected to feature heavily as it does, with sites of crisis—Bosnia/Herzegovina/Kosovo/ Serbia all appearing regularly. However, this is also the case for more peaceful areas of former Eastern Europe such as Hungary—which of course is notable for the issue of linguistic diversity remaining a burning topic.

Finally, preliminary examination of the coverage of Turkey (13 locational instances) seems to be linked to the issue of religion (a topic which features highly in Table 3), and Turkey's position on the current periphery of "Europe" as defined by policy makers.

"Tangible concerns" from within the Gaelic perspective

The editorial decisions made over an extended period of 14 years are complex. Clearly a European current affairs programme might be expected to deal with topics related to the economy and economic environment, given their interrelationship with other aspects of life. They do feature heavily with almost 150 items on issues of "economics" and almost 200 around aspects of the "local economy", including 52 on aspects of land, 41 on fishing, 20 on crofting and 37 on tourism—all to be expected in a programme that seeks to put the current affairs of much of the Gaelic community at its heart. Similarly, there are few surprises in terms of the prevalence of cultural issues (119), music (212) and matters dealing with language as such (76). Again 162 instances where cultural issues in minority communities feature and 44 dealing with aspects of customs would seem appropriate, when the relationship between culture and language has previously been flagged up as important for minority language communities (Scottish Arts Council 2003).

Of particular interest however was the unexpectedly high coverage of issues such as racism (43 instances); fascism (29); immigration (73) and refugees (67). Although it might be argued that these were common to many current affairs programmes over this period, detailed examination of the perspective from which these items handle these issues suggested that a more empathetic and less xenophobic treatment of topics such as refugees and immigration is in evidence than is common in some English language programmes (and certainly in much of the tabloid press). In the programmes examined, stereotyping tended to be rejected and with it the narrow set of ideological values associated with such approaches (Lacey 2009, 157). Also rejected was any automatic reliance on governmental views, which can tend to see immigration and the issue of refugees as limited to "problems" for the host nation. Instead a more individual-focussed and refugee/immigrant-focussed perspective tended to be adopted—suggesting a presumption of sympathy with refugee/immigrant communities and those within them.

Finally, in terms of treatment of topics, it was of interest to note, in relation to sexual or gendered politics, only three programmes in 14 years dealing with homosexuality and only two with Aids. Clearly this merits further investigation, but preliminary discussions with one member of staff suggested that this was not primarily to do with religious sensibilities or similar concerns, but rather with the time slot on the TV schedule at which *Eòrpa* had traditionally been transmitted—7 pm on a weekday, immediately after Gaelic children's programmes.

To make complete sense of this wealth of data, clearly much more research remains to be done. However, some tentative conclusions may be offered.

As a general approach to the issue of reporting and journalism, Allan (2007, 76) suggests that "Journalists are among the pre-eminent story-tellers of modern society". He points out that journalists construct news accounts against a backdrop of assumptions about the social world which they expect the readers to share. They are more likely to select news items that conform to the "maps of meaning" held in common with their imagined audience. Some of the elements chosen by the programme's producers which may construct "maps of meaning" for Gaelic viewers have been suggested above, and the general choice of topics and locations seen in *Eòrpa* does not seem to contradict this view.

What of the role of Gaelic current affairs in creating a proper public sphere[17] in which meaningful public debate takes place? Manning is highly critical of what he sees as a general failure of news and of journalism to create this successfully: "The interface between private experience and public power is structured through the public sphere" he says, and while "contemporary political news media offer the potential to involve and engage audiences in political debate at a deeper level than ever before, this potential is rarely realised" (Manning, quoted in Burton 2010, 266).

Can it be argued that Gaelic programmes such as *Eòrpa* help create this public space for a minority community which until recently was badly served by television or where, extrapolating from MacLean's view quoted earlier that there could be no public sphere since there was "no real Gaelic Television to speak of"? According to *Eòrpa* staff, the general consensus in research carried out for the BBC would tend to reflect this view, and that is re-enforced by the public recognition given to *Eòrpa* by the British Academy of Film and Television Arts and the Scottish Broadcasting Commission.

Might it be argued, however, that Gaelic speakers who are linked through their common culture and language are served in terms of a media public sphere through their fluency in English and thus their access to the media public sphere is achieved in the English language? All Gaelic speakers save the very young are fluent in English. However, evidence suggests that it would be difficult to find any English language programme that consistently deals with the range of topics and geographical areas in the manner that *Eòrpa* clearly does.

Perhaps a useful approach might be to consider television's provision of a "public sphere" as being less uniform than is sometimes assumed. Adopting this approach, Cunningham (2001), looking at migrant groups' experience of transnational television, argues that what is experienced by minority communities is less of a common public sphere and more

---

[17] In the Habermasian sense of the public sphere being a space which mediates between civil society and the state, and in which "individuals and groups discuss and argue about public matters" (Harrison 2000, 25).

multiple public spheres. He refers to them as public "sphericules"—which undermines the common assumptions of television as providing one single and common public sphere:[18]

> Instead it points to forms of citizenship which exist alongside a nationally based civil society. These are 'do-it-yourself' forms which are based on 'culture, identity and voluntary belonging' rather than based on rights derived from, and obligations to, a state. To explore the public sphere in these terms, is to look at those whose 'civitas' connects communities in dozens of countries while also embracing their situatedness in a given one (Sinclair and Cunningham 2000: 28).

While it would be wrong to simply compare Gaelic speaking communities to transnational dispersed communities, there does seem to be some evidence that a common "civitas" and shared outlook can connect Gaels (through common values) with others who have experienced similar histories—such as dispersion, discrimination, marginalisation—issues that do not form part of the "public sphere" for the majority communities. In some ways it can be argued that this reflects a broader European outlook, not necessarily shared by the majority English speaking UK community.

Cormack recently argued that indigenous minority language communities are not victims of post-modernity (in the sense that many were victims of modernity), but—at least in some aspects—examples of it.

> Minority languages are not a remnant of some out-of-date world-view, fragments of now superseded linguistic, political or cultural structures. Rather they fit in with the current global structure very easily, with their emphasis on cultural choice and their focus on identity. Those who use, defend and adopt minority languages are better seen as the prototypes of the new global citizens of the twenty-first century, rather than as atavistic cultural dinosaurs (Cormack 2005, 120).

When asked about whether the issues routinely dealt with in *Eòrpa* were peripheral or core to the concerns of communities such as Gaels in Scotland, the head of BBC Alba recently suggested that these issues "May seem peripheral to the mainstream ... but in our view they are core to those who are concerned".[19]

---

[18] Although of course press, radio and other forms of debate could contribute to other forms of a wider media "public sphere".

[19] Discussion with myself at the Rannsachadh na Gàidhlig (Gaelic Research) conference 2010, Aberdeen.

Works Cited

Allan, S. 2007. *News Culture* (2nd Edition). Maidenhead: OUP.

Anderson, B. 1991. *Imagined Communities*. London: Verso.

BBC/MG Alba Partnership *BBC Alba Performance, Partnerships and Future Strategy*. October 2009. London: BBC Trust.

BBC Scotland. 2009. *BBC Scotland Audience Report*. November.

Beveridge, C. and R. Turnbull. 1989. *The Eclipse of Scottish Culture*. Edinburgh: Polygon.

Briggs, M. 2010. *Television Audiences and Everyday Life*. Maidenhead: OUP.

Burton, G. 2010. *Media and Society: Critical Perspectives*. New York: McGraw Hill.

Chalmers, D. and M. Danson. 2006. Language and Economic Development. In *Revitalising Gaelic in Scotland*, edited by Wilson McLeod. 239-256. Edinburgh: Dunedin Academic Press

Chalmers, D. 2009. The Promotion of Arts and Culture as a Tool of Economic Regeneration: An Opportunity or a Threat to Minority Language Development?—The Case of Gaelic Scotland. In *Rights, Promotion and Integration Issues for Minority Languages in Europe*, edited by Susanna Perton, Tom Priestly and Colin H Williams. 141 – 164. London: Palgrave.

Compass Management Resource Partnership. 2002. Review of An Comunn Gaidhealach and The Royal National Mod. Inverness: HIE.

Cormack, M. 1994. Programming for cultural defence: The expansion of Gaelic Television. *Scottish Affairs*. 6: 114-131.

—. 2005. The cultural politics of minority language media. *International Journal of Media and Cultural Politics*. 1(1): 107-22.

—. 2008. Gaelic the Media and Scotland. In *The Media in Scotland*, edited by Neil Blain and David Hutchison. 213 – 227. Edinburgh: EUP.

Crisell, A. 2006. *A Study of Modern Television–Thinking inside the Box*. New York: Palgrave.

Cunningham, S. 2001 Popular media as public 'sphericules' for diasporic communities. *International Journal of Cultural Studies* 4 (2) http://ics.sagepub.com/content/4/2/131.full.pdf+html. Accessed 17 August 2010.

Daiches, D. 1996 *The Scottish Enlightenment 1730–90*. Edinburgh: Saltire Society.

Davie, G. 1999. *The Democratic Intellect: Scotland and Her Universities in the Nineteenth Century*. Edinburgh: EUP.

Dhòmhnallach, R. 2005. *Gaelic Arts Strategy 2005–2009.* Glasgow: An Lochran.

Glazer, K. 2006. Reimagining the Gaelic community: ethnicity, hybridity, politics and communication. In *Revitalising Gaelic in Scotland,* edited by Wilson McLeod. 169–185. Edinburgh: Dunedin Academic Press.

Grierson, J. 1979. *On Documentary,* ed. Forsyth Hardy. London: Faber and Faber.

Harrison, J. 2000. *Terrestrial TV News in Britain: The Culture of Production.* Manchester: Manchester University Press.

Herman, A. 2003. *The Scottish Enlightenment: The Scots' Invention of the Modern World.* Edinburgh: Fourth Estate.

Home Office 1978. *Broadcasting White Paper.* London: HMSO.

Hutchinson, R. 2005. *A Waxing Moon–The Modern Gaelic Revival.* Edinburgh: Mainstream.

Jenkins, B. 2008. *Viewers verdict: TV news is too shallow.* 31 May. http://www.heraldscotland.com/viewers-verdict-tv-news-is-too-shallow-1.881597. Accessed 17 August 2010.

Lacey, N. 2009. *Image and Representation: Key concepts in Media Studies.* Houndmills: Palgrave.

MacInnes, J. 2006. *Dùthchas Nan Gàidheal.* Edinburgh: Birlinn.

MacKinnon, K. 1991. *Gaelic-a past and future prospect.* Edinburgh: The Saltire Society.

MacLean, M. 2000. Parallel Universes: Gaelic Arts Development in Scotland 1985–2000, in *Aithne na nGael: Gaelic Identities*, edited by Gordon McCoy and Maolcholaim Scott. Belfast: Queens University

Manning, P. 2001 *News and News Sources: A critical introduction.* London: Sage

Moffat, A. 1995. Annual Sabhal Mòr Ostaig Lecture. Skye: SMO.

Oliver, J. 2007 Where is Gaelic? Revitalisation, language, culture and identity. In *Revitalising Gaelic in Scotland*, edited by Wilson McLeod. 155-169. Edinburgh: Dunedin Academic Press.

Scottish Arts Council. 2003. *Gaelic Arts Policy.* http://www.scottisharts.org.uk/1/information/publications/1000305. aspx. Accessed 17 August 2010.

Scottish Executive. 2001. *Gaelic: Revitalising Gaelic a National Asset.* Edinburgh: Scottish Executive.

Sinclair, J. and S. Cunningham. 2000. Go with the flow: Diasporas and the Media. *Television and New Media* 1 (1). http://tvn.sagepub.com/content/1/1/11.full.pdf+html. Accessed 17 August 2010.

Walsh, J. 2009. Ireland's Socio-economic Development and the Irish Language: Theoretical and Empirical Perspectives. In *Language and Economic Development*, edited by John Kirk and Donall P O'Baoill. Belfast: Queens University.

Wilson, P. and M. Stewart, eds. 2008 *Global Indigenous Media—cultures, poetics and politics.* London: Duke University Press.

PROVINCIAL INSIDERS OR METROPOLITAN EXPATRIATES? THE STRANGE CASE OF SCOTTISH JOURNALISTS IN LONDON

DAVID STENHOUSE

Introduction

One of the most famous portraits of Scottish journalists working in the belly of metropolitan journalism appears as an aside in H. V. Morton's 1928 travelogue *In Search of Scotland.*

Morton was a newspaperman by trade and his travel books were as popular in their time as Bill Bryson's are in ours. Like Bryson, Morton combined detailed research lightly worn with wit, comic panache and a talent for sweeping generalisation. By the time he came to Scotland, Morton had already completed *In Search of England* and *In Search of Wales. In Search of Ireland*, which would complete the set, would be published in 1929. His travel book about Scotland was billed as the first Scottish travelogue of the 20th century, "Looking to close a travel-writing gap of over a hundred years" (1928: xii).

After a leisurely journey through the Borders by motor car, and after chapters on Edinburgh, Glasgow and Dundee, Morton reached Aberdeen. Though he had never been to the Granite City before, Morton had already encountered some of its citizens:

English Journalism is red with the hair of Aberdonians. Newspaper proprietors feel better when these hard-heads are about, because they reduce to the lowest minimum the risk of libel actions. The dreadful blue pencils of the Aberdonians travel cautiously over the world's news, cutting out the cackle and getting down to the bare bones of reality. A pencil in such hands ceases to be a pencil: it becomes a surgical implement ... I hit up against the Aberdeen mentality when, as a young journalist from the provinces, I took the post of junior sub-editor on one of the big London dailies. One night a reporter wrote a short article stating that the fig-tree in

> St Paul's Churchyard had given birth to seven figs. In the course of a long night's work I sub-edited this and put a headline on it and forgot it. Three days later I was carpeted by an Aberdonian night editor.
>
> 'Did you do this?' he asked, flinging a clipping at me.
>
> 'I did.'
>
> 'Don't you know,' he cried, hitting his desk at every word, 'that the fir-r-st-requirement-in-your-profession-is-accuracy? ... St Paul's is five minutes' walk from this office! Did ye not think of running down to count the figs?' (1928: 133).

The punctilious and picky Scottish fact checker is a familiar British character, a variant of those other archetypal Unionist Scottish *personae*, the engineer, the policeman and the "upper servant" like the Scottish butler Hudson in the 1970s television series *Upstairs Downstairs*. But Morton was also nodding to another stock idea, the metropolitan perception that London journalism was run by Scots, a perception which by the 1920s was already more than a century old.

The novelist and social critic Thomas Carlyle had left Scotland for London in 1834 and others, like the Ibsen critic William Archer, who was considered to be the most important theatre critic in London before the First World War, followed as the century went on. In their wake went many others whose departure was not noted in Scotland because they had not yet made their names, but who were attracted to London for the same reason that striving provincials always have been, because it seemed to hold out the possibility that there they would find fame. For journalists, London held a particular appeal: it offered a wider range of potential employers than existed in Scotland, a wider range of topics to cover and, potentially, much larger salaries.

The perception that Scots were disproportionately represented in London journalism is how a brain-drain appears from the other end of the drain: if London journalism was "red with the hair of Aberdonians" it was because of the number of Aberdonian journalists who had left Aberdeen behind and relocated south, preferring the subeditors' desk of the *Evening Dispatch* to that of the *Evening Express*. The dominance of Scots within certain British institutions (medicine, the army, the consular branches of the foreign service) is of course a key Unionist *trope*, and one which devolution has problematised in a number of interesting ways. But the media are not just one modern estate amongst others, they constitute the dominant cultural force of the 21st century, the arena in which public discourse is defined and debated, in which political arguments are addressed or ignored, elided or engaged, and the institution which, after Anderson (1983), we routinely think of as both constructing and articulating notions of national community. Journalism allows its practitioners an enviable licence to comment, critique and occasionally preach to their readers on matters of public policy and political controversy.

London-based Scottish journalists challenge easy categorisation within paradigms of centre and periphery: Scottish-based journalists, especially but not exclusively political journalists and commentators, are key actors in Scottish civic life, interpreting the nation back to itself and contributing to a discourse centred on Scotland's history, culture and geography. What role do, and should, Scottish journalists who are based outside Scotland play in the debate about the direction of Scottish society and culture?

This chapter examines a series of key interventions by London-based Scottish journalists into Scottish public discourse between 1998-2002 and asks if London-based Scottish journalists should be seen as careerists, hyper-conforming provincials, "sophisticated" Scots who have slipped the bonds of parochial Scottish media culture, or, ironically, as the last British journalists, able to offer a "national" perspective to an increasingly metropolitan and London-centric media?

Finally, it will ask how the longer term cultural effects of devolution will impact on the position of Scottish journalists working in London: will it cast Scottish voices working out of London adrift from the Scottish body politic, or could it paradoxically afford them greater legitimacy and authority to comment on what is happening North of the Border?

Home Rule for Scottish Journalists?

In the 1970s those who opposed the creation of a Scottish Assembly described it as a job creation scheme for Glasgow trades unionists and Edinburgh lawyers. They might have included Scottish journalists. Newspaper journalists like Neal Ascherson and George Rosie were significant figures in the devolution movement of the 1970s, and in the 1980s arguments for devolution were advanced strongly by figures like Joyce MacMillan who eventually took part in the broadly based Scottish Constitutional Convention which devised The Claim of Right for Scotland. In the 1990s, it's only a slight exaggeration to say that the creation of the Scottish Parliament in 1999 served as a remarkably effective job-creation scheme for London-based Scottish journalists. London newspapers whose interests in Scotland had previously been confined to a narrow and repetitive repertoire of stories and investigations (whisky, golf courses, Edinburgh as the HIV capital of Europe) commissioned a series of London-based Scottish writers, many of whom had left their homeland some decades before, to produce lengthy authored pieces about Scotland's changing political culture.

The remit of these pieces was to "explain" Scotland to an implied metropolitan readership.[1] As subsequent surveys showed (Trench 2001) the finer details of the devolution project were imperfectly understood by many in England, and even the political journalists who covered the Westminster beat were far from certain about how the creation of a Scottish Parliament and a Welsh Assembly would impact on the way Britain was governed and administered. But the mechanics of how the devolutionary settlement would work, baffling though they seemed, were structural questions with factual answers. They were easier to explain than the emotional and cultural drivers within Scottish society which had given the devolution campaign much of its force.

Many of the pieces commissioned to explain *why* Scots were so in favour of devolution fell into an autobiographical mode in which the journalist who had removed himself from Scotland chose to explain the story of Scotland's experiment in devolution in terms of the personal narrative of their own life. In *The Guardian* of 24 April 1999 Kevin Toolis wrote a long essay, "Scotland the vainglorious", which anatomised the political attitudes he was brought up with:

> It is fair to say that I grew up hating England and the English. Even the sound of their toffee-nosed English voices on the television was enough to define them as the enemy—limp-wristed, half-pint-drinking English poofs. I knew that, even though I had never met an English person in my life. I was Scottish [...]

> Us Scots were better than the English in some not entirely expressible way, but we were. We were not impressed by all the silly baubles, titles, the Royal Family, the aristocracy and all that rubbish. We believed we lived in a more meritocratic society. We were truer, and Scotland an altogether more beautiful country. Sure, there was poverty, but it was 'good poverty', where no neighbour ignored a hungry child and everyone was happy eating their fish suppers. Our national myth was evoked each week in the reactionary *Sunday Post* newspaper, in the cartoon section. The Broons were a sprawling inter-generational Glaswegian family [sic], all living happily on top of each other in a Gorbals tenement circa 1950. The Broons

---

[1] Hobson's (1984) description of how, after the American Civil War, Northern journalists toured the Southern states and wrote pieces explaining the exotic, atavistic, unreconstructed South to an implied Northern readership is directly relevant here.

battled, they argued, grandad drank, but it was like us Scots, just one big happy national family.[2]

Toolis' piece ingeniously skewers many of the comforting conceits which were at the heart of what could be termed the "tactical national reimagining" of Scottish identity in the 1980s and 90s, that period in which certain aspects of Scottish society were rediscovered or worked up, and others played down, erased or effaced in order to argue that the country's culture was intrinsically collectivist, social democratic and "fair", a reconstruction which placed it in contrast, and Manichean opposition, to the individualistic, free market and "selfish" ideology of Thatcherism.

Toolis' tone is best described as "rueful regret": once (presumably before he was disabused of the delusion by an immersion in the clearer air of the South) he believed such things. Now he has put away the childish delusions associated with his upbringing in Scotland. But the piece is also a moral challenge, speaking to those shadow aspects of Scottish culture which are hidden, unexplored, dangerous, and which, by extension Scottish political culture is unwilling to acknowledge in itself. It may also perhaps be motivated by a desire to critique the normative nature of much of the debate, or puncture its occasionally sanctimonious tone. Its pay-off leaves little doubt that the author now dismisses the beliefs he was brought up with, and expresses the hope that the entire country could follow the journey he has been on:

But will it be the same in Scotland in ten years' time? What is Scottishness? No one, as yet, has the answer. I hope, as a Scot, that it is something more than the bundle of myths and hatred that I grew up with.

I wish we had no need for it at all.

This rather disobliging piece about the direction that Scottish culture seemed to have taken during much of the twentieth century was not unique. One of the hopes expressed for devolution was that it might offer an opportunity for Scotland to put its own cultural house in order. In August 1999 in a speech at the Edinburgh International Festival, the composer James MacMillan addressed what he saw as endemic anti-Catholic sentiment in Scottish civil society. Though most coverage of his comments focussed on the detail of his remarks about religious intolerance,

---

[2] The Broons (Browns), who feature every week in the *Sunday Post* to this day, are, of course, like the publisher of the newspaper, from Dundee.

his speech also took aim at the normative construction of Scottish national identity:

> at the heart of this malaise is a very Scottish trait—a desire to narrow and to restrict the definition of what it means to be Scottish ... "this country's national religion is Protestant and Presbyterian, and the Scottish Parliament is duty bound to reflect this fact."

> This tendency to restrict, to control and to enforce conformity and homogeneity is an obsessive and paranoid flaw in the Scottish character. It is not confined to the Presbyterian mind. It has eased effortlessly into the collective psyche of much secular discourse, so that even the humanist arid liberal objections to religious belief (and to Catholicism in particular) are motivated by the same urge to restrict, control and enforce.[3]

MacMillan's comments provoked a range of journalistic responses. But amongst the comment pieces from church leaders, arts critics and others it also provoked responses from Scots outside the country, who often couched their critiques in personal narratives which looked back, critically, on their childhoods in Scotland.[4] Andrew O'Hagan noted his approval of the MacMillan critique of Scotland's sectarianism in a piece entitled "'A nation scarred by bigotry'. Ring a bell?" published in the *Sunday Herald* newspaper (15 August 1999), in which his own childhood experiences are taken as talismanic:

> Scotland is a divisive, bigoted society, and this week James MacMillan, the country's best composer, felt the need to come out and say so. Good on him.

> Scottish cultural life is a kind of ongoing guerrilla warfare—a struggle to touch something real in a time of abstraction; to express truth, to give form to what you know or imagine, against an inclination of blood and bone, which serves to render you quiet. The local sites of religious zeal in everyday Scottish life—sport, marriage, education, architecture, the newspapers, the pubs—are pervaded with a notion of the Catholic underdog.

---

[3] James MacMillan, The Bigotry that Shames Scotland, EIF lecture, August 1999.

[4] It was not ever thus: the early-twentieth-century Kailyard school of Scottish writers were, mostly, émigrés in the South: they tended to look back on the Scotland they had left behind with sometimes cloying, sentimental affection. Even the newspaperman and novelist Lewis Grassic Gibbon, writing from Welwyn Garden City with very mixed feelings about the Mearns that he had left behind as a young man, saw the place as harsh, closed, small minded, but not childish.

The culture of Scotland had been marshalled during the 1980s and 1990s as an explanation and justification for devolution. Now that devolution was a reality, it seemed to have become fair game for aggressive, even hostile critique from those who set themselves up as mediators between the hopeful, and suddenly perplexing, devolved country and the sceptical metropolis which eyed Scottish devolution with bemusement and sometime overt hostility.

Implicit in these critiques was also the idea of filling a void, speaking the unspoken, even the unspeakable. The position taken by these London writers was that they were impelled to speak out in the absence of internal Scottish debate. Unspoken was another assumption: that their perspective from London was clearer than that of those who were still mired in the small country politics and concerns of the place they had left behind. They had put aside childish things, and the childish thing they had put aside was Scotland.

A forceful critique of the childishness of Scotland and its new parliament came from Michael Gove, Secretary of State for Education after the 2010 UK general election, then a polemical columnist in *The Times*. In his regular column on 20 August 2002 Gove took aim at the Scottish Parliament in a piece provocatively entitled "Peter Pan Scotland—a country that never grew up":

> Top of the Parliament's political agenda at the moment is a measure which would levy £2,500 fines on restaurants and bars that do not allow public breast-feeding. Few of us would want to deny Scotland's children their own mother's milk but the proposal raises questions. If we are to overturn one of the basic foundation stones of liberty, that those who own private property should be free to set the rules for those who enter it, might we not need a higher justification than breast is best? And if we are to defend the principle that Scotland requires a legislative assembly, might it not be easier if its members appeared to have more pressing priorities than regulating the nation's suckling arrangements?...
>
> The breast-feeding Bill may be trivial, but it is sadly all too typical of the prevailing Scottish political culture. It is a self-regarding politically correct gesture, backed by lobby groups but far from the main concerns of most voters. It requires a grotesque and intrusive extension of state powers, plays to the political elite's belief that they are a progressive vanguard and ignores the basic principle of property rights on which prosperity and liberty depend.

The facts behind this piece were soon shown to be in doubt. The following week Magnus Linklater, writing in the Scottish edition of *The*

Times, offered a corrective not just to the sentiments of the Gove piece but also to the facts—the breastfeeding legislation was a private member's bill which was unlikely to gather enough support to come before the parliament. But nonetheless Gove's column is an interesting piece of writing. Its theme is infantilism, a theme emphasised by the headline about the "Peter Pan nation" that never grew up, and part of a whole series of tropes which emphasised the difference between the Mother of Parliaments in Westminster and the stripling parliament in Edinburgh.

The pro-devolutionary movement in Scotland had enjoyed a relatively clear run within Scotland at expressing its version of Scottish politics and identity throughout the late 1980s and 1990s. By 2004, that narrative was looking so exhausted that another Scottish émigré, John Lloyd, was able to write a piece in *Prospect* Magazine called "Not so Canny" which proclaimed the end of the Scottish moment:

> In the 1980s and 1990s, the Scots made a bid for greater power within the United Kingdom. That bid has failed.
>
> The bid for power may better be represented as several bids—though these were strongly interlocking, and at times could combine. A sense of grievance was the unifying feature, and this grievance was largely directed at the English. It was combined with a strong sense of superiority—which could, itself, take differing forms, though with a common theme.
>
> Among the most pervasive beliefs was that of moral superiority. It was devoutly believed—and devoutly is the word, since it derived from the presumed greater virtues of a flinty Presbyterianism over an accommodating Anglicanism. The late John Smith was among those who believed that "the Scots are a more moral people" (as he once told me) than the English whom he aspired to govern. He shared this belief with that other gifted and self-sacrificing Scots politician, Donald Dewar who had for much of his political life drawn the appropriate conclusion: that Scotland should have a separate parliament.
>
> Moral superiority could and did coexist perfectly well with a desire to remain British. "Here's tae us, wha's like us?"[5] was a toast which could be either grudge-filled or giggling, depending on the speaker or the time, as could the derisive adaptation of the patriotic song, "There'll always be an England," with the second line "As long as Scotland's there." In his oddly titled *The Day Britain Died*, Andrew Marr writes of what he gathered of the Scots/English relationship as a child in his moderately Conservative,

---

[5] A toast sometimes heard in Scotland, and expressed in Scots. The English equivalent would be "Here's to us, who's like us?".

proud-to-be-British, middle-class Scots home—"we Scots lost, but we were nobler and braver and more tragic than the English, who were dull and smug. We were rough, they were smooth. We were gritty, they were suburban."

Between Toolis' rueful autobiographical self-laceration and Lloyd's magisterial meta-analysis lay a set of shared assumptions: the political fate of Scotland and the arguments used to support its experiment in self-government were neither above criticism nor purely a matter for debate within Scotland. They also raised the interesting idea that whilst the argument for self-government had emphasised, for rhetorical reasons, the coherence of Scottish society and its collectivist rather than competitive nature, that argument had come at a cost: intellectual dissent. The unionist argument had been successfully marginalised within Scottish civic society during the 1980s and 1990s, even whilst, at a UK level, it continued to enjoy electoral support. Could effective criticism of Scotland's prevailing ethos now only be expressed by those outside the country?

The presence of Scottish-identified writers writing about Scotland for London-based newspapers and a British readership introduced a level of complexity to the relationship between different spheres of the British media which goes beyond the centres and peripheries model. Should Scottish-identified writers who choose to write about Scotland from outside the country be seen as peripheral irritants to the Scottish body politic, or as an expression of the legitimate opinions of a Scottish community of interests which exists outside the country's borders?

One effect of devolution was that both the Scottish Parliament and Scottish civic society became increasingly interested in the perspectives of diaspora Scots, and increasingly keen to involve them in the affairs of the devolved country. It would be profoundly ironic if, whilst welcoming the views, and tourist dollars, of Americans, Canadians or Australians who increasingly identified as Scots, the devolved country were to discount the views of first generation Scots who chose to live and work outside Scotland, but within Britain.

The views, sometimes contrarian, of Scottish journalists who are based in London and who offer, in different ways, non-conformist opinions on Scottish civic culture, represent peripheral voices which articulate the concerns of the British periphery back to the Scottish centre. But as devolution becomes the settled model of Scottish government will the voices of Scottish journalists become more or less significant?

Conclusion

The (re)establishment of the Scottish Parliament in 1999 offered a number of explicit and implicit promises to Scottish civic society. One central promise was that the devolved parliament would lead to the re-centring of Scottish politics, the revival of domestic Scottish political institutions and the rejuvenation of Scottish civic society. Behind these lay a political assumption too: that Scotland's domestic political institutions could now be run according to a political agenda more in tune with "Scottish" values and more resistant to British Governments of an unsympathetic character that might wish to impose "alien" values on Scotland. In the immediate aftermath of the 1999 settlement, it was possible to believe that this argument held force: the Scottish media, especially newspapers in Scotland, benefited from devolution in two ways.

Firstly, Scotland's constitutional experiment became major Scottish, British and international news. The recreation of the parliament led to a surge of interest in Scotland and its political identity. The escalating costs and delays in the construction of the parliament building, the rainbow array of small parties elected to the first parliament, (thanks in large part to the complex voting system employed), the death of First Minister Donald Dewar, the resignation of First Minister Henry McLeish, all ensured that Holyrood got, and deserved front page coverage, and that there was an increased appetite on the inside pages for analysis, discussion and "think pieces" about Scottish affairs.

Secondly, at the institutional level, many newspapers in Scotland benefitted from a temporary financial surge. The *Sunday Herald* was created in February 1999 on an explicit agenda of reporting and representing the new Scotland. The Scottish section of *The Sunday Times*, which had been created in response to the 1988 launch of *Scotland on Sunday,* was given greater prominence, and the Scottish edition of *The Times* took on Scottish staff and writers with an agenda to represent Scottish life in greater breadth and depth than before.

In the world of the print media in Scotland it seemed that the argument of devolution was working: news outlets which had, pre-devolution, been provincial or peripheral to the powerful metropolitan centre were now becoming meaningful centres in their own right, commissioning work from indigenous journalists on Scottish topics. The gravitational pull exerted by the new parliament was enough to recentre key parts of Scottish civic society, and metropolitan voices which had once seemed so central seemed to be becoming increasingly peripheral to Scottish reality. Logically, the role of London-based, though Scottish-born or identified, writers would diminish as devolution settled in and became the established norm. Scotland would become the story and the Scottish story would be told most compellingly from within the country.

This has not happened, and the reasons why it has not happened need some exploration. The most important is economic: one effect of the seismic and deep-rooted structural changes in the Scottish newspaper industry has been that the range, depth and extent of Scottish coverage has been severely curtailed. As *The Herald/Sunday Herald* and *Scotsman/ Scotland on Sunday* roll into seven days a week operation by contracting their newsrooms, the depth, breadth and the very viability of the Scottish newspaper model is under threat as it is hit by the double whammy of declining circulations and declining market share as Scottish editions of London titles woo customers from indigenous papers (Hutchison 2008). This has meant that, far from being at the centre of re-energised civic cultures, Scottish newspapers have withered since devolution, their long term structural decline masked by the few good years which followed the creation of the Parliament

The structural decline of the Scottish newspaper industry has already had a major effect on journalism and journalists in Scotland. The contraction of staff, the conflation of roles, the collapse in the freelance market and other forces have made some commentators like Professor Philip Meyer, who predicted that Scotland's major quality newspapers may not survive beyond 2018,[6] question the long term viability of Scottish newspapers altogether. That has meant, perhaps paradoxically, that at the very time that the devolved parliament enters its second decade of life, the civic institutions which it once promised to revive are struggling for their very existence. In such a context Scottish commentators in London-based newspapers, who once seemed peripheral irritants to the Scottish body politic, are likely to become *more* important, with the role of articulating and explaining Scotland to an implied British readership, but also, as the Scottish print media struggles to survive, to interpret Scotland through the centre and back to itself.

At one time it seemed likely that a devolved Scotland would mark the end of the kind of punctilious Aberdonian subeditors that H. V. Morton wrote about in *In Search of Scotland*. The role of subeditor may not survive the institutional revolution in newspapers. But there is no sign that London-based Scottish columnists, commentators or news editors will be out of a job soon.

And as for the expatriate Scots occupying prominent positions on the airwaves—Gavin Esler, Eddie Mair, Andrew Marr and James Naughtie

---

[6] Interviewed in BBC Radio Scotland, *The Investigation*, 15th May 2008.

spring immediately to mind—they too appear to face a prosperous future. Like all broadcast journalists, they are obliged to operate within the constraints of impartiality and balance still required in British radio and television, so how they have presented Scotland to the rest of the UK is a fascinating and rather different story which is beyond the scope of this chapter.

Works Cited

Anderson, B. 1983. *Imagined Communities: Reflections on the Origin and Spread of Nationalism*. London: Verso.

Huchison, D. 2008. "The History of the Press" in *The Media in Scotland*, edited by D. Hutchison and N. Blain. 55-70. Edinburgh: EUP.

Morton, H. V. 1928. *In Search of Scotland*. London: Methuen.

Hobson, F. 1984. *Tell about the South: the Southern Rage to Explain*. Louisiana State University Press.

Trench, A. ed. 2001. *The State of the Nations 2001: The Second Year of Devolution in the United Kingdom*. London: Imprint.

LONDON RULES—
THE MYTH OF A NATIONAL MEDIA

HOWARD TUMBER

Recent UK "national" newspaper stories (Gallagher 2010) have highlighted the discontent felt by some BBC journalists and executives about the proposed move outside of London of some of the BBC's production and programmes. The Corporation is moving five departments—sport, children's, Radio 5 Live, learning and parts of the future media and technology department—to MediaCity, currently being built at Salford Quays, Greater Manchester, and due for completion in 2011. In 2008 the BBC Trust approved the BBC Executive's recommendation for a new target for production "Out of London" of 50% by 2016. The BBC plan was to achieve growth in the Nations (Scotland, Wales and Northern Ireland) from the 2007 figure of 6% of network spend to 17% by 2016, with an interim target of 12% by 2012. In the English Regions growth was planned to increase from 26% in 2008 to 33% in 2016.

How much these BBC changes will change the London "bias" of the media in Britain remains to be seen but one thing we can question is whether Britain actually has a national media.

The "National" Press

Through an examination of how the so-called national press has been defined by academics and regulatory agencies, its current unbalance in terms of production, circulation and readership becomes more apparent. A UK national newspaper, for instance, is understood by the media industry agency ABC[1] as "one which is widely distributed in *at least* one of the following: a) England, Wales and Northern Ireland; or b) Scotland; or c) the Republic of Ireland" (my emphasis). The number of wholesalers

---

[1] Source: National Newspapers ABC Reporting Standards (2010). The Reporting Standards are the industry-agreed rules by which ABC/ABCe data is prepared. For more details see:
http://www.abc.org.uk/Corporate/AboutABC/Reporting_standards.aspx

handling the newspaper determines, according to ABC, the level of the distribution, so that if a newspaper is available at the majority of the wholesalers in a particular region, its distribution is considered wide and its scope national. Yet a question then arises: what if a newspaper is distributed widely in one region other than England, for instance the Republic of Ireland? Would that newspaper be considered national? Surely not, as the following extract on the Scottish press market explains:

> Putting politics, semantics and national pride to one side, it should be noted that the ABC, the Audit Bureau of Circulation, includes the major Scottish newspapers in its monthly audit of UK national newspaper circulations. This highlights the empirical fact that a key component of newspaper purchase in Scotland is the London-based national press. It could be argued that in terms of newspaper description 'national' implies availability all over the country, and the London-based nationals meet that criterion, while the Scotland-based papers do not. However, they are available all over Scotland, and thus meet the criterion if Scotland is regarded as a nation (Cole and Harcup 2010, 51).

Similarly, the ambiguities of the concept "national press" were examined by Seymour-Ure (1991) in his study of the British press and broadcasting, whilst highlighting the common London base and uneven circulation pattern of most daily newspapers. The concentration of the printing plants[2] in England and the fact that most of the dailies had their base in London have made the nationwide circulation of newspapers "a fiction" (Seymour-Ure 1991, 19). The consolidation of the newspaper wholesale sector reinforced the centrality of England and Wales, countries which in 1992 had 78 wholesalers and fifteen years later only fifteen (and a further seven operating in other parts of the UK) due to acquisition and/or loss of independent wholesalers.[3] This regional concentration is comprised of three large multiple wholesalers—of newspapers and

---

[2] Printing plants in the UK have been closing in the last few years with the accompanying losses of jobs resulting from cost reduction initiatives. The purchase of a new mega printing plant in north London (the Broxbourne plant) by News International, which left its Wapping headquarters recently and reduced its printing staff considerably, exemplifies this restructuring process. Equally illustrative is the dismissal of 1500 staff from the Daily Mail & General Trust as a result of the closure of regional printing plants during 2009. For more information, see the Press Gazette: http://www.pressgazette.co.uk/

[3] Office of Fair Trading (2008) *Newspaper and magazine distribution in the United Kingdom Introductory overview paper on the newspaper and magazine supply chains.* Available online at:
http://www.oft.gov.uk/shared_oft/reports/comp_policy/oft1028.pdf

magazines—and independent wholesalers. The three main wholesalers are: Dawson News (with its depots in the South and West of the UK); Menzies Distribution (including almost all of Scotland, northern England and parts of Wales, East Anglia, London and the South East); and Smiths News (territories and depots are mainly in central England).[4]

The fundamental role played by London in the national press market is not new. During the late nineteenth century, despite the fact that London-based leading newspapers were circulated throughout Britain and Ireland, they were mostly perceived as fundamentally London, rather than national, papers (Potter 2004, 39). In his analysis of the British press during the First World War, McEwen (1982, 461) defined the "national press" as comprised by those newspapers which had a national readership, excluding provincial, Welsh, Scottish and Irish newspapers, and focusing upon the London papers and *The Manchester Guardian*, including the latter only in view of the influence it exercised in the capital city. This is not surprising if one considers that the biggest national newspaper press in Western Europe is found in London and the leading publications in the UK are all London daily newspapers (Tunstall 1996). Even today the very definition of the national press is underpinned by those newspapers which are published in London and readily available across the UK, for London remains the source of most news ranging from parliament, senior courts, the royal family to financial institutions (Cole and Harcup 2010, 19). As the capital city of the UK, London's central dominance rendered the British press a particular European case by being dominated by national newspapers published in one city (Tunstall 1996, 2).

In terms of circulation, in 1995 the leading ten titles that made up the national daily press accounted for 69 per cent of all daily newspapers distributed in the UK and were edited in London and then circulated throughout the country (Sparks 1999, 42). In the past the production of a national newspaper required a variety of elements. Seymour-Ure (1991, 21) argues that the recipe for a national paper was comprised of a mixture of national reputation, geographical reach and breadth of content. He further explains that before 1945 the ingredients were different because a dynamic provincial press managed to co-exist with a London-based metropolitan press without being overshadowed by the latter in terms of circulation or editorial authority.

---

[4] Office of Fair Trading, op. cit.

**Table 1. Readership profiles in Great Britain during April 2009 –
March 2010**

	Unwtd Sample	Est. No. Of Readers	London & SE	SW & Wales
		(000's)	%	%
Estimated percentage of population aged 15 +	36856	49675	36	14
Daily Newspapers—6 Day AIR				
The Sun	4707	7751	41	11
Daily Mirror/Record	2933	4288	28	12
Daily Mirror	2126	3381	35	15
Daily Record	834	952	2	0
Daily Mail	4029	4881	42	16
The Daily Telegraph	1805	1840	48	18
The Times	1503	1768	56	13
Daily Star	903	1617	24	10
Daily Express	1281	1529	35	15
The Guardian	935	1124	57	10
The Independent	486	635	57	12
Financial Times	330	418	69	5
Sunday Newspapers				
News of the World	4718	7642	35	13
The Mail on Sunday	4163	5213	43	15
Sunday Mirror	2322	3826	34	14
The Sunday Times	2842	3219	48	13
The Sunday Telegraph	1601	1677	47	17
Sunday Express	1319	1622	33	15
The People	833	1331	30	12
The Observer	1031	1212	54	11
Sunday Mail	1020	1118	3	0
Daily Star Sunday	519	950	28	9
The Sunday Post	911	832	2	1
The Independent on Sunday	470	600	57	12
Scotland on Sunday	211	190	3	1
Sunday Herald—Scotland	170	125	1	1

	Midlands	North West	NE & North	Scotland	Greater London
	%	%	%	%	%
Estimated percentage of population aged 15 +	16	11	14	9	13
Daily Newspapers—6 Day AIR					
The Sun	17	6	13	11	16
Daily Mirror/Record	11	13	14	22	12
Daily Mirror	14	17	18	2	15
Daily Record	1	1	0	96	1
Daily Mail	16	10	10	6	11
The Daily Telegraph	12	9	10	3	10
The Times	11	8	9	3	23
Daily Star	14	17	25	9	9
Daily Express	14	12	15	9	7
The Guardian	9	8	11	4	35
The Independent	10	7	10	4	25
Financial Times	11	6	6	3	37
Sunday Newspapers					
News of the World	18	10	14	9	13
The Mail on Sunday	17	10	11	4	12
Sunday Mirror	16	18	16	3	14
The Sunday Times	14	9	11	5	19
The Sunday Telegraph	13	10	11	3	13
Sunday Express	15	13	17	7	8
The People	17	18	20	3	11
The Observer	13	9	8	4	28
Sunday Mail	1	0	1	94	1
Daily Star Sunday	14	22	19	9	13
The Sunday Post	2	5	14	75	1
The Independent on Sunday	10	8	10	3	28
Scotland on Sunday	2	0	4	89	1
Sunday Herald—Scotland	1	0	0	97	1

"National" Readership

An examination of readership profiles for the period April 2009-March 2010, shown in Table 1,[5] indicates that London and the South East (SE) concentrate the highest proportion of readers of national newspapers in Britain (36%), followed by the Midlands which only has 16%. All of the newspapers, except for the *Daily Star*, have the highest number of their readers in London and the SE. Moreover, all of the broadsheets have more than a half of their readers in that area. The *Financial Times* has almost 70% of its readers concentrated there. Similarly, Sunday national newspapers have the highest number of their readers located in London and the SE. The quality papers are more read in that region, where they have around 50% of their readers. *The Independent on Sunday* and *The Observer* have more than half of their readers in the area.

Together with the degree of circulation and readership, the variety of content and the biases of newspapers have also been considered points of reference for measuring their national relevance. Papers such as *The Scotsman* and *The Glasgow Herald* (retitled *The Herald* in 1992) were labelled "too Scottish to be national" and the *Financial Times* was criticised for having too specialised content (Seymour-Ure 1991, 19). In the same vein, reading London-based newspapers became crucial for those interested in national political affairs, such as the doings of parliament and the city in London, and the economic life of the country (Sparks 1999, 45).

The situation, as Anthony King (2008) remarked in a report for the BBC Trust, is now even more London-centric:

> Few London-based newspapers now have full-time correspondents based in Northern Ireland and fewer, if any, have full-time correspondents in Wales. The London-based daily papers do have full-time staffs in Scotland, but the members of those staffs are, in most cases, principally concerned with producing the Scottish edition of the paper they work for; they find it increasingly difficult to place stories about Scotland in the south-of-the-border editions of their own paper. The effect is that news of Wales, Northern Ireland and Scotland has become increasingly ghettoised in the print media. It is largely confined to newspapers published in those nations (e.g. the Glasgow-based *Herald,* the *South Wales Echo,* the *Belfast Telegraph*) and to the editions of the London-based newspapers that are distributed there (King 2008, 25).

---

[5] Source: the National Readership Survey (NRS Ltd.), April 2009-March 2010.

Nowadays with the introduction of devolution of power from Westminster to Scotland, Wales and Northern Ireland in 1999, the way the media report political news has witnessed some changes; however, Westminster continues to be the base for the political editors and therefore the impact of the new devolved assemblies on the political reporting in London has been insignificant (Barnett and Gaber 2001, 132):

> Scottish newspapers and the Scottish editions of London-based papers continue to report news of events and developments taking place in England, but it is becoming harder and harder for newspaper readers outside Scotland, including in England, to follow what is going on elsewhere in the UK (King 2008, 25).

The most damning indictment of the dominance of London in the UK news profile is evident in the research for the BBC Trust conducted by Cardiff University (Cushion, Lewis and Ramsay 2010). With the aim of measuring how devolution stories were reported by the media in order to examine issues of accuracy, impartiality and coverage of the four nations within the United Kingdom, a review of the BBC coverage was carried out in 2007 and updated in 2009. The detailed content analysis of 5,177 news items across a range of BBC programmes revealed that there was an improvement of the coverage of devolution items over that period, and that the BBC was noticeably more sensitive to those issues and other stories about Scotland, Wales and Northern Ireland than other broadcasters. The report points out that there was also a tendency in most broadcasters to present stories concerning England and Wales as if they applied to the UK as a whole, and that, despite the geographical distribution of the audience, there was a primacy (and bias) of England as a source of information. Equally, the report argued that most of the policy-related stories focused on Westminster as a political institution although the BBC slightly increased the number of news items related to Scotland, Wales and Northern Ireland.[6] This is not a situation that the various audience groups are satisfied with, as shown by the BMRB Media research (2008) which indicated that the majority of the UK population were interested in news concerning not only England, but also other nations in the UK in order to have a better understanding of political processes elsewhere.

---

[6] Specifically the report states that in 2007 only one piece of news out of 160 dealing with the key devolved areas of health and education was not on England; a greater spread across the four nations was registered two years later (BBC Trust 2010, 14).

The BBC Executive (BBC Trust 2008) responded to the Cardiff University initial research by accepting the criticism of the failure to provide the audience with political stories that represent more accurately the diversity of the UK, and by announcing that steps would be taken towards producing a better coverage of the devolved nations, provided that those stories were strong and relevant.

In response to Cardiff University follow-up research, the BBC Trust announced (July 2010) that the improvements already made by the BBC had been visible in the increase of: the proportion of news items relating to the devolved nations; the number of BBC television reporters broadcasting from Scotland, Wales and Northern Ireland; the number of news items and references relating to devolved powers; and the comparison between the policies of the devolved nations. The review also identified areas where further progress is needed:

> Some BBC news items still do not make it clear which part of the UK they are referring to, and hence are reported as if they apply to the whole of the UK, when in fact stories apply to England.

and secondly:

> There are some areas where there is a continued bias in favour of stories about England. For example, of 112 BBC items about health and education, 104 related to England and eight to the other three nations. However all news stories about the arts and policing related only to England (BBC Trust 2010).

The London dominance then is not just confined to political news. In a recent blog in the *Guardian*, Toby Frow, the theatre director, complained that plays he had directed in major regional theatres got less medium coverage than those in the tiniest London venues. He made a plea for arts and culture critics to move out of their metropolitan comfort zone. He complained that the national press had only reviewed his out-of-London work where he had directed productions at Birmingham Rep, West Yorkshire Playhouse and Northampton's Theatre Royal, a total of six times during the past seven years. In contrast every show he had directed in London, whether at a fringe venue or west end theatre, had received near-universal coverage (http://www.guardian.co.uk/stage/theatreblog/ 2010/may/ 26 /regional-theatre-media-coverage.).

Despite the BBC move out to the regions and in particular the creation of its new media hub in Salford, any real change in London's dominance as the centre of journalistic activity is very doubtful. Apart from the structural constraints of source-journalist relations, the chances of media companies employing more journalists and/or redistributing existing ones outside London in the current economic crisis are very remote.

References

ABC. 2010. *National Newspapers ABC Reporting Standards.* http://www.abc.org.uk/Corporate/AboutABC/documents/nn.pdf. Accessed 12 July 2010.

Barnett, S. and I. Gaber. 2001. *Westminster tales: the twenty-first century crisis in British political journalism.* London: Continuum.

BBC Trust. 2008. http://www.bbc.co.uk/bbctrust/our_work/other/nations_ conclusions.shtml. Accessed 12 July 2010.

—. 2010. *BBC Network News coverage of the four UK Nations: follow-up.* http://www.bbc.co.uk/bbctrust/our_work/other/nations_follow_up. shtml. Accessed 12 July 2010.

BMRB Media. 2008. *BBC Trust – Nations' Impartiality Review.* http://www.bbc.co.uk/bbctrust/assets/files/pdf/review_report_research/ impartiality/appendix_b_bmrb_research.pdf. Accessed 12 July 2010.

Cole, P. and T. Harcup. 2010. *Newspaper Journalism.* London: Sage.

Cushion, S., J. Lewis and G. N. Ramsay. 2010. *Four Nations Impartiality Review Follow-up: An analysis of reporting devolution*, Cardiff University. http://www.bbc.co.uk/bbctrust/our_work/other/nations_follow_up. shtml. Accessed 12 July 2010.

Frow, T. 2010. London arts editors: get out more. http://www.Guardian.co.uk/stage/theatreblog/2010/may/26/regional-theatre-media-coverage. Accessed 12 July 2010.

Gallagher, I. 2010. I'm not moving up North, says BBC HR boss: £190,000-a-year executive quits as he joins growing number of BBC 'refuseniks' who want to stay in South. http://www.dailymail.co.uk/news/article-1305133/Im-moving-North-says-BBC-HR-boss--190-000-year-executive-quits-joins-growing-number-BBC-refuseniks-want-stay-South.html. Accessed 22 August 2010.

McEwen, J. M. 1982. The National Press during the First World War: Ownership and Circulation. *Journal of Contemporary History*, 17 (3): 459-486.

Office of Fair Trading (2008) *National newspapers: A review of undertakings relating to the supply of national newspapers in England and Wales (the Code of Practice).*

http://www.oft.gov.uk/shared_oft/reports/comp_policy/oft1026.pdf. Accessed 12 August 2010.

Potter, S. J. 2004. Empire and the English press, c. 1857-1914. In *Newspapers and Empire in Ireland and Britain. Reporting the British Empire 1857-1921*, edited by S. J. Potter. 39-61. Dublin: Four Courts.

Seymour-Ure, C. 1991. *The British Press and Broadcasting since 1945.* Oxford: Blackwell.

Sparks, C. 1999. The Press. In *The Media in Britain. Current Debates and Developments*, edited by J. Stokes and A. Reading. 41-59. London: MacMillan Press Ltd.

Tunstall, J. 1996. *Newspaper power: the new national press in Britain.* Oxford: Clarendon Press.

EUROPEAN PERSPECTIVES

JOURNALISM IN CONTEMPORARY FRANCE

RAYMOND KUHN

The practice of journalism in France is currently at a low ebb. Domestic news media markets are characterised by hyper-competition for audiences and revenue; media consumers are less loyal than in the past to any particular media outlet, while the young are a particularly difficult clientele to attract and retain; new technology poses an economic challenge to the established mainstream media, notably digital channels in the television sector and the internet in the case of the press; traditional journalistic practices are having to adapt, sometimes reluctantly and frequently with considerable tension, to media organisations' need to have both an online and offline presence; and sources, both commercial and political, often seem to have a resource advantage over journalists in the process of news agenda construction and issue framing. It is of little consolation to French journalists coping with these changes in their domestic news media environment that journalism in other developed societies is having to face up to a similar set of economic and professional challenges.

This chapter provides a broad overview of the state of journalism—metropolitan and non-metropolitan—in contemporary France. It begins with a section on key features of the news media landscape and in particular the balance between national and provincial news outlets. This is followed by a section on the scale and scope of the problems currently facing French journalism, while Part Three considers some of the responses made to address these concerns.

The news media landscape

The relationship between metropolitan and non-metropolitan journalism in contemporary France is heavily influenced by the structural configuration of the news media landscape. The balance here is strongly in favour of national media outlets, with some significant sources of local/regional strength, notably in the newspaper sector. Among print media, for instance, magazines are usually produced in the greater Paris area, while in the broadcasting sector it is national radio stations and television channels that are the most important market players. In contrast, the dominant outlets in the newspaper sector in terms of circulation are to be found at the regional level. The result is that the majority of French journalists—well over 60%—work for media based in and around Paris. Nationwide just under 70% of journalists work in the press, 14% in television and under 10% in radio, with the remaining 6% employed across other sectors such as film, graphics, publishing, advertising and education.

The daily newspaper sector consists of two distinct markets: national titles produced in Paris and provincial (i.e. local and regional) papers (Albert 2008). The big regional titles, often centred on a provincial conurbation, dominate sales nationwide: of the 8 million total print run of daily newspapers in France, just over 6 million are regional titles and fewer than 2 million are national. In any particular French region a single title frequently enjoys a de facto monopoly position and is usually well able to protect its territorial fiefdom against potential competitors (Martin 2002). The biggest selling daily is *Ouest-France* (Rennes) with a circulation of 786,000 in 2009. In 2006 the Ouest-France group published no fewer than 42 local editions of its main daily newspaper, employed around 1,200 journalists and had a network of about 5,000 correspondents who provided local information to the newsdesk (Tessier and Baffert 2007, 38). Other high circulation regional dailies (2009 figures) include *La Voix du Nord* (Lille: 282,000), *Sud-Ouest* (Bordeaux: 304,000), *Le Progrès* (Lyons: 218,000) and *Le Dauphiné libéré* (Grenoble: 242,000). In contrast, the national titles sell mainly in the greater Paris area. In 2009 *Le Monde* had a circulation of 323,000, *Le Figaro* 331,000 and *Libération* 117,000. The most obvious gap on the supply side among national dailies and the main reason for their low total circulation nationwide is the absence of a popular title with tabloid journalistic values: France notably lacks the equivalent of *The Sun* in Britain or *Bild* in Germany. Similarly, none of the regional newspapers bases its appeal on tabloid-style journalism.

The great importance attached to local identity in France has contributed to the powerful position of provincial papers in their particular geographic localities. Strong identification with heterogeneous sub-national cultural traditions and local communities has helped underpin the strength of local and regional newspapers in their competition with the national dailies. Despite the creation of ever faster and more efficient communication and transportation networks, many French people cling strongly to their local roots, taking a great interest in information relevant to events and personalities in their particular locality or region. The provincial papers have been well placed to satisfy this demand, with their extensive coverage of local and regional information. They also tend to be cheaper to buy than the national dailies as well as being more successful in securing regular readers through subscription and home delivery, both of which all newspapers are increasingly keen to encourage as means of distribution because of the low number of newsagents per head of population in France.

The structures of the French political system have also helped the provincial press. Top national politicians generally seek to legitimise their position through control of a local/regional power base: for instance, Martine Aubry, leader of the main opposition party (the Socialist party) is mayor of Lille, Alain Juppé, a leading member of the governing party (the Union pour un Mouvement Populaire), is mayor of Bordeaux and Ségolène Royal, the defeated Socialist candidate in the 2007 presidential election, is head of the regional council of Poitou-Charentes. Well-known national politicians are thus locally embedded in a way that directs at least some media attention away from a purely metropolitan focus. As a result, politicians of national standing are obliged to take a keen interest in their mediation by the relevant local/regional news media. More generally, French politicians are always keen to harness the support of the non-metropolitan media in their election campaigns, with Jacques Chirac even declaring his candidacy for the 1995 presidential election via a regional newspaper, *La Voix du Nord*.

The sales superiority of provincial titles does not mean that national newspapers have a lower status or exert little influence. Whereas in some other European countries, such as Italy and Germany, large non-metropolitan urban centres publish high quality, prestige newspapers, this is not the case in France. As far as the publication of elite opinion-forming newspapers is concerned, there is no French equivalent of Milan or Frankfurt. On the contrary, despite their comparatively low circulations, in key respects the national dailies are the dominant players in the French press system. Whereas the provincial dailies may be important sources of information for the mass of society, it is the national dailies that reflect the concerns of elites. In particular, the quality national dailies such as *Le Monde*, *Le Figaro* and *Les Echos* exercise an influence among key political and economic decision makers, as well as acting as a major forum for the discussion of new ideas in social and cultural matters. This privileged position of the national press among elites is scarcely surprising, given that the capital is the centre of French political, economic and cultural life. As a result, even provincial titles based far from the capital complement their local and regional content with stories that have a national resonance. In contrast, the national titles largely ignore local and regional news, except when this has a strong human interest dimension, such as a natural disaster.

While circulation of daily newspapers is low by European standards, in contrast France has a healthy magazine sector, even if it has been adversely affected by the economic downturn of recent years. Indeed, the French magazine market is Europe's biggest both in terms of revenues and advertising, while France has one of the highest levels of magazine readership in the world (Charon 2008). Young people are particularly avid readers of magazines, while the weakest readership is among the elderly: the opposite age profile of newspaper readers. Two groups of magazine titles are, albeit in very different ways, important in terms of political journalism. The first consists of news magazines approximating to the style of the US *Time* or *Newsweek*. France has four main weekly news magazines—*L'Express*, *Le Nouvel Observateur*, *Le Point* and *Marianne*— covering political, economic, social and cultural issues for their educationally highly qualified and socially upmarket readerships. The news magazines fill a gap left by the lack in the French media landscape of quality Sunday newspapers which in Britain, for example, have long provided a rich source of political analysis and commentary. They compete for readers not just against each other, but also with the more generalist of the business magazines such as *Le Nouvel Économiste* and *Challenges* as well as the quality national dailies. The combined circulation of the four news magazines has grown steadily to exceed 1.5 million per week. The second group of magazine titles whose journalism is of political importance includes the photonews weekly *Paris Match* and celebrity magazines such as *Gala* which allow politicians to market themselves to audiences under conditions of "controlled mediation".

In the broadcasting sector the major radio stations and television channels are predominantly national. Radio provision is dominated by four major national networks: RTL, Europe 1, NRJ and France Inter (Cavelier and Morel-Maroger 2008). In television the dominant players since the economic liberalisation of the sector in the 1980s have been the commercial channels TF1 and M6 and the two main public service channels France 2 and France 3. In addition to the news output of these generalist channels, France also has three national rolling news channels: i-télé, LCI and BFM TV. As part of its regional remit France 3 programmes different regional news programmes nationwide and thus serves alongside the regional press and local radio as a significant source of non-metropolitan news for provincial audiences. The regionalisation of French television is, however, not as developed as in Germany or Spain:

this reflects the lower status of the region within the French political system, the absence of strong regionalist political parties and the original institutional development of television in France as a highly centralised medium, with strategic decision-making based in Paris. Moreover, even in the more variegated and segmented provision that has resulted from the implantation of digital television in recent years, the main channels in terms of both supply and demand are still national.

Television is the primary source of national and international news for French citizens (57%), followed in order of importance by the radio (20%), the press (14%) and the internet (8%) (La Croix 2010). Thus television is a more frequent primary source for national and international news than radio, press and internet combined. It should be noted, however, that among the 18-24 age group the internet (19%) is the second most important source of national and international news after television (63%), while for all those under 35 the internet comes ahead of the press. For many young people the internet's combination of visual and audio text, its interactive functions, its accessibility for users on the move via mobile phones and other handheld devices and its capacity to allow users to be producers and not just consumers of information make newsprint newspapers look tired and out of date.

Journalism in crisis

Journalism in France is in a parlous condition. This may seem a paradoxical assessment, since as recently as 2008 there had never been more people officially employed as professional journalists in France. Indeed the growth in numbers since 1975 has been nothing short of prolific (see Table 1). A closer inspection of the figures shows, however, that the rate of growth has slowed down significantly in recent years: 60% between 1980 and 1990; just under 20% between 1990 and 1999; and 13.5% between 2000 and 2008, with more than half of this latest increase taking place in the first two years of the millennium alone. Between 2006 and 2008 the rise in the number of journalists in France was negligible, while in 2009 there was even a slight fall in the overall total.

Table 1   Number of officially recognised journalists in France

Year	Number of journalists
1975	13,635
1980	16,619
1985	22,621
1990	26,614
1995	28,000
2000	33,314
2005	36,828
2006	37,423
2007	37,738
2008	37,811
2009	37,390

Sources: Observatoire des métiers de la presse (2009, 2); Commission de la Carte d'Identité des Journalistes Professionels (2010).

Yet while employment statistics are essential quantitative indicators of the state of the profession, they reveal nothing about the qualitative condition of journalism in contemporary France. Like its counterparts in other developed societies, this has been profoundly affected by wide-sweeping changes in the news media environment in recent years. As elsewhere, one of the main drivers of change has come from the rapid spread of new information and communication technologies in a process that has come to be dubbed "the digital revolution". Journalism is affected by these developments at two distinct levels: first, in terms of the economic viability of traditional news media outlets—the *business* of journalism and, second, in terms of the occupational practices of journalists—the *profession* of journalism. The rest of this section examines each of these two aspects in turn.

The business of journalism, especially in its traditional newsprint form, is now confronted with a huge economic challenge. While the spread of the internet has had an impact on all traditional news media, it has posed a particularly acute problem for newspapers. The problems are particularly severe for general information titles, whose print circulations and advertising revenue are both in a decline that some commentators regard as terminal. Yet the transfer of newsprint newspapers' information function to the internet poses the problem of how to monetise web-based content in the face of the availability of free news from a wide range of different providers. As is the case in other Western countries, there is as yet no clear business model that guarantees the commercial viability of general information newspapers on the net.

Meanwhile, newsprint newspapers are finding it increasingly difficult to attract readers. For many French citizens reading a newspaper remains a daily ritual. Observance of this ritual is, however, less widely maintained than previously. According to official government statistics, in 2008 69% of French citizens above the age of 15 sometimes read a daily newspaper (compared with 73% in 1997), but only 29% did so (almost) every day (36% in 1997) (Donnat 2009, 6). Only 11% read a *national* daily more than once a week (13% in 1997), while 32% read a *regional* daily with the same frequency (38% in 1997). Of all the sociological variables—educational qualifications, gender, ethnic origin, employment status—potentially linked to the decline in newspaper reading, age is the most important. In 2008 58% of 15-24 year olds sometimes read a daily newspaper (70% in 1997), but only 10% did so (almost) every day (20% in 1997) (Donnat 2009, 6). There is evidence that young people in particular have become accustomed to not paying for access to certain media and entertainment services (for example, the downloading of music) and that this is creating a new relationship between provider and user in the online world. Young people are particularly resistant to paying for a newspaper and there is a fear among newspaper owners and journalists that the current generation of young people may never properly acquire the habit of regular reading even as they grow older.

For instance, a recent study of readership of the regional press in France revealed the extent to which young people were not just less interested than their elders in reading newspapers, but also that this represented a generational rather than simply an age effect (Rouger 2007). One of the main reasons given was that this particular generation was less attached to the locality than its predecessors, with the result that what had previously been a strong aspect of the journalism of regional newspapers—a focus on local news—was much less valued by this new generation. In similar vein, the attractiveness for young urban professionals of free newspapers such as *Métro* and *20 minutes* (both of which are available in different local editions in major French towns and cities) has been attributed in part to the way in which the journalistic content and format of the newspaper are more suited to a postmodern lifestyle where media usage is characterised by mobility, free access to information and soft news (Rieffel 2010). In short, one of the key drivers of change in the relationship between the public and journalism in contemporary France is to be found in the modifications undergone by French society in recent years.

In addition to circulation problems, the other major issue of concern for the newspaper industry relates to finance, particularly advertising revenue. The share of media advertising taken by the press has been on the decline for many years and this trend is set to continue as television and, even more so, the internet increase their market share. The expansion of the internet has led to advertising revenue moving away from the established media, as advertisers chase changing patterns of media usage among their target audiences in the purchase of goods and services. Regional newspapers, for example, have been badly affected in recent years by the loss of classified advertising to the internet, while for the national titles Google has become an unwanted competitor for brand advertising. These structural changes in the media advertising market were compounded in 2008-09 by the cyclical downturn in the performance of the French economy. The combined impact was catastrophic for the financial well-being of the daily newspaper sector across both national and regional markets and for the employment prospects of journalists.

The economic difficulties of journalism as a business are compounded by problems facing the practice of journalism as a profession, resulting in widespread concern among journalists about their occupational role in the age of digitised information production and distribution. Technology now allows for the production and distribution of new forms of journalism that originate from outside of the established mainstream media. Journalists' traditional professional status based on claims to authority, expertise and objectivity has been undermined by the rise of new practices of news gathering and distribution, including the growing input of ordinary citizens, while mainstream media have to cope with the growing information function performed by a range of social, alternative and participatory media such as Facebook, Twitter and YouTube.

While the internet can be seen to democratise information production and distribution, it may also de-professionalise the activity of journalism. Blogs at their worst become sites of unsubstantiated rumour and gossip where the rules of ethical journalism do not apply—evidenced in the unsubstantiated revelations of the alleged extramarital affairs of President Sarkozy and his wife Carla Bruni on the website of the Sunday newspaper *Le Journal du Dimanche* in March 2010. In contrast, one major advantage that some (though certainly not all) press outlets have in the eyes of the French public is their relative credibility as suppliers of accurate information. These enjoy a strong brand image which is already serving them well in the online world. It is not surprising, therefore, that some newspaper and news magazine websites such as Le Monde.fr, Le Figaro.fr and L'Express.fr feature among the most popular in terms of usage.

Yet in general public confidence in the journalistic product is not high in France. Radio is the most trusted media outlet (60%), followed by the press (55%) and then television (48%), with the internet in last position (35%) (La Croix 2010). Confidence in the internet as a source of reliable news is highest among the young and declines with each successive age segment of the population. Moreover, public perception of the independence of journalists is low in France. A significant majority (66%) consider that journalists are not politically independent (only 25% think that they are), while 60% of the public judge that journalists are prone to financial influence (compared with a mere 26% who take the opposite view).

New ways forward or simply firefighting?

Different modes of response have been made in recent years to address the challenges facing the practice of journalism in France, notably in the newspaper sector. Four are briefly outlined in this section: changes to journalistic content, upping the online presence, independent news websites and public policy initiatives.

The first response is aimed at modifying the content and format of the journalistic product to make it more attractive and user-friendly. The elite national dailies continue to emphasise the depth of analysis and quality of their columnist journalism, while incorporating different supplements— economy, finance, literature, the arts—to boost sales on specific days of the week. Certain genres of coverage—such as sport, culture and lifestyle—now occupy greater space than in the past, as do stories and features aimed at women readers. Even in traditional genres, such as domestic politics, there is a tendency towards the inclusion of a more "human interest" approach to political coverage that emphasises the concerns of "ordinary voters" and the personal attributes of politicians. In addition, coverage of popular culture, including television chat shows and reality programmes, has become an integral part of coverage, as newspapers attempt to attract younger readers. Yet tweaking content and format in search of new readers may be a high risk strategy. Not only may changes in content designed to attract a younger readership fail to bring in additional new readers, but they also risk alienating older age groups that currently constitute the most faithful clientele of many newspapers, especially the regional titles.

A second response by traditional news media outlets is to adapt to the technological challenge of the internet. There has certainly been a growth in the quality of the web presence of French newspapers in both national and provincial markets, with a concomitant reorganisation of newsrooms to incorporate both newsprint and online versions of the journalistic product. Several newspaper titles, especially the national dailies, have invested significant resources in creating multi-faceted websites which serve to propagate the newspaper brand, while at the organisational level newsrooms are increasingly integrated in the production of both hard copy and on-line material. One of the most successful online media ventures in France is the website Le Monde.fr, which provides archival resources, discussion sites for users and links to other relevant websites. Newspaper titles are also seeking to distribute content via mobile telephones and the iPad. For instance, in 2009 a digital version of *Libération* was available to iPhone users for a monthly subscription of €12 (compared with €1.30 per day for the newsprint version).

Third, several new independent websites have been created outside of the traditional mainstream media, with news content available only (or principally) via the internet. Rue 89, Bakchich, Mediapart and Arrêt sur image, for example, provide alternative sources of news, information and comment for their users. They try to provide a different perspective on news items from the mainstream media, focus on particular topics of interest to their users and, in the case of Rue 89, make significant use of contributions from non-professional journalists. They are currently niche players in the direct provision of online news to the public, coming well behind the general portals such as Google News and the websites of the mainstream offline media. Moreover, like the web versions of established media outlets, their commercial viability has not yet been secured. These sites are, however, frequently cited by mainstream media and they have become an integral part of the world of online journalism in France.

The final level of response to the problems affecting French journalism has come from outside the world of the media. Faced with the possible collapse of several newspaper titles, President Sarkozy has pledged to provide additional financial support on top of the significant state assistance already provided to the press sector. In 2009 the French government agreed to commit about €200 million of extra aid per year for three years. A large proportion of the additional subsidy was allocated to improving distribution networks—with a significant planned increase in household delivery and the freezing of postal tariffs—as well as additional assistance to modernise printing works. To avoid discrimination between online and print journalism, electronic newspapers would henceforth benefit from state assistance, and a new status of online press publisher was created by legislation. In addition, a new legal framework for the exercise of intellectual property rights for journalists across different media was announced. Finally, it was agreed to give every

French teenager on their 18th birthday a year's free subscription to a newspaper of their choice for one day per week: newspapers cover the cost of the free copies, while the state finances their delivery.

Conclusion

The imperative of "adapt to survive" facing the business and the profession of journalism in contemporary France embraces both metropolitan and non-metropolitan media outlets. It would be misleading to argue that the national media are in an overall stronger position than their provincial counterparts (or vice-versa) to make the necessary adjustments to the new conditions created by a combination of technological, economic and social change. Weekly news magazines seem to be faring better than daily newspapers, specialist newspapers (finance, sport) appear to be more successful than general information titles, and some media companies, such as Ouest-France, have a more coherent multimedia strategy, a more attractive journalistic product and greater resources than others to cope with the contemporary challenges. Overall, however, the combined force of these challenges makes the state of French journalism as a whole over the next few years very hard to predict with any sense of certainty and in this respect the French situation has much in common with that of many other developed societies.

Works Cited

Albert, P. 2008. *La presse française*. Paris: La documentation française.
Cavelier, P. and O. Morel-Maroger. 2008. 2nd edition. *La radio*. Paris: Presses Universitaires de France.
Charon, J.-M. 2008. 2nd edition. *La presse magazine*. Paris: La Découverte.
Commission de la Carte d'Identité des Journalistes Professionels. 2010. http://www.ccijp.net/
Donnat, O. 2009. *Les pratiques culturelles des Français à l'ère numérique: Éléments de synthèse 1997-2008*, Paris: Ministry of Culture and Communication.
http://www.pratiquesculturelles.culture.gouv.fr/doc/08 synthese.pdf
La Croix. 2010. *Baromètre de confiance dans les média*. Paris. http://www.la-croix.com/illustrations/Multimedia/Actu/2010/1/20/ barometre- medias.pdf
Martin, M. 2002. *La presse régionale*. Paris: Fayard.
Observatoire des métiers de la presse. 2009. *Photographie de la profession des journalistes*, Paris.

http://www.metiers-presse.org/pdf/1255448008.pdf

Rieffel, R. 2010. *Mythologie de la presse gratuite*. Paris: Le Cavalier Bleu.

Rouger, A. 2008. What future for local news? The crisis of the French regional daily press. *Journalism Studies*, 9 (5): 822-31.

Tessier, M. and M. Baffert. 2007. *La Presse au défi du numérique*. Paris: Ministère de la Culture et de la Communication.
http://www.culture.gouv.fr/culture/actualites/rapports/tessier/rapport-fev2007.pdf

JOURNALISM IN CATALONIA:
CREATING A PERSPECTIVE ON THE WORLD

ENRIC CASTELLÓ

Constituting a dialogue

Catalan communication research most often attempts to explain the current state of the journalism and communication systems in that part of the world by tracing their roots back to the historical period known as *la transición*, or "transition".[1] Of course, there was "life" before Franco's death but, as a number of analysts have pointed out, the demise of his dictatorship was based much more on economic progress)—starting with the period known as *desarrollismo*[2] (Vilarós 2005, 31)—than on social progress. Even so, his death in 1975 meant the end of a specific historical period and the starting point of a new project for Spanish society.

As regards the media landscape, several authors have noted that at the end of the sixties and the early seventies there was already a certain amount of space appearing in the state television monopoly RTVE—despite it being still controlled by the Francoist regime—for greater openness and a certain relaxation of censorship, a situation which facilitated the emergence of new discourses on pluralism. However, it seems clear, as I have argued elsewhere (Castelló and O'Donnell 2009b, 175-176), that it was not until the passing of a new law on RTVE following the establishment of democracy (Estatuto de la Radio y Televisión, 1981), and the launch of the "autonomous"[3] channels in the Basque Country (1982)

---

[1] The democratic transition is usually taken as spanning the period between the death of Francisco Franco in 1975 and the first democratic elections in 1977, although discussion of its exact timeframe remains on-going; some authors argue that Spain is still in a kind of "post-transitional" era.

[2] This word is based on the Spanish noun *desarrollo*, meaning "development".

[3] This is the term used to described the television companies set up by the so-called Autonomous Communities which were themselves constituted in the early nineteen-eighties, replacing the old "regions" of the Franco regime. Spain is

and Catalonia (1983), that significant sections of the Spanish population had access to an alternative set of "national discourses" on television to those managed from the political centre, Madrid. It was not by chance that the first autonomous television stations were launched in the territories of two of the so-called "historic nationalities",[4] the Basque Country and Catalonia, where there was already a demand for alternative perspectives (or for the establishment of new hegemonic ones) on the "national" and for the circulation of discourses of the national which were not mediated by centralist institutions in Madrid.

TVE (the television arm of RTVE) had previously included opt-outs from Spanish national broadcasting which had allowed its regional Catalan branch, TVE-Catalunya, to screen a small number of programmes in Catalan. But it was not until 1973 that TVE-Catalunya aired the first current affairs programme in this language (*Giravolt*). In the final years of the dictatorship, TVE-Catalunya only had 17 hours of Catalan programmes per month (Binimelis et al 2009, 100), most of them offering a "regionalist" or "culturalist" version of Catalanness and softening or hiding any sense of social and political struggle. The creation of an independent public Catalan Broadcasting Corporation in 1983 was driven by two aspirations: on the one hand a social demand for democratic initiatives in the field of communication and on the other the inability of the Madrid-based Spanish media to include a wider range of national discourses on society and politics. As Binimelis et al. point out (2009, 102) "in its fifty years of existence, it seems clear that TVE has been unable to envisage a clear project and continuity for its Catalan studios, despite TVE Catalunya's enormous contribution as both a factory for new programmes and a training ground for television professionals".

In the eighties, a group of scholars led by Josep Gifreu focused on the theorisation and promotion of what came to be called a Catalan Communicative Space which would have two aims: the development of strategies for action to strengthen the Catalan cultural space, and of mechanisms for monitoring the results of such strategies both internally (bringing together the various Catalan-speaking territories) and externally (acknowledgement from outside Catalonia of its "difference" from the rest

---

divided into seventeen such communities, of which a dozen now have their own television channel.

[4] The Spanish Constitution of 1978 named the Catalans, the Basques and the Galicians as Spain's three "historic nationalities" (each of these has its own language, making Spain a country with one official language for the whole territory—Spanish—but two in those regions with their own language). They were later joined by Andalusia and Valencia following referendums there.

of Spain) (Gifreu 2009, 88). It is possible to argue that the Catalan media space is characterised (at least in the Spanish context) by a number of specificities, these including not only its language but also its strong local media spaces—often based on a single county—the leading role played by regional newspapers and, though this point is much more open to debate, the existence of a certain way of doing things—a sense of moderation in the coverage of news—and, politically and economically, a "self-centred" approach to news stories. That is to say: while for American news Washington and New York are centres, for British news London is the centre, so for Catalan news Barcelona constitutes the political and economic centre. But, as will be argued here, the fact of belonging to a larger state whose central government's writ also runs in Catalonia offers rich possibilities of dialogue between political centres.

The creation of these kinds of "self-centred" messages is possible thanks to economic structures and cultural specificities, but more importantly the availability of Catalan media and journalism has produced a wide range of discourses regarding definitions of the "national" and an alternative imaginary which gives the public access to a collective perspective of the world which is recognisably different from that emanating from Madrid. The Catalan media have not succeeded in effacing Spanish-centred messages; they have enabled the establishment of a richer dialogue between Catalan and Spanish perspectives. This dialogue is clearly an unequal one based, in Salvador Cardús's words (2006, 52), on an asymmetrical relationship, but it also offers significant opportunities.

Do Catalan media create a "centre"?

A productive concept which can be borrowed from sociolinguistics when discussing this topic is "self-centring" (*autocentrament* in Catalan). For Bernat Joan (1998, quoted in Gibert 2000, 22), self-centring is a key element in nation-building processes. It is important not to mistake self-centring for ethnocentrism, which is more related to the cultural and ethnic group. In using the term "self-centring" I am referring to the location of the social and political focus of news. The constitution of a "self-centre" can be understood as the concerted action of specific social groups (through policies fostered by parliaments but also through the actions of non-governmental organisations and individuals) to forge a structure (corporations, media companies, social associations, infrastructures, human resources) which takes as one of its objectives the circulation of a way of seeing things which conceives the world from a certain ideological definition of a centre, in dialogue with competing definitions from other social groups (as this approach to "self-centring" is closely related to the geopolitical dimension of the news, these social groups are in addition usually territorially-based).

Putting the accent on action brings our view close to Alberto Melucci's social constructionism, according to which collective identity is constituted through a process of construction arising from a "system of action" (Melucci 1996, 70). But the flow of communication and influence, the task of construction, is not simply a top-down one; it is a more dynamic system that must be understood in its complexity. As a result, the focus here will be both on the structure of the Catalan media landscape, and on an evaluation of the particular way of seeing things it offers, through a case study. To do so, we will need to look at both the material structure and at the ideological work carried out by media workers.

Of the thirty most consumed forms of media in Catalonia,[5] more than half have their headquarters in Madrid, thirteen in Catalonia and one in a foreign country. This media-consumption structure is not so very different from that of other Autonomous Communities in Spain in which we find a strong local press and radio stations and in most cases one autonomous television channel (which does not, however, always top the audience ratings). An important point in Catalonia is that the public corporation owns the top radio station and television channel in the list of most followed media. In other words the availability of Catalan-based media in radio and television is heavily dependent on public funds—the only privately owned channels in the list are the radio stations RAC 1 and Segre Ràdio and the television channel 8TV.

However, this list could give a biased picture of the complexity and richness of the Catalan media system. Particularly noteworthy are the presence of a strong local press, radio and television channels serving single counties, and magazines which cater for limited but loyal audiences. The strength of local and small-scale media is one of the characteristic features of the Catalan media landscape. Astonishing though it may sound, thirty-six newspapers are published on a daily basis in Catalonia—which has a population of around 7.5 million—most of them (twenty-six) in Spanish, with those in Catalan mainly addressing a single county or a broad local area. As López states (2009), only 13.1% (by circulation) of the daily press distributed in Catalonia is written entirely or mostly in Catalan. These figures are more balanced for the radio audience, which is almost half and half Catalan (46.9%) and Spanish (53,1%).

What can be understood from these figures is that there is indeed a Catalan media structure—a weak and publicly funded one—existing

---

[5] Source: Baròmetre de la Comunicació (first wave 2009).

alongside stronger Spanish media corporations and public media, and that these Catalan media do not always occupy the top positions in the audience rankings. The existence of such a "material structure" is a necessary condition for the consolidation of a self-centred discourse, but is not enough on its own to guarantee its success: the practices carried out within this media structure (the "symbolic structure") have to work in that direction.

So, are Catalan journalists working towards the creation of such a symbolic centre? It seems clear that there are indeed self-centring discourses on the world circulating in the Catalan media. However, these discourses are in permanent dialogue with a stronger centre, the Spanish one. Thus the creation of a Catalan-centred idea of the world is, at the same time, strengthening the Spanish-centred frame, from which these media discourses are not able to escape. The media cannot constitute an independent system isolated from the social and political context in which they are developed and, despite the banners which can sometimes be seen in the stands of Barcelona Football Club's stadium, the Camp Nou, demanding independence for Catalonia, Catalonia is (still) Spain.

Media reporting: politics and sports

Using a small case study from the press, I will present here an example of how a "self centre" is constituted in media discourse and the unavoidability of doing this in a dynamic of dialogue.

On 10 January 2008 the then Catalan Vice-president Josep Lluís Carod Rovira (a leading figure in Esquerra Republicana de Catalunya)[6] visited Scotland for a meeting with First Minister Alex Salmond to exchange information about the referendum processes in both countries. This meeting attracted significant coverage in the Catalan press: both Barcelona and Madrid-based newspapers (most of the latter in their "Catalonia" sections) offered broad information about the encounter.[7]

---

[6] Republican Left of Catalonia, a pro-independence and leftish party.

[7] In the Scottish press I found only one brief commentary in one newspaper: Douglas Fraser's "Catalan visit fosters friendship" (*The Herald,* 11 January 2008: 7).

Table 1. Headlines about Carod-Salmond meeting (11 January 2008)

Barcelona-based newspaper headlines	Madrid-based newspaper headlines
La Vanguardia: Carod links the [Catalan] Government with Scottish plans for independence[8]	*El País*: Carod demands Spain learn from British democratic culture[9]
El Periódico de Catalunya: Carod criticises Spanish democracy and praises the British[10]	*El Mundo:* "Catalonia is like Scotland, but Spain is not like England"[11]
Avui: Carod urges referendum in response to the failure of the Statute[12]	*ABC:* Josep Lluis "Wallace"[13]
El Punt: Carod states that the failure of the Statute can only lead to independence[14]	*La Razón:* Carod envies England[15]

Table 1 shows the corresponding headlines which are in fact concise indicators of the main thrust of the full reports. The discourse of *La Vanguardia* is self-referential to the extent that the journalist focuses not on the Spanish but on the Catalan Government. The word used is *Govern*, the only Catalan word in an otherwise Spanish-language headline: this is the term currently used to distinguish the Catalan government from the Spanish one, the latter being routinely referred to by the Spanish term *Gobierno*. The journalist frames the visit as controversial in that it links the Catalan Government (led by the Catalan Socialist Party, which does

---

[8] "Carod implica al Govern con el plan escocés para la independencia" (*La Vanguardia*, 11 January 2008: 18).
[9] "Carod pide a España que aprenda cultura democrática británica" (*El País,* Cataluña Section, 11 January 2008: 5).
[10] "Carod menysprea la democràcia espanyola i exalça la britànica" (*El Periódico de Catalunya*, Catalan version, 11 January 2008: 23)
[11] "Cataluña es como Escocia, pero España no es como Inglaterra" (*El Mundo, Catalunya*, 11 January 2008).
[12] "Carod impulsa el referèndum davant el col·lapse estatutari" (*Avui*, 11 January 2008: 8). The Statute of Autonomy is the document which specifies the powers devolved by the Madrid government to the Catalan government. Attempts to renegotiate it in 2005-6 were widely viewed in Catalonia as a failure.
[13] "Josep Lluis 'Wallace'" (*ABC*, 11 January 2008)
[14] "Carod certifica que el «col·lapse» estatutari només porta a la independència" (*El Punt*, 11 January 2008)
[15] "Carod siente envidia de Inglaterra" (*La Razón*, 11 January 2008).

not support independence) with Scottish National Party plans for an independence referendum. *El Periódico*, on the other hand, locates its headline in a Spanish frame—along the same lines as *El País*—announcing that Carod criticises *Spanish* democracy. Meanwhile *Avui* and *El Punt* are also located in a Catalan frame, talking about the failure of the Catalan statute in terms of "the process having come to a standstill". As for the Madrid papers, *El País, El Mundo* and *La Razón* all present Spanish-centred messages underlining the comparison made by Carod between Spanish and British democracy. *ABC* also offers this frame, though in an ironical way, the first sentence of the report referring to the harmless envy (*envidia sana*) Carod confesses to profess for Scotland regarding its independence process. These headlines give us a good example of how, by offering a controversial image of the *person* (it is Carod who "envies", "despises" or is even sarcastically described as "Wallace"), the Spanish-centred discourses displace the political meaning of the visit, even in those headlines in which Carod asks Spain to learn from Britain about democracy. The Catalan-centred headlines, on the other hand, focus much more heavily on the political agenda, while *El Mundo, ABC* and even *El País* highlight the controversial statements made by Carod.

A second illustration of self-centring journalism relates to sport, which is a fruitful field for observing how public Catalan media construct a particular perspective on the world. Let's look at two examples: reporting on Spanish football success in the European Championship (2008) and reporting on the American NBA. When Spain won the European Championship in June 2008, TVC (Catalan television) and TVE (Spanish television) reported the celebrations in the streets of Madrid very differently. The Catalan channel covered the parade in the centre of Madrid in the news,[16] but the time they dedicated to this and the way they reported the event were far removed from the narrative provided by Spanish television. To describe the massive parade in Madrid (one million people in the streets), the Catalan channel used the expression "Madrid, de cap per avall" ("Madrid, upside-down"), which in fact has the meaning of "chaotic". The two and a half minute live report from Madrid was a short one inserted in the sports section of the news programme and depicted "the people as masses". In addition to this, the Catalan channel also reported the celebrations in Catalonia in another report: "Molta celebració arreu

---

[16] Source: http://www.3cat24.cat/video/524059/esports/La-festa-a-Colon. Accessed 20 April 2009.

d'Espanya" ("Lots of celebrations all around Spain").[17] This piece includes expressions such as the reference to the "wild euphoria" (*eufòria desfermada*) among some supporters in Tarragona, expressions which are repeated to explain the reaction in Madrid. The term "desfermada" (literally "unleashed") implies some kind of uncontrolled force, an image of some kind of beast liberated from the cage coming to our minds. In the piece, supporters of the Spanish team are seen lighting sparklers in Tarragona, driving through Girona waving Spanish flags and tooting their horns, or are depicted *en masse* as an anonymous multitude in Madrid. The only news about celebrations in Barcelona is about German supporters, peacefully eating sausages while watching the match. The Catalan channel also reported on the disturbances and vandalism during some of the celebrations, which in some way links the Spanish national euphoria with these kinds of problems, and stressed that the Spanish team had not won this championship in 44 years.[18]

TVE, on the other hand, dedicated a huge amount of resources to covering the triumphant journey of the Spanish national team through Madrid. Its first channel provided live coverage throughout the afternoon from the Plaza Colón in Madrid in a special edition of *España directo*[19] (Spain Live), and also reported from several other Spanish cities and towns.[20] The empathy with which the TVE presenters covered the parade was evident—visibly happy in comparison with the Catalan ones and through the use of expressions like "todos con la selección" ("everybody with the team"). Spanish television also reported on the special resources they had mobilised for covering the championship and for a couple of days used an on-screen logo in the form of the national strip together with the motto: "Bienvenidos a casa" ("Welcome home").[21] They also broadcast speeches by the players, the reactions of the supporters, all of this commented on by the journalists in a very positive tone. Here the celebration, in the journalist's words, "is in Madrid because it has to be

---

[17] Source: http://www.3cat24.cat/video/522719/esports/Molta-celebracio-arreu-dEspanya. Accessed 20 April 2009.
[18] Source: http://www.3cat24.cat/noticia/291538/esports/Euforia-i-alguns-aldarulls -en-les-celebracions-per-la-victoria-de-la-seleccio-espanyola and http://www.3cat24.cat/video/522649/altres/I-44-anys-despres-Espana-aixeca-lEurocopa. Both accessed 20 April 2009.
[19] Source: http://www.rtve.es/mediateca/videos/20080630/seleccion-espanola-llega -madrid-con-copa-europa/200593.shtml. Accessed 20 April 2009.
[20] Source: http://www.rtve.es/mediateca/videos/20080630/espana-echa-calle-para-festejar-eurocopa/198093.shtml. Accessed 20 April 2009.
[21] Source: http://www.rtve.es/mediateca/videos/20080630/trabajo-tve-eurocopa/19 9795. shtml. Accessed 20 April 2009.

somewhere, but this is a thank-you from the Spanish team to the whole of Spain, to all the supporters". The focus on the massive numbers taking part was also evident, presented here as proof of the happiness of the people. Here, the reports depicted "the masses as people".

In terms of this football event we can conclude that Catalan journalists working in the public channel have a "problem" insofar as there is no "Catalan team" representing Catalonia in international matches and championships and, at the same time, national football teams are usually a highly successful television topic in terms of audience, especially when they win important events.[22] Spanish national success is, then, also Catalan success, for example through the presence of Catalan players playing in the Spanish team. This is the reason why some journalists are so insistent on reporting how many Catalans are included in Spanish national teams. A good example is *Avui*'s headline "The Spanish water polo team, made up of eleven Catalans, is already leading group A".[23] This paper also used the news heading "Olímpics Catalans" ("Catalan Olympics") to put special emphasis on the participation of Catalan sportsmen and women in the Beijing Olympics.

Perhaps the best example of this self-centring is the news reports on the NBA (the United States National Basketball Association), specifically reports on those teams with Catalan players. Catalan television had provided Catalan basketball fans with specialised programmes reporting on NBA news for some time, mostly scheduled in late night slots or on their second channel (C33), but "NBA fever" began in earnest in season 2001-02 when the Catalan player Pau Gasol was selected to join the Memphis Grizzlies. At the moment of writing this chapter, Gasol is playing for the Los Angeles Lakers, his brother Marc is playing for the Memphis Grizzlies, Rudy Fernández—a player born in Mallorca who had played for the Catalan team DKV Joventut de Badalona—is playing for the Portland Trail Blazers, and Juan Carlos Navarro—who had already played for the Grizzlies—and Ricky Rubio have announced their intention to join the NBA. The arrival of so many Catalan players in the NBA has led to a great deal of coverage of their careers, their successes and failures. The NBA is the centre of the basketball world: having the opportunity to report on the Catalan contribution to any centre is to become, for the duration of a two minutes news item, part of that centre. But this self-

---

[22] Catalan journalists substitute the lack of a Catalan team with abundant coverage of FC Barcelona, which has taken on the representation of hegemonic national discourses on Catalonia.

[23] Source: http://www.avui.cat/article/esports/38101/waterpolistes/catalans/tomben /montenegro/amb/la/seleccio/espanyola.html. Accessed 23 April 2009.

centring can also be done from a "Spanish perspective" when the media talk about Spanish players in general, irrespective of their place of birth. Thus one of the reports in *La Vanguardia* began "Cara y cruz de entrada para los equipos españoles en los playoffs de la NBA" ("Opening Toss of the Coin for the Spanish Teams in the NBA playoffs"),[24] in which "Spanish teams" are those in which a Spaniard is playing.

A result of this complex situation is that Catalan public television has been attacked from both sides, by both Spanish and Catalan nationalisms, being accused on the one hand of having a Catalan nationalist "skin"[25] and on the other of being a tool for the "Spanishing" (*espanyolització*) of Catalan culture (Aleixandre 2006). However, if we step back a little from the at times quite heated debate, neither of these suggestions seems appropriate. Its journalists are simply doing what BBC or TVE journalists do: talking about their countries and contextualizing the world from a perspective determined by the social, political and cultural context in which the journalists live and work. This is not necessarily a nationalist perspective, but it does create community-centred messages. News is not simply about "the world", but about how big events can affect the community and how its members are present in the world, are constructing it. It is when collectively a group or community has the chance to explain the world through a particular prism that this group can draw a line between it and other centres and, then, constitute itself as its "own" centre. Thus, self-narratives are the key to escaping the status of periphery.

Maintaining a double periphery

Any centre needs a periphery. Because the periphery is the zone in which "we" begin to blur into others, its "existence" is the clearest proof that there are other centres, and "otherness"—a constitutive need for self-construction—becomes evident. Your centre is as strong as the discourse of your periphery is robust. Keeping a periphery in "good working order" means feeding some kind of narrative about it on a regular basis. Thus, the most obvious danger for a centre is to "lose" its periphery—thereby

---

[24] Source: http://www.lavanguardia.es/free/edicionimpresa/res/20090420/53685 578497.html?urlback=http://www.lavanguardia.es/premium/edicionimpresa/20090 420/53685578497.html. Accessed 23 April 2009.

[25] The expression used by socialist politician Joan Ferran in December 2007 was "crosta nacionalista". See: http://www.elperiodico.com/default.asp?idpublicacio PK=46&idioma=CAS&idnoticia_PK=464276&idseccio_PK=1008. Accessed 2 February 2010.

becoming a periphery itself—as happens when a cultural periphery becomes "someone else's" periphery or when it constitutes itself as a centre.

From a cultural point of view, traditional Catalan nationalism has cultivated a discourse about a periphery composed by the greater Catalan-speaking area inhabited by Valencians, Balearic Islanders and North-Catalans (from Roussillon in France).[26] But this is a conflictive space, a site of struggle, for two reasons. It is a periphery, parts of which are already "claimed" by two stronger centres (Valencia by Spain and Roussillon by France) and, in the case of the Autonomous Community of Valencia (directly south of Catalonia), it could also be described as its own proto-centre in a constant "discursive swing" between two larger "domestic" centres (Spain and Catalonia), its constitution as a full-blown centre being very much "work-in-progress". The pan-Catalan nationalist discourse which locates Valencia as part of a broader national (i.e. Catalan) culture centred on Barcelona has little resonance among the Valencian population, especially in the city of Valencia itself, capital of the Autonomous Community (Castelló and Castelló 2009). In fact, it is not particularly attractive to find yourself defined as someone else's "cultural periphery" and, in such a case, the population is more likely to join forces with the most powerful centre, in this case Spain: hegemonic (Spanish) discourses have more appeal than alternative (Catalan) ones and in any case the "Catalan discourse" emanates from an area which also has a strong and now well-established Spanish culture.

There is no communication system operating throughout the whole Catalan linguistic area. Each part of this area has its own newspapers, television channels and radio stations; also public media in each area depend on different political structures (as opposed to the Madrid-based ones, which are broadcast throughout Spain). Media operating from Barcelona are almost exclusively followed by Catalans living in Catalonia, and few people in Valencia and Mallorca follow them, with the possible exception of a couple of on-line experiments.[27] The non-existence of such a media system is not only due to political reasons but also to its very poor economic prospects. Moreover, the Valencian government has been

---

[26] The Catalan language is not confined to Catalonia, but is also spoken in areas to the south (Valencia), the East (the Balearic Islands), and the north (Rousillon).

[27] TVC had a 0.5% audience share in Valencia in 2008 (Source: TNSofres, published in http://www.levante-emv.com/cultura/2009/01/23/cultura-dispersion-audiencia-deja-canal-peores-registros-historia/546363.html. Accessed 22 March 2010. I should mention the on-line news initiative http://www.vilaweb.cat, which I would say is the only media offering with a clearer "pan-Catalan" focus which enjoys any success.

working for decades against the installation of any Barcelona-based media in its territory, even to the extent of blocking TVC's signal in 2007, although a group of people mobilised by cultural associations and political parties tried to prevent the police from disabling the antenna.[28] This cancellation aroused a popular campaign to restore TVC broadcasts in the region.[29]

On the other hand, it must be said that hegemonic discourses in Catalan news give a relatively negative image of the Valencian Autonomous Community. As the periphery is the place where "we" blur into "them", it is also a constantly problematised field. News broadcasting on TVC about Valencia displays the typical coverage of the periphery by the centre, focusing on corruption, natural disasters, social injustices, cultural conflict, economic crisis and the like. Entering "País Valencià" (the formal name of the Valencian Autonomous Community) into the search engine for TVC news reports produces a list of primarily negative headlines. Of the 50 results obtained in a recent search almost 35 related to negative news broadcast from 29 February 2008 to 21 April 2009: crises, crime, bribery, floods, cultural policies against the Catalan language, town planning excesses, demonstrations against the Government and popular protests, problems with the educational system, and so on (this, of course, could be at least partially down to the "bad news" syndrome, but even so the pattern is clear).

While this periphery is unclear, or in dispute, the Catalan media also circulate a discourse on an "internal periphery" which is univocal. We are referring to regions *within* the country which are *symbolically* constituted as "the Catalan periphery". This is not ordered in a geographically concentric logic with Barcelona at its centre. The Catalan centre is based in Barcelona because that is where political and economic power are concentrated, but the centre-periphery logic referred to here is a symbolic one, based on historical and contextual reasons. Catalan elites have traditionally worked in Barcelona and spent their holiday time on the coast to the north of the city (Maresme, Costa Brava and the Girona coast) or in the nearest part of the Pyrenees (Cerdanya and Ripoll). Other industrial areas inland like el Vallès are important economic centres. None of these

---

[28] The episode in which a group of people block the Spanish police force as they try to disconnect the aerial can be viewed on http://www.vilaweb.tv/?video=4850&canal=30 (accessed 24 April 2009) as can the demonstrations in Alacant and Valencia against the blocking of Catalan channels on http://www.3cat24.cat/video/402099/societat/Milers-de-persones-cont ra-lapagada-de-la-Carrasqueta. Accessed 24 April 2009.

[29] Source: http://www.televisiosensefronteres.cat/. Accessed 2 February 2010.

counts as a "periphery". What constitutes the Catalan "territorial periphery" in symbolic terms are the areas around Lleida and Tarragona, especially the regions near the River Ebro.

Each of the four Catalan provinces (as the territory is divided by the Spanish administration) has its own leading newspaper(s) (Barcelona, *El Periódico de Catalunya* and *La Vanguardia*; Tarragona, *Diari de Tarragona*; Lleida, *Segre*; and, Girona, *El Punt*).[30] This four-part structure is an expression of the complexity of Catalonia and its failure in terms of creating collective representations of a "shared national interest". In fact, in Lleida and Tarragona there is a strong discourse of Barcelona-centric inequality, even a kind of "victim mentality". We can find this discourse in relation to a wide range of media products from news to sit-coms. Thus viewers in both Tarragona and Lleida have complained about the extent to which both their regions are ignored in weather forecasts broadcast from Barcelona,[31] while the County Council of Lleida complained in 2005 about the sit-com *Lo Cartanyà* (TVC) claiming it presented their region as an "rural nightmare" (*esperpent rural* in Catalan[32]). Well established discourses relating to Tarragona (and to a lesser extent the Ebro region) stereotype it as an area of intense industrial activity (it is home to two nuclear plants and a large petrochemical complex) or ridicule the popular *correbous* ("bull running") festival, which has received intensive coverage since the banning of bullfighting in Catalonia in 2010.[33]

Stereotyping discourses of the rural have been softened in recent years by television programmes such as *A pagès* (In the Countryside, TVC, 2008) and soap operas like *Ventdelplà* which have tried to offer a more complex imaginary on daily life in small villages, avoiding a postcard image "where everything seems to have been designed for the tourist" (Castelló and O'Donnell 2009a, 53). Despite this, reporting on Tarragona and Lleida relates mostly to minor cultural and traditional festivities, local

---

[30] Source: Baròmetre de la Comunicació. First wave 2009.

[31] Source: http://blogs.ccrtvi.com/defensor. Accessed 16 September 2010.

[32] Source: http://www.vilaweb.cat/www/elpunt/noticia?p_idcmp=1565533. Accessed 16 September 2010. "Esperpent"—"esperpento" in Spanish—is a Spanish literary genre based on the grotesque representation of reality.

[33] Source: http://www.ebredigital.cat/amposta/les-festes-taurines-de-lebre-al-punt-de-mira-dels-mitjans-estatals/?id=414. Accessed 16 September 2010. "Correbous" consisting in running along the streets with one or several bulls. There are a number of variations such as "bou embolat" in which people place two burning torches on the bull's horns, or "bous a la mar" in which the bull ends up swimming in the sea. Various animal rights associations have denounced this kind of treatment.

social life and events, accidents and crime, and *faits divers*.[34] In quantitative terms, Table 2 shows the results from TVC's news report search engine using the keywords "Barcelona", "Tarragona", "Lleida" and "Girona" compared with the population in 2007. Barcelona is over-represented while the area with the greatest under-representation is Tarragona. For Girona and Lleida there are acceptable deviations in the news.

Table 2. Comparison News vs. Population

	News reports		Population (000s)		Dev.
Barcelona	3860	77.1%	5333	74.0%	+3.2%
Girona	445	8.9%	706	9.8%	-0.9%
Tarragona	363	7.3%	758	10.5%	-3.3%
Lleida[35]	336	6.7%	414	5.7%	+1.0%
TOTAL	5004		7211		

Sources: raw data obtained from http://www.3cat24.cat/videos (accessed April 2009) and IDESCAT. The analysis is my own.

Media discourses in Catalonia (and only the Barcelona-based media have a complete geographical spread) construct, then, a double peripheral system, like a protective enclosure consisting of a double wall. Closer to the centre is an internal periphery consisting of spaces controlled by the autonomous government. The second periphery is made up of areas outside Catalonia but claimed as being under its cultural influence. This periphery does not function as a "regular" periphery for the reasons outlined above.

Final remarks

Centre-periphery relationships in Spain are a complex issue. As Brassloff (1996) noted in this regard, the same words take on different

---

[34] This impression was confirmed by the results of a study carried out by a group of students at the Universitat Rovira i Virgili, Tarragona, in 2007-08 regarding representations of Tarragona in television news on the Catalan public channel (Georgina Giné, Núria Pons, Albert A. Sunyol (2008) *El tractament de Tarragona als informatius de TV3*. Unpublished).

[35] I obtained the results on "Lleida" by subtracting the figure from those obtained with the word "Duran", as there is an important Catalan politician whose surname is "Duran i Lleida" and the entire surname is always mentioned in the news.

meanings depending on who is uttering them. The commonest approach to the topic is a large-scale one, focusing on the radial structure of Spain and the relationships between the central government in Madrid and the Autonomous Communities. But Spain is a multi-centric reality and each political, economic and cultural centre also has sub-centres or even diverse peripheries of its own.

In Catalonia we have seen how the media construct a self-perspective through news reporting and cultural production. This logic can be seen at work not only in international news, but also in news related to Spain or even just to Catalonia. This perspective works as a filter, selecting themes, constructing the agenda, but also framing the information. The constitution of a self-centre means also the production of a periphery, and a new set of unequal cultural and communication relationships.

Lluís Calvo points out in a recent essay that Barcelona still has a great deal of work to do as a city to gather together all the efforts in the cultural field throughout the Catalan territory. The city itself "needs to be both centre and periphery" (Calvo 2010), a situation which would require it to be open to new ideas from outside, but also to integrate the complexity of Catalonia. This would require enhanced participation, in both quantitative and qualitative terms, of the cultural and social peripheries, to make them participate in the centre. This is a complex process in which representations of the rural and the urban must be rethought, discourses about towns and cities reconsidered, and more space for the cultural system to display this complexity provided: in other words, putting the periphery in the centre and displacing the "traditional" centre to the periphery. Today, a successful self-perspective on the world requires a kind of fluid and ductile system which can better adapt to social complexity. It is time for academics, journalists and politicians to leave behind unfruitful discussions about what is more "Catalan" or more "Spanish" and to embrace an open debate about the cultural projection of any society which takes proper account of its richness and complexity.

Acknowledgements

This article is part of the research project funded by the Spanish Ministry of Science and Innovation CSO2010-20047, "The media construction of political and territorial conflicts in Spain: a study on discourses and narratives".

Works Cited

Aleixandre, V. 2006. *TV3 a traïció. Televisió de Catalunya o d'Espanya?* Barcelona: Proa.

Binimelis, M., J. Cerdán and M. Fernández-Labayen. 2009. TVE Catalunya. Fifty ycars of light and shade. *Catalan Journal of Communication and Cultural Studies*, 1 (1): 97-103.

Brassloff, A. 1996. Centre-Periphery Communication in Spain. The Politics of Language and the Language of Politics. In *Language, Culture, and Communication in Contemporary Europe*, edited by Ch. Hoffman. 111-123. Bristol. Multilingual Matters.

Calvo, L. 2010. Barcelona: centre and periphery. *Catalan Journal of Communication and Cultural Studies*, 2 (1): 109-118.

Cardús, S. 2000. Les relacions asimétriques entre identitats. In *Identitats*, edited by G. Sanginés and À. Velasco. 34-53. Afers: València.

Castelló, E. and R. Castelló. 2009. One Country, Three National Days. Nations, Citizenship and Media Discourses in Valencia. In *National Days: Constructing and Mobilising National Identity*, edited by D. McCrone and G. McPherson. 181-196. Palgrave McMillan.

Castelló, E. and H. O'Donnell. 2009a. Stateless Fictions. Soap Operas in Catalonia and Scotland. In *The Nation on Screen: Discourses of the National on Global Television*, edited by E. Castelló, A. Dhoest and H. O'Donnell. 45-64. Cambridge: Cambridge Scholars Publishing.

Castelló, E. and H. O'Donnell. 2009b. Historias de Cataluña. Ficción y memoria histórica en TVC. In *Historias de la pequeña pantalla*, edited by E. Cueto, F. López and D. George. 175-196. Iberoamericana-Veuvert: Madrid-Frankfurt.

Gibert, Q.. 2000. Aproximació al conflicte identitari català. In *Identitats*, edited by G. Sanginés and À. Velasco. 15-36. Afers: València.

Gifreu, J. 2009. The Catalan Communicative Space: still a strategic objective. *Catalan Journal of Communication and Cultural Studies*, 1 (1): 87-95.

Joan, B. 1998. *Un espai per a una llengua*. València: Tres i Quatre.

López, B. 2009. La llengua. In *Informe de la Comunicació a Catalunya 2007-2008*, edited by M. de Moragas, I. Fernández, N. Almiron, J. J. Blasco, J. M. Corbella, M. Civil and O. Gibert. 251-262. Bellaterra: Publicacions UAB.

Melucci, A. 1996. *Challenging Codes: Collective Action in the Information Age*. Cambridge: Cambridge University Press.

Vilarós, T. M. 2005. Banalidad y Biopolítica: La transición española y el nuevo orden del mundo. *Desacuerdos.* 2: 29-56. On-line version: http://www.arteleku.net/4.0/pdfs/vilaros.pdf. Accessed 18 March 2009.

STRUCTURAL SHIFT
AND FUNCTIONAL STABILITY:
GERMAN JOURNALISM
IN THE "BERLIN REPUBLIC"

SIEGFRIED WEISCHENBERG, MAJA MALIK
AND ARMIN SCHOLL

Introduction

The state of a society's journalism reflects to a certain extent the collective historical experiences of the culture which journalists belong to. German history includes the tradition of a strong and authoritarian state that largely restricted freedom of expression and collapsed in the catastrophe of the Nazi era. The first time the German press became a relevant factor in politics was during the suppressed and eventually failed revolution of 1848/49, when newspapers could be published freely and without substantial interference by the state. Karl Marx among others worked as a journalist, becoming editor of the *Neue Rheinische Zeitung* in 1842. In the second half of the 19th century the German press became professional and commercial. The first Press Law of 1874 granted some limited press freedom and—even more important—offered a degree of stability to the emerging newspaper industry. As in commerce in general, journalists then became workers in offices, these being characterised by internal hierarchies, strict structures and a strong division of labour (cf. Bücher 1917). The increasing professionalisation created many new jobs in the fast growing newspaper industry.

But the new professionals often had a rather limited educational level, which contributed to their low social status. For that reason, in his lecture on "Politik als Beruf" (Politics as Vocation) sociologist Max Weber (1968 [1919]) called them a "pariah caste". However, by the end of the *Kaiser* era (1918), Germany had a fully developed media system with numerous quality newspapers, particularly in its capital Berlin, but also in other centres of the country. But the Nazi era ended all promising developments in German press and radio. Immediately after Hitler's seizure of power, top media personnel were forced to resign and were replaced by party propagandists (cf. Frei and Schmitz 1989).

After the Second World War, the most important aim of the military rulers of West Germany was to establish a new democratic press. The allies started to hand out licences to young journalists who knew the country but were not burdened by Nazism. Most of the print media that are prominent today—*Der Spiegel, Die Zeit* and *Frankfurter Allgemeine Zeitung,* for example—were launched during the years before 1949. In broadcasting, the allies introduced the public service system, mostly following the British BBC model. Unlike the BBC however, the German approach to public service was characterised by responsibility being given to the *Länder* (federal states), thus ensuring a decentralised system. In their respective broadcasting laws setting up the broadcasting corporations the governments of the *Länder* assigned an important role to political parties.

Even nowadays the role of political parties has not disappeared in public service broadcasting, although fierce competition from commercial radio and TV since the middle of the 1980s has meant that economic influences on journalism are now more important than political ones. Moreover, public broadcasting has also felt the effects of commercialisation and has included elements of infotainment in order to make its programmes more attractive to a broader public. Furthermore, politicians have followed the American approach of utilising popular entertainment. Chancellor Gerhard Schröder (1998-2005) offers an excellent example of this strategy: he appeared in a soap opera, in TV-films and in the top Saturday evening quiz show.

Schröder was the first politician-protagonist of the so-called *Berlin Republic*, established in the summer of 1998 when the location of the German capital moved from the somewhat "boring" and provincial city of Bonn to the more glamorous and upcoming Berlin, by far the largest urban centre in the country. In Bonn, political communication was focussed on a kind of family of correspondents reporting for newspapers and broadcast corporations with headquarters far away. Today the government quarter in Berlin is dotted with newspaper offices and journalists—their number is estimated to be 3000. They follow every step of the "political heavyweights". It does not seem to be accidental that at the end of 1999 journalists started to uncover by far the most serious scandal in Germany's post-war history to date. Details became publicly known of an illegal web of "secret bank accounts" with leading figures of the conservative party CDU, and especially former Chancellor Kohl, involved. In general, it seems that reporting has become much faster and more investigative since Berlin became the new capital.

Summing up the latest developments in politics, economics and media, it can be said that journalism and media coverage have changed dramatically simultaneously. Commercialisation has made media coverage more attractive to a broad public by the inclusion of entertainment elements in journalism. Journalists' proximity to the government and to leading politicians has made them more aggressive and more investigative. The removal of the capital to Berlin has centralised the former de-centralised politics and polity as well as the media industry, which for the most part has moved to Berlin too. If these shifts actually do affect German media, German journalists can be expected to reflect this change in their professional attitudes.

The following findings on the characteristics of German journalism are based upon a representative study "Journalism in Germany II", a survey of 1536 German journalists which the authors of this chapter conducted between 2003 and 2005. The study replicates the precursor study carried out in 1993 (cf. Weischenberg et al. 1998). With the help of the data gained from the two studies it is possible to describe the current structure of journalism in Germany as well as the structural changes which took place between the 1990s and the 2000s. Unfortunately we are not able to compare the journalists in the centre (Berlin) with the journalists in the peripheries. For reasons of data protection the polling firm which carried out the study was not allowed to make accessible the names and headquarters of the media organisations the journalists actually work for. Therefore our argumentation is based on a comparison in time rather than on a regional comparison: The first study in 1993 covers the more de-centralised period of the Bonn republic, whereas the second study in 2005 covers the more centralised period of the Berlin republic.

Methodology

The study draws on a theoretical framework (cf. Görke and Scholl 2006; Scholl and Weischenberg 1999) and defines journalism on three different levels:

1) Within *society*, journalism is defined as a social system that enables society to observe itself, as it provides the public independently and periodically with information and issues that are considered newsworthy, relevant and fact-based. Thus, journalism can be distinguished from public

relations, which is neither independent nor necessarily relevant or fact-based in all cases (cf. Scholl and Weischenberg 1998; Scholl 1996).

2) On the *organisational* level journalistic organisations can be distinguished from other organisations by their contribution to journalistic coverage. Thus, the definition of journalistic media includes media which are independent units, not published by political parties, associations, trade unions or other professional organisations, or public authorities, which are published periodically and at least six times a year, and which include journalistic coverage (not just advertising, fiction, music, games and puzzles). With this definition, non-periodical media (e.g. books, quarterly published journals) are excluded as well as fictional media (e.g. paperback novels, motion pictures) or media without sufficient distribution, which are considered to be of little public relevance. As professional observers of others, journalistic media are distinguished from public relations media, which are produced on behalf of companies, associations, unions etc. and serve primarily as creators of a client's positive public image (cf. Scholl 1996; Malik 2005).

3) On the level of *individuals* journalists are conceptualised as the system's actors. They fulfil professional roles for which they are prepared by training and work in the newsrooms. Journalistic roles are defined by their main activities and duties within the process of producing journalistic coverage—both as full-time or freelance staff. A member of a newsroom is considered a journalist if he or she is predominantly engaged in producing journalistic coverage and thereby influencing the content of the media. This includes the anchors of TV news shows and the editors of online news as well as freelancers for magazines.

Drawing on this definition of journalism the population of the survey was identified in four steps: (1) The universe of journalistic media in Germany was determined by listing all print, television, radio and online-media as well as news agencies and media services. In this way 2890 journalistic media organisations were identified. (2) A stratified random sample of 1768 media was surveyed with a written questionnaire including questions about the number of journalists working as full-time employees or as freelance journalists, the number of male and female journalists, and the number of journalists working for various editorial departments and in various hierarchical positions. (3) On this basis, a population of 48,000 professional journalists could be estimated in total and distinguished by several parameters. (4) A multi-stage stratified random sample of 3600 journalists was drawn from this population. The stratification was carried out on the level of different media types (e.g. small and big regional daily newspaper, nationwide daily newspaper, small and big weekly newspaper), state of employment (full-time vs. freelance), position in newsroom hierarchy, gender and editorial departments (such as politics, economics, sport, culture, local/ regional department, etc.).

Finally, a stratified random sample of 1536 journalists was surveyed by telephone between February and April 2005 (return rate: 73 percent). The questionnaire included questions about professional status and professional career, role perceptions, ethics of reporting, image of the journalists' audience, perceived influences on journalists, job satisfaction and socio-demographic characteristics.

Structural Shift

In 2005 about 48,000 journalists worked for almost 3000 media organisations in Germany. 12,000 of them were professional freelancers, who we define as journalists either deriving more than half of their income from journalistic work (rather than from public relations activities) and/or spending more than half of their working time on journalistic tasks (rather than for public relations or any other tasks). If we compare the data with the precursor study in 1993, we observe an increase in the number of media organisations (plus 500) but a decrease in the journalistic workforce (minus 6000) although full-time or permanently employed staff numbers have remained stable (36,000 journalists). Firstly, we can conclude from these findings that the journalist's job has become more stressful because fewer journalists provide (more) coverage for more media. Secondly, an unknown number of non-professional freelancers and/or journalists with hybrid roles (working both as journalists and as public relations practitioners) hide behind the decreasing number of professional freelancers, compensating for the increasing journalistic workload.

More than a third of all German journalists (including the professional freelancers) continue to work for daily or weekly newspapers, followed by journalistic personnel working in broadcast media and magazines of all kinds. Less than five percent are employed in online media, showing that professional online journalism is still a minority business.

Table 1: Number of journalists* by type of media organisation

type of media organisation	number of journalists	percentage
daily and weekly newspapers	17,113	35
freesheets	2,876	6
magazines	9,419	20
news agencies and media services	1,428	3
public and commercial radio	8,003	17
public and commercial television	7,215	15
online media	2,325	5
total	48,379	101[1]

* Includes both full-time/permanently employed staff and (professional) freelancers.

Most German journalists work for local or regional departments of media organisations (27 percent) or for the politics department (15 percent). One in ten journalists works for the cultural department (10 percent) or for a specialist department (10 percent). The remaining categories are the lifestyle department (8 percent), the sports department (6 percent) and the business journalism department (5 percent).

There are a considerable number of journalists who cannot be assigned to an editorial department (18 percent). This demonstrates a significant change in German media organisations which have altered the structure of editorial departments to the typical structure of Anglo-Saxon journalism.

The structure of journalism in Germany outlined above manifests a decrease in professionalism in parts of the journalistic system. There are considerably fewer professional journalists working for an increased number of publications. Newspapers, freesheets and news agencies have not only reduced or outsourced their full-time and permanently employed staff, but also cut back the number of freelancers significantly. These findings testify to a quantitative reduction of journalistic manpower with the risk that accuracy is reduced too, if more tasks have to be completed by fewer journalists. Thus, quantitative reduction leads to a loss in quality.

Functional Stability

While the structural constraints of journalistic work have changed significantly, central aspects of journalists' attitudes remain stable.

---

[1] The final percentage of 101 is due to rounding.

Role perception and role performance

Journalists' professionalism is closely related to their roles, which can be measured both in an objective and in a subjective dimension. Although both dimensions can be distinguished empirically, they belong together theoretically because role perceptions do not simply consist of journalists' subjective professional attitudes, being as a result irrelevant for the objective description and analysis of the journalistic system. Rather, role perceptions also reflect journalists' actual roles and professional rules in a contingent (non-deterministic and non-causal) manner.

In order to combine subjective role perception with (an estimation of) objective role performance we asked journalists what their professional intentions were and whether they were able to achieve these professional goals. Thus, we sought to establish what the main professional goals in journalism are, and whether these goals are mere professional "ideology" or real practices (of course only as self-reported to us by journalists).

As we argued in an earlier publication (Scholl and Weischenberg 1998, 166ff.), apparently contradictory role perceptions should not necessarily be considered mutually exclusive. Rather, they seem to be hierarchically ordered and complex. There is in fact no contradiction if a journalist aims to be both a neutral disseminator of facts and a critic of public affairs because on the basis of a neutral collection and presentation of information he/she may additionally criticise what is going wrong. Therefore, we prefer to conceive role perceptions as having various dimensions (in a factor analytical sense) rather than as self-contained categories (in a logical sense of exclusiveness, completeness, etc.).

The most relevant group of aims refers to the key concept of objective reporting. Theoretically objective reporting can be considered a four-dimensional construct: the first dimension can be termed *substantial* because information should be objective (reflecting reality), neutral and precise; the second dimension is more *formal* because information should be presented in a simple (complexity reducing), analytical and interpretative way; the third dimension is *temporal* because information should be disseminated quickly; and the fourth dimension is *social* because information should be of interest to the broadest possible audience or public.

Table 2: Role perceptions: targeted and achieved (N=1536)

Professional roles	agree*	achieve**
get information to the public neutrally and precisely	89	76
provide analyses and interpretations of complex problems	79	75
get information to the public quickly	74	79
present reality as it is	74	67
concentrate on news which is of interest to the widest possible public	60	74
criticise public affairs	58	43
give ordinary people a chance to express their views on issues of public interest	34	57
stand up for the disadvantaged	29	43
Scrutinise politics, business, and society	24	27
influence the political agenda and getting issues on the political agenda	14	39
present new trends and convey new ideas	44	58
convey positive ideals	44	43
help people in their everyday lives	44	69
present one's own opinion to the public	19	67
provide entertainment and relaxation	37	79

* Percentage of respondents who entirely agree or mostly agree with the professional aim
** Percentage of respondents who entirely agree or mostly agree with the professional aim *and* who entirely agree or mostly agree that they are able to achieve this aim in their job

　　The findings provide evidence for both the theoretical and practical importance of objective reporting. German journalists' role perceptions are dominated by strong approval of objective reporting (information journalism). The vast majority entirely or mostly agree with the aims of "getting information to the public neutrally and precisely" (89 percent), "providing analyses and interpretations of complex problems" (79 percent), "getting information to the public quickly" (74 percent), "presenting reality as it is" (74 percent), and "concentrating on news which is of interest to the widest possible public" (60 percent).

　　Another result supports the interpretation that information journalism is the basis (and basic agreement) of the journalistic profession: on average about three out of four journalists approving of these items also report that they can entirely or mostly achieve the roles in question. This approval and achievement of objective reporting is even stronger than it was in 1993 (cf. Weischenberg et al. 1998, 243). We can either assess this finding as an impressive confirmation of objective reporting, which is the professional ideal not only of Anglo-Saxon journalism and which represents journalists' independence from particular interest groups, or we can regard it as a mere indicator of a more or less passive journalistic role of disseminating information.

Another group of aims is used to operationalise active, political, or advocacy journalism. Journalists were asked whether they want to criticise public affairs, to stand up for the disadvantaged, to scrutinise politics, business and society, or to influence the political agenda. Here too, we can theoretically distinguish between different dimensions: *critique*, *advocacy*, and *scrutiny*. The order of these three dimensions represents an order of commitment. As criticism is rather unspecific, it can be applied to all kinds of phenomena, whereas advocacy is clearly related to a certain group (disadvantaged people) but is still an everyday phenomenon. Scrutiny should demand the highest commitment because it requires an oppositional attitude towards powerful people and groups. But even this very political attitude need not be interpreted as partisanship—the support of a certain political party or lobby group—but is still covered by the professional rules that investigative watchdog journalism follows.

Empirical data reveal that approval of active journalism roles correlates negatively with commitment. More than half of German journalists aim to criticise public affairs (58 percent), but only about one third perceive themselves as persons who give ordinary people a chance to express their opinions about issues of public interest (34 percent) or who stand up for the disadvantaged (29 percent). Approval of scrutiny is even lower: only one in four journalists aims to scrutinise politics, business, and society (24 percent), and only one in seven aims to influence the political agenda (14 percent). This low degree of approval can partly be explained by the sample of journalists itself: it includes not only typical news journalists but also lifestyle, entertainment and society journalists. In fact local journalists and journalists covering political issues *are* somewhat more interested in criticism, advocacy and control (between 5 and 10 points more than overall sample). Not only do few journalists perceive their professional role as a critique, advocacy or scrutiny function but also those who approve of these roles are sceptical about the possibility of achieving them.

A third cluster of aims seems to be additional to the core demands of journalism but nonetheless belong to a modern understanding of the profession. Again, these aims can be described theoretically in more than one dimension. The first dimension is best labelled *lifestyle* journalism. It includes aims like "convey positive ideals" and "present new trends and convey new ideas". The second dimension can be labelled *service* journalism. It includes aims like "help people in their everyday lives" and "present one's own opinion to the public", which should not be interpreted in the context of political debate but in the sense of orienting the audience and performing a kind of service in everyday matters. The third dimension includes *entertainment* journalism and is represented by the aim "providing entertainment and relaxation".

The findings reveal that lifestyle journalism is approved of by almost half of German journalists. Four out of ten want to present new trends and convey new ideas (44 percent) and to convey positive ideals (40 percent). With respect to service journalism, they are split. Again four out of ten approve of helping people in their everyday lives (44 percent), but only two in ten want to present their own opinions to the public (19 percent), which they may consider involves making up the audience's mind for it. More than a third of the journalists under study want to entertain their audience and help it relax (37 percent). Interestingly, these roles have not become more popular since the 1990s, as there is no increase in their approval (cf. Weischenberg et al. 1998, 243f.; Weischenberg et al. 2006, 111).

These results again are partly due to the broad definition of journalism used which includes lifestyle magazines and entertainment roles performed in media organisations (insofar as they belong to journalism and not to the entertainment business). Indeed we find that journalists working for magazines or covering soft news and soft topics approve of the service role, the lifestyle role and the entertainment role to a higher degree than the overall sample does (cf. Weischenberg et al. 2006, 280-285).

Journalists who perceive their role as entertaining or service-oriented are convinced that they can achieve these roles. It seems easy to entertain the audience (79 percent), to give advice to the audience (69 percent) or to present one's own opinion (67 percent), whereas fewer journalists are able to achieve their aim of conveying new trends and ideas (58 percent) or positive ideals (43 percent) because it is harder to affect the audience with coverage in these fields than it is in the field of entertainment or presenting service-oriented facts and opinions.

Reporting practices

If professional aims represent what journalists *want* to do, ethical considerations are indicators of what journalists are *allowed* to do. Ethics can be observed with the help of reporting practices because they are both specific with respect to certain cases and situations and general in terms of overall rules for "dos and don'ts".

The overall impression of German journalists' ethical attitudes is that they are very cautious in adopting unusual reporting practices. Only a few entirely or mainly justify any of these practices. It is only the use of confidential government documents without authorisation which is justified by a substantial minority (25 percent). Still, a minority (11 percent) justifies getting employed in a firm or organisation to gain inside information or pretending to hold an opinion or attitude to inspire an informant's confidence, but all the other practices are much less approved of. In comparison with the data of 1993 these findings document a significant loss of courage or of growing ethical sensitivity—depending on whether one regrets or appreciates this development (cf. Weischenberg et al. 1998, 247f.).

Table 3: Approval of unusual reporting practices (N=1536)

Reporting practices	Justify mostly/ entirely	depends on circum- stances	do not justify mostly/ entirely
using confidential government documents without authorisation	25	59	16
getting employed in a firm or organisation to gain inside information	11	49	40
pretending to hold an opinion or attitude to inspire an informant's confidence	11	45	44
claiming to be somebody else	8	32	60
paying people for confidential information	6	27	67
using hidden microphones or cameras	5	28	67
badgering unwilling informants to get information	1	12	87
agreeing to protect confidentiality and not doing so	1	3	96
making use of personal documents without permission	<1	8	92

The high percentage of journalists who report approval of certain unusual reporting practices dependent on the circumstances indicates that ethical rules are not considered fixed norms but flexible props. Even so, some of the strategies seem to allude to a topic which is almost taboo. German journalists refuse to treat informants in a way they consider unfair (badgering unwilling informants or breaking confidentiality). Furthermore, they clearly distinguish between the use of unauthorised documents with official information—which some of them do justify—and personal information, which hardly a journalist justifies because privacy is a very strict norm in German culture.

Conclusions

Taking all the results together, we observe a creeping decrease in professionalism in the *structure* of German journalism (the number of journalists and freelancers) but a stabilisation regarding the *function* of journalism for society (cf. role perceptions and reporting practices). Although the media have changed dramatically since the 1990s, there are no dramatic shifts in journalists' professional attitudes and performances. In this respect journalism in Germany turns out to be a stable profession with a distinctive professional culture. On the one hand, the profession is differentiating increasingly with respect to different media types (universal vs. special interest; old vs. new; small vs. large; etc.), and in some parts it intermingles with other forms of public communication, such as public relations, advertising, entertainment and user-generated content. On the other hand, traditional values and professional norms are still central for the journalists' self-perception and their role performances.

The Berlin republic has obviously altered German journalism (in structure) but this has not led to a completely different journalism compared to the journalism that had developed in the Bonn republic (with respect to its function for society). Thus far, the results outlined above can be explained by social system theory (cf. Görke and Scholl 2006): system theory on the one hand predicts a certain stability of the functions accomplished by societal systems (here the profession of journalism, journalistic media coverage), which is accompanied by structural adaptations (characteristics of journalists and media organisations) to new developments within society. On the other hand, systems within society autonomously fulfil their exclusive function for society (here journalism, the media) and cannot be determined by their environment (politics, economy, etc.). The new circumstances of the Berlin republic have not (yet?) altered journalism in a way that it cannot be recognised anymore as the profession which we are used to accept as journalism. However, the question as to whether further structural shifts may result in functional shifts too remains, for the moment, unanswered.

Works Cited

Bücher, K. 1917. *Die Entstehung der Volkswirtschaft. Vorträge und Aufsätze. Erste Sammlung* (The emergence of national economics. Lectures and articles. First collection). 10th edition. Tübingen: Laupp Buchhandlung.

Frei, N. and J. Schmitz. 1989. *Journalismus im Dritten Reich* (Journalism in the Third Reich). München: Beck.

Görke, A. and A. Scholl. 2006. Niklas Luhmann's theory of social systems and journalism research. *Journalism Studies* 7 (4): 644-655.

Malik, M. 2005. Heterogenität und Repräsentativität. Zur Konzeption von Grundgesamtheit und Stichprobe der Studie "Journalismus in Deutschland II" (Heterogeneity and representativeness. Population and sampling procedure in the study "Journalism in Germany II"). In *Auswahlverfahren in der Kommunikationswissenschaft* (Sampling methods in communication science), edited by V. Gehrau, B. Fretwurst, B. Krause, and G. Daschmann. 183-202. Köln: Halem.

Scholl, A. 1996. Sampling journalists. *The European Journal of Communication*, 21 (3): 331-343.

Scholl, A. and S. Weischenberg. 1998. *Journalismus in der Gesellschaft. Theorie, Methodologie und Empirie* (Journalism in society. Theory, methodology, and empirical results). Opladen, Wiesbaden: Westdeutscher Verlag.

Scholl, A. and S. Weischenberg. 1999. Autonomy in journalism: How it is related to attitudes and behavior of media professionals. *Web Journal of Mass Communication Research* 2 (4). http://www.scripps.ohiou.edu/wjmcr/ vol02/2-4a.HTM.

Weaver, D. and G. Cleveland Wilhoit. 1996. *The American journalist in the 1990s. U.S. news people at the end of an era.* Mahwah, NJ: Erlbaum.

Weber, M. 1968. *Politik als Beruf* (Politics as vocation). 5th edition (1st edition 1919). Berlin: Duncker & Humblot.

Weischenberg, S., M. Löffelholz and A. Scholl. 1998: Journalism in Germany. In *The global journalist: News people around the world*, edited by D. H. Weaver. 229-256. Cresskill, NJ: Hampton Press.

Weischenberg, S., M. Malik and A. Scholl. 2006. *Souffleure der Mediengesellschaft: Report über die Journalisten in Deutschland*

(Prompters of media society: Report on journalists in Germany). Konstanz: UVK.

"THE ISLAND OF LONELINESS"?
LITERARY JOURNALISM
FROM THE AZOREAN PERIPHERY

ISABEL SOARES

In 2007 the feature documentary *Wild Rose*[1] was aired to much public acclaim on the major commercial Portuguese television channel SIC. In it Pedro Coelho, the author of the programme and its on-screen reporter, promoted a young shepherd girl called Rosa ("Rosa" is also the Portuguese word for "rose") to the status of TV star of the moment. The blonde teenager represented a naïve portrait of youth from a lost and provincial part of northern Portugal which time had passed by, and which was hardly known to the coastal urban masses who constitute the bulk of the country's metropolitan population. Rosa, whose main ambition was to carry on her studies amid her time-consuming chores around the family's farm, quickly became an exotic and interesting figure, metonymically taken for a whole neglected population living in the most remote, or peripheral, areas of the country. The success of the programme was huge and was followed by the publication of a book entitled *Wild Rose, Shepherd of Dreams and Other Stories*, a compilation of three *reportagens*[2] Coelho had shot for SIC and which was sold out by Christmas. Both "Wild Rose", an obvious pun on Rosa's name, and the "Other Stories" were the result of Coelho's in-depth reporting on subjects whose common denominator is their location on the fringes of either geographical or social centres. They were all originally broadcast on television before appearing in print and, due also to their controversial

---

[1] Since the corpus consists of texts and television programmes originally in Portuguese, all titles and quotations will be translated into English.

[2] The noun *reportagem* in Portuguese does not have a literal translation into English. It can, however, mean literary reportage *latu sensu* or feature story. In everyday usage it stands for pieces of in-depth reporting aired as news specials on television or published in the print media. For further details on the meaning of the word *reportagem* see Soares (2009, 29).

contents and success with the public, they established Coelho (born 1966) as one of the leading Portuguese television reporters of his generation.

Reporting from the periphery—from a plural and vast uncharted periphery—in his book, Coelho tells the story of Rosa and her wild, yet innocent, dreams of meeting Prince Charming and of being able to flee from the cold, desolate, northern mountains of Trás-os-Montes where her herds of sheep graze. Along with the story about Rosa, the book also includes many stories Coelho found behind the bars of prisons, broadcast in 2004 under the title *Bar Code*. By focusing attention on the lives of inmates, most of whom were men and women doing time for drug trafficking and consumption and for petty theft, the reporter raises controversial questions about the Portuguese judicial system while opening up the gates of prisons to let primetime audiences have a glimpse of what goes on in that seemingly hermetically closed and segregated world. Finally there is the narrative set on the Azorean island of Corvo, or the "Island of Loneliness" as the journalist termed it when it was shown on TV in 2006.

If all three televised programmes were the work of a well-trained, well-researched and unbiased reporter who raises awareness of issues not usually subjected to public scrutiny and rarely given media attention, the book, on the other hand, is a first-person account, a narrative of the journalist's quest for, and encounter with, the subjects about whom he is going to report. And this not only transcends the mere factuality and impartiality we so often associate with journalism but also bears an imprint of originality in Coelho's work. In fact, on committing "Wild Rose" and "Other Stories" to paper, the reporter/author becomes a literary journalist because he is unable to remain detached from what he is reporting. This is clear in "The Island of Loneliness", an instance of in-depth reporting leading to the entanglement of the journalist and his topic.

The purpose of the following analysis is, then, to consider Pedro Coelho as a literary journalist by focusing particularly on his feature story regarding the island of Corvo. Corvo is an ultra-peripheral Portuguese island (Europe's westernmost territory), afloat in the middle of the North Atlantic, forgotten by central administration and recipient of special EU subsidies on account of its extreme remoteness. In Corvo, Coelho is therefore the journalist reporting from a geographic periphery and his account a piece of literary journalism, a genre whose most admired figures include, among others, Norman Mailer, Truman Capote and, more recently, Anna Politovskaya.

However, in order to argue that "The Island of Loneliness" falls within the category of literary journalism, we need, firstly, to locate this genre within journalism itself and to discard the assumption that it is journalism about literature or literary criticism. The adjective "literary" is being used here, then, not in relation to content but to form, so as to characterise a particular type of journalistic writing which resorts to literary devices such as scene depiction, dialogue and character description. Indeed, if one could define literary journalism in just a single sentence it would be "it reads like a novel"—a statement that, as Norman Sims declares, "has been used to compliment and unintentionally to insult literary journalism" (2007, 1). Detractors accuse it of a close connection to fiction that can dangerously question its commitment to the truth, while its champions regard it as a type of journalism free from the trappings of too much objectivity and too little personalisation.

Notwithstanding a long line of practitioners that can be traced back to Daniel Defoe and his *A Journal of the Plague Year* (1722), literary journalism first emerges as a distinct journalistic genre in the mid-nineteenth century with the investigative work of Henry Mayhew for the *Morning Chronicle*, later to be popularised by the—sometimes sensationalist and always controversial—articles W. T. Stead wrote as editor of the *Pall Mall Gazette* in the 1880s and 1890s.[3] The innovative character of the journalism that not only Stead but also Andrew Mearns and Charles Booth were producing on the social peripheries of great urban centres such as London's East End was characterised by the critic Matthew Arnold in 1887 as "New Journalism". Unaware of course that the expression would come to define a whole journalistic genre—and would be used in 1973 in Tom Wolfe's seminal book *New Journalism*—Arnold adopted an ironic tone in order to characterise what he considered an impertinent, because personalised, way of presenting news which broke with the orthodoxy of impartial factuality. As Kevin Kerrane (1997, 17) comments:

> The term "new journalism", in fact, was originally coined ... to describe the style of Stead's *Pall Mall Gazette*: brash, vivid, personal, reform-minded and occasionally, from Arnold's conservative viewpoint, "featherbrained." The Victorian social reporters ... aimed at a factual literature of modern industrial life. Their literary touches came less from

---

[3] In 1885, W. T. Stead published what came to be regarded as his most controversial and thought-provoking articles for the *Pall Mall Gazette*, "Maiden Tribute of Modern Babylon". In this series, he revealed to a bewildered audience all the horrors of prostitution as a business involving little girls, and how he had managed to purchase a thirteen-year-old girl to serve as apprentice in one of the many brothels in London. However, more than its controversial contents, the "Maiden Tribute" constitutes a cornerstone in late nineteenth-century New Journalism. See Dudek (1961, 128-129).

artistic design than from the writer's sense of moral or political urgency: a determination to dramatize the reality of poverty, prostitution, and prejudice.

The New Journalism of the late-nineteenth century cannot be considered straightforward literary journalism, but it had the merit of introducing the interview and making headlines more appealing, even sensational. Inevitably such an approach helped sell newspapers at a time when literacy levels were increasing. Nevertheless, and more importantly, New Journalism, because of its treatment of "subjects ... unfamiliar to middle-class readers" (Hollowell 1977, 40), was concentrating attention on the plight of the disenfranchised, ostracised masses who lived below the poverty line in the dimly lit and dirty neighbourhoods of affluent cities. This was a kind of journalism that intersected closely with another emerging field of study, sociology, in the way it dissected and interpreted the numerous social/peripheral/marginalised urban Others. And its practitioners could also be regarded as proto-sociologists while they were disguising themselves as paupers and vagrants in order to study those communities through participant observation methods or, as far as journalism is concerned, immersion reporting.

Besides, new journalists were writing about reality as it was individually and subjectively apprehended by them, without the constraints of canonical journalistic impartiality. By 1903 New Journalism was so popular that Jack London's monumental *The People of the Abyss*, an account of his experience as a vagrant in the streets of the East End, became an instant best-seller upon publication and also his most renowned and timeless piece of journalism. And this is another characteristic of literary journalism, its time-defying capacity or, as Phyllis Frus terms it, the "endurance criterion" (1994, 2). In fact, texts of a literary journalistic nature resist time and the dimming of the newsworthiness of their contents, which explains why works such as *The People of the Abyss* or Truman Capote's *In Cold Blood* (1966) have never been out of print. That is, the literariness of these texts allows them to be read long after the events they deal with have happened.

In the early 1970s, it became evident that a "new" journalism would have to be acknowledged both by the journalistic community and the Academy. In the "Introduction" to *New Journalism*, Tom Wolfe, however, states his dislike for any expression including the adjective "new" to characterise any movements, parties or theories (1973, 23) and then begins to lay out the theoretical ground of literary journalism. Quite simply he had come to the conclusion that:

It was possible to write accurate non-fiction with techniques usually associated with novels and short stories. ... It was possible in non-fiction, in journalism, to use any literary device ... and to use many different kinds simultaneously, or within a relatively short space... to excite the reader both intellectually and emotionally (*ibid*, 15).

And furthermore, what was really worth noticing was that there were already many journalists like Wolfe himself treading the path of that New Journalism which went under the names of "literary non-fiction", "literary journalism", "the non-fiction novel", "journalistic non-fiction", "art-journalism" or even the more imaginative "the other literature". In time, and when academics started dissecting this genre, the term "literary journalism" gained, if not universal acceptance, at least predominance over all other attempts at naming this alluring and non-canonical journalism.[4] Throughout the 1980s and 1990s books like Norman Sims' *The Literary Journalists* (1984), Thomas Connery's *A Sourcebook of American Literary Journalism: Representative Writers in an Emerging Genre* (1992) or Kevin Kerrane and Ben Yagoda's *The Art of Fact: A Historical Anthology of Literary Journalism* (1997) helped popularise this expression which would finally come to be accepted as the more or less universal denomination of the genre at the dawn of the new century with the appearance of John Hartsock's *A History of American Literary Journalism: The Emergence of a Modern Narrative Form* (2000) and the creation in 2006 of the International Association for Literary Journalism Studies. It is entirely appropriate then to attempt the analysis of "The Island of Loneliness" under the theoretical auspices of literary journalism and to include Pedro Coelho in the stream of literary journalists.

Coelho starts by defending the proposition that Corvo, a rocky island of roughly 17 square kilometres and 400 inhabitants, is an island unto itself and for this purpose he deconstructs the idea put forward by the English poet and cleric John Donne in the seventeenth century and adopted by Ernest Hemingway in *For Whom the Bells Toll* (1940) that "No man is an island, entire of itself; every man is a piece of the continent, a part of the main" (2007, 59). Corvo is, on its own, an instance of resilient independence from both country and continent as is proven by its history of defying mainland legislation, for example by providing shelter for

---

[4] Although in Europe academic tradition has commonly connected "literary journalism" to journalism concerned with literary criticism, it is now widely acknowledged that the expression is used to name and define that journalistic genre in which journalists not only resort to literary devices but also do not shy away from revealing their own judgements and opinions on any given subject. See, Hartsock (in press).

pirates when buccaneers ruled the seas and by not conforming to the imposition of modern traffic rules. But, more than the distance separating the island from any continent, there is, as the journalist discovered throughout his sojourn, the distance that separates the islanders from one another, so that Donne's assumption becomes even more problematic because in Corvo every man is indeed an island.

Revealing the sources he used to prepare himself before going to Corvo to shoot his documentary, which included major Portuguese writers and ranged from "the distanced realism of Raul Brandão, the historic narrative of António Ferreira de Serpa [to] the romantic vision of Fernando Dacosta" (*ibid*, 62), Coelho is led to conclude that nothing he had learned in the books he read had prepared him for the reality he encountered. As he says: "Distance has united the *Corvinos* [inhabitants of Corvo] and together they survived it; but progress, subsidies, the internet, have transformed each one of the ... inhabitants into islands of themselves" (*ibid*). With the help of João Cardigos, the only resident doctor on the island, who acts as the journalist's guide and who is a continental foreigner never accepted by the islanders, Coelho loses the romanticised notion of a self-sufficient island in the Atlantic, a notion which would be further shattered when, after the broadcast of "The Island of Loneliness", he received e-mail messages from almost every single one of the 400 *Corvinos* who did not see themselves reflected in the documentary and forbade Coelho to set foot on the island again. And, in a very personal tone which sets Coelho aside from the merely factual journalist, he confesses: "In the whole process, that is what upsets me the most. I do not know many pieces of land which seduce me as much as Corvo" (*ibid*, 63). This confession can, consequently, be interpreted as a clear indicator of the journalist's feelings as a man, someone who has been dealt a heavy blow and is saddened by it. Conversely, the presence of the journalist's self in the narrative reflects what Hartsock defines as "a writing subjectivity" (2000, 17), a prerequisite of texts which fall within the category of literary journalism. Coelho is writing "The Island of Loneliness" with the purpose of revealing his own apprehension of the island rather than replicating the images and impressions fabricated by others. It is his interpretative imprint which is being stamped on the pages of the book.

Nevertheless, what lifts "The Island of Loneliness" above being the mere script written by a reporter on a commission to shoot a documentary on a given remote region is the fluidity with which Coelho intersects the factual account with personal interpretation. When the journalist describes the island as "the most remote of all the Azorean islands, also the most distant and isolated national territory" (*ibid*, 69), he is performing the journalistic mission of informing the public objectively. However, when he lets his readers into his subjective apprehension of the island and islanders he becomes a character in his own narrative, a process that can also be termed "participant observation reporting" and which is one of the particular features of literary journalism (Sims 2007, xviii). This technique of immersion is visible throughout the interviews he conducts on the island as he offers his own thoughts at the moment of interviewing the islanders. For example, there is his conversation with Sara, a teenage girl whom he wants to ask about her expectations for the future (Coelho 2007, 100):

> "And you, would you leave the island?"—I asked Sara, all the while thinking she was freer [than the other islanders] to acknowledge a full divorce from the island and the answer seemed to reproduce that most typical *Corvino* feeling: an immense will to leave, which obviously the majority refuses to surrender to by not leaving.
> "If I had the chance to leave, I would. But I'd come back. I'd always come back. This soothes me, so to say."
> "And doesn't this tire you?"—I insist, thinking to myself that if this young lady had a safe path to follow outside the island, she would not hesitate for a second. The answer, however, sounded sincere.
> "I don't do much here, but I'm used to it. Sometimes I get sad, but I could also get sad someplace else."

More than the interview itself we are struck by the fact that Coelho is himself thinking about the answers he would like to get, which reveals his biases and preconceived ideas: the islanders are people who would gladly leave the remoteness of Corvo. Instead, the answer the *Corvinos* always offer is that something stronger than their will, something of a shared umbilical chord, ties them to the harsh small piece of land which they call home.

Also, as would a travel writer—and travel writing bears a great resemblance to literary journalism (see Soares 2009, 18)—Coelho describes the gastronomic delights the island has to offer the continental traveller:

> Judging by the healthy colours of *Corvino* pigs, bred naturally without preservatives, and tasting the flavour of the meat transformed into steaks at the island's only restaurant, the writer's observation becomes an unquestionable truth (Coelho 2007, 78).

Sentences like this, in which opinion is entangled with the representation of the journalist's self as a writer, hardly allow readers to be aware that "The Island of Loneliness" is, first and foremost, a piece of journalistic writing *per se*. Furthermore, humour and character depiction also contribute to the sense of literariness that transforms the book into an example of literary journalism.

In order to enhance the peculiarities of Corvo that highlight its peripheral status, setting it aside from a national/continental shared identity, Coelho uses the example of João Garcia, farmer, politician, regional MP, and the island's mailman. Garcia's ability to juggle numerous activities seems an almost genetic characteristic of the islanders. In the case of Garcia "letters and cows have different schedules; and letters have proved the best political instrument on the island" (*ibid*, 65-66) because Garcia managed to win nomination for the Azorean Parliament. As for the rest of the islanders, "the biological clock of cows is compatible with that of every *Corvino*, irrespective of all other occupations they might have: they milk the cows at daybreak, they milk the cows in the evening before light goes out" (*ibid*, 66) and thus all *Corvinos* are keen on multitasking in seemingly not remotely-related activities that puzzle continentals and transform the islanders into instances of national otherness. In fact, taken at face value, literary journalism "is about embracing an understanding of the social or cultural Other" (Hartsock 2000, 22) and what Coelho is revealing in his account is that *Corvinos* are a sociocultural Other of the continental Portuguese just as much as if they were foreigners.

The revelation of the Other, and the inclusion of the writer's opinions, are distinctive features of literary journalism present in the pages of "The Island of Loneliness" as are the passages of dialogue, with their colloquialisms which Coelho captured while talking with the *Corvinos* he met. But where the author reveals himself as a true literary journalist is when he describes the islanders almost as if they were characters in a novel. There is the priest, Alexandre Medeiros, "tall and slim up to his chin … with a vibrant and exuberant voice. [And who is] free from anguish, remorse or sadness" (Coelho 2007, 70-75) for not having married. There is Celso, the civil servant, whose continental wife left him on account of not enduring Corvo's remoteness, and whose love of the island keeps him "hostage of a *Corvino* philosophy" tied to the pier like some broken ship (*ibid*, 86). There is the Mayor, a *Corvino* by birth but different from his fellow islanders and not liked by them, something which perplexes Pedro Coelho: "If everybody already knew Fernando Pimentel [the Mayor], in all his failings and virtues, why did they elect him by such a significant margin? … Could he afterwards have lost, in a single blow, all that was good about him?" (*ibid*, 88-89). Coelho thinks not. As an outsider he believes Pimentel is a good man, someone who looks "disconnected from everything around him, even from himself" (*ibid*, 89), smoking cigarette after cigarette, speaking at a different speed from the other *Corvinos*, "forgetting syllables, leaving some unverbalised" (*ibid*, 87). His family is one of the few most influential on the island but he is prey to something that, natural and usual in all communities, gains monstrous proportions on this forsaken dot in an immense ocean: gossip and hearsay.

It is Coelho who explains that "the island lives unto itself, eternally mulling over the same conversations, the same criticisms" (*ibid*, 88) and, what is more, even if *Corvinos* do not speak ill of their island and do not allow strangers to do so, they live by speaking ill of each other. As a result "Corvo is one of the regions in the country where the consumption of anti-depressives substantially exceeds … the national average" (*ibid*, 89). Out on the street people are forced to see endlessly those whom they love and those they hate and consequently conflict arises frequently. Now, in order to avoid this excessive contact, the islanders have learnt to shut themselves within four walls and surf the internet to take themselves beyond their oppressive island. And now as Celso, another of the island's internet addicts recognises, because of the World Wide Web which allows *Corvinos* to sail other remote seas "there is no time left in Corvo for other things" (*ibid*, 76) like socialisation so that the islanders truly become islands unto themselves. They are, in fact, able to milk their cows and have other occupations but, in the end, and no matter how they resist admitting it, they try to flee from their claustrophobic island. And as Coelho melancholically concludes: "Where else can people be islands unto themselves other than on the island of loneliness?" (*ibid*, 107).

If among the topics most covered by literary journalism are those which reflect "patterns of social organization that deviate from the mainstream culture" (Hollowell 1977, 40) clearly Coelho is giving ample coverage of a whole community living on both geographic and social fringes. Corvo is thus depicted as a case of the otherness within, in this case the insular and strange Other of continental Portugal. And, unconstrained by the shackles of mere factual reporting, Coelho is the literary journalist allowing his readers to see a reality as it is individually apprehended by him. Ultimately, it is through the writing of this literary journalist that Corvo is transformed from a peripheral geographic location, pervaded by the endless social problems which come with that remoteness from the mainland, into a sad, isolated, and lost island of loneliness.

Works Cited

Coelho, P. 2007. *Rosa Brava, Pastora de Sonhos e Outras Histórias.* Dafundo: Oficina do Livro.

Dudek, L. 1961. *Literature and the Press: a History of Printing, Printed Media, and Their Relation to Literature.* Toronto: Ryerson Press.

Frus, P. 1994. *The Politics and Poetics of Journalistic Narrative: The Timely and the Timeless.* Cambridge: Cambridge University Press.

Hartsock, J. C. 2000. *A History of American Literary Journalism: The Emergence of a Modern Narrative Form.* Amherst: University of Massachusetts Press.

—. In press. Tracing the Historical Outlines of 'Literary Reportage': The 'Other' Literary Journalism. In *International Literary Journalism: Historical Traditions and Transnational Influences*, edited by John Bak. Amherst: University of Massachusetts Press.

Hollowell, J. 1977. *Fact and Fiction: the New Journalism and the Non-Fiction Novel.* Chapel Hill: University of North Carolina Press.

Kerrane, K. 1997. Making Facts Dance. In *The Art of Fact: A Historical Anthology of Literary Journalism*, edited by Kevin Kerrane and Ben Yagoda. 17-20. New York: Touchstone.

Sims, N. 2007. *True Stories: A Century of Literary Journalism.* Evanston: Northwestern University Press.

Soares, I. 2009. *South.* Where Travel Meets Literary Journalism. *Literary Journalism Studies.* 1 (1): 17-30.

Wolfe, T. 1973. Seizing the Power. In *The New Journalism: With an Anthology*, edited by T. Wolfe and E. W. Johnson. 23-36. New York and London: Harper and Row.

BEYOND EUROPE

ABANDONING THE COUNTRY:
THE FAILURE OF CENTRALIZED OWNERSHIP
AND CONTROL OF THE CANADIAN MEDIA

CHRISTOPHER WADDELL

The English-language Canadian media are currently undergoing a process of rapid change.[1] Global Television, the over-the-air television network owned by Canada's largest media conglomerate Canwest Global, entered bankruptcy protection in October 2009. Canwest's national newspaper chain followed the same route in January 2010. As a result, the conglomerate will be broken up with new owners for each part likely to operate the businesses without the debt load that killed Canwest. At the same time the two major private networks, Canwest and CTV, have closed television stations in some smaller communities while new buyers have bought others in conjunction with employee groups in efforts to keep local television alive. Canada's broadcast regulator, the Canadian Radio-television and Telecommunications Commission (CRTC), also rejected for the third time a request from over-the-air broadcasters that they be paid by cable and satellite companies for their redistribution of the over-the air signals that they now provide for free to cable and satellite.

The recession of 2008-09 was less severe and shorter in Canada than in most other industrialized nations. No banks failed or required government assistance, the increase in bankruptcies was less than in previous recessions, the housing sector suffered none of the mortgage crisis or steep price declines of other countries such as the United States and unemployment rose from under 6 per cent to a peak of 8.6 percent, still almost four percentage points lower than at its worst in the last major recession of the early 1990s. While the recession largely bypassed Canada, the upheaval that has affected the worldwide media did not miss the country. Both a recession-driven decline in advertising revenue and the more substantive changes facing all media as they try to cope with the

---

[1] This chapter is an extended version of a keynote address given at the Centres and Peripheries conference held in Glasgow Caledonian University in May 2009. It has been expanded to take account of developments since then.

immediacy, influence and income-threatening power of the internet hit Canadian news organizations as well. They all face challenges although in different ways that reflect Canada's unique situation of extreme concentration of ownership in the hands of half a dozen companies of almost all the country's television, radio, newspapers, satellite and cable distributors, mobile phone and internet service providers.

This chapter focuses on changes in the English-language print and broadcast media in Canada. It will review the regulatory and ownership structure, highlight how centralized and conglomerate ownership have changed the content of media outside the major cities, examine the current status of newspapers and television in Canada and then conclude with some comments about where we could be headed. It does not deal with French-language media in Canada, which are very active largely in Quebec and just as concentrated in terms of ownership as in the rest of the country. The major difference, in addition to content, is that the public broadcaster Radio-Canada has a much larger share of the French-language television audience in Canada than the CBC (Canadian Broadcasting Corporation) has of the English-language audience in the rest of the country.

The chapter also ignores the magazine sector and radio. CBC Radio does very well with its news and information programming. Unlike CBC television, CBC Radio carries no advertising and is near the top in audience numbers in many of Canada's major cities. It produces distinct morning and evening programming in those major centres, although to cut costs, increasingly elements of daily programming are syndicated from Toronto. By contrast, in private radio much of news or information programming and content is linked to phone-in talk programmes.

In Canada newspapers are unregulated other than through voluntary membership in press councils in some provinces. The councils have no ability to apply sanctions or to enforce whatever decisions they reach in response to public complaints but must rely on voluntary compliance from their members. By contrast, television in Canada is highly regulated by the CRTC which is a federal government agency that oversees all aspects of broadcasting and telecommunications in the country. It grants licenses for radio and television, sets all the rules for broadcasting, including cable and satellite television distributors, specialty and pay-TV channels as well as regulating the telephone, mobile telephone and telecommunications sectors. The CRTC does not regulate the internet although it is increasingly interested in the shift of broadcasting to the internet and the impact of that on the ability (or lack of ability) to enforce Canadian content requirements for radio and television that exist as part of the regulator's issuance of broadcasting licenses.

Toronto is the media centre of English-speaking Canada and most of the country's news organizations are based there. It is also the country's largest market. In dealing with the peripheries, newspapers and television in Canada have largely adopted similar strategies. In addition to the CBC, five conglomerates control the media in Canada. They are:

Ctvglobemedia—It owns Canada's dominant national newspaper, the *Globe and Mail*, the largest private TV network, CTV, with stations in twenty-eight communities as well as thirty-two specialty channels, including some of the country's most popular such as the leading sports channel, business and music channels. Its stock is privately held with the major shareholders being pension funds and the Thomson family.

Torstar owns the country's largest newspaper, *The Toronto Star*, three papers in mid-size cities in southern Ontario, a national network of more than 100 weekly and bi-weekly rural and suburban community and special interest newspapers and websites, a share of the Toronto edition of *Metro*, the daily free paper published in more than seventy cities around the world, Harlequin Romances and 20 per cent of ctvglobemedia. It is a publicly-traded company and was initially a leading but ultimately unsuccessful bidder for the newspaper chain once owned by Canwest.

CanWest Global owns Global Television, the other private television network in Canada, with seventeen stations across the country as well as Canada's second national newspaper the *National Post*, daily newspapers in ten major metropolitan centres and twenty-one specialty television channels. Prior to going bankrupt it was a public company operating through several subsidiaries. The over-the-air broadcaster entered bankruptcy protection in October 2009 and has been sold under court direction along with the specialty channels to Shaw Communications, a western Canada-based cable television, mobile phone and internet service provider (ISP). The *National Post* was bundled with the other newspapers which entered bankruptcy protection in January 2010 and is currently operated by a company created by its secured lenders led by the Bank of Nova Scotia. The lenders sold the entire newspaper chain as one package for $1.1 billion in early May to a group of hedge funds who were primarily the CanWest newspaper division's unsecured creditors. They hope to resell the company to investors in an initial public offering on the Toronto Stock Exchange some time in 2010 or 2011.

Rogers Communications is the country's major cable company and ISP, one of three dominant mobile phone network operators; it also owns five local TV stations, six specialty channels, more than fifty radio stations and publishes Canada's leading consumer and trade magazines. It is a publicly traded company.

Quebecor owns TVA, the dominant private French language TV network, the major French-language tabloid daily newspaper in Quebec, *Le Journal de Montréal* and the English-language tabloid *Sun* newspaper chain in seven other large cities across Canada, as well as daily, weekly and bi-weekly newspapers in more than sixty smaller communities across the country. It also owns Quebec's largest cable company and internet service provider Videotron. Quebecor is also a publicly-traded company.

Consolidation of ownership in the Canadian media started decades ago and there have been numerous studies and reports from parliamentary committees and commissions warning about the risks to public discourse created by the lack of diversity in editorial content and comment that came with concentration of ownership. Federal governments, both Liberal and Conservative, ignored the issue and in fact have openly supported more concentration. In the late 1990s the Liberal federal government eliminated restrictions that had prevented cross-ownership—the same company owning both television stations and newspapers in the same community or market. The conglomerates that quickly emerged were partly regulated and partly not. The CRTC still regulated the broadcast assets of the conglomerates but newspapers remained outside regulation, leading some to wonder whether newspaper editorial positions would in future be dictated by the desire to ensure favorable views by regulators and easy treatment at license renewal time for their broadcasting operations.

A new round of mergers and concentration followed as common owners bought and consolidated newspaper and television ownership. That set the stage for convergence based on the theory that a reporter is a reporter whether he or she works in television, print or radio so the same person could turn out stories for all these different media owned by the parent. It was the perfect solution for an accountant, as in theory the result would be more in terms of content produced, since fewer journalists would be needed if every journalist was filing for all the media a company owned. At the same time, the convergence model foresaw a time when a television station and newspaper that used to compete in editorial content fiercely in the same market under separate owners would now happily share information, stories and what in the past had been exclusives, simply because they now shared the same ultimate owner.

The CBC employed a similar consolidation strategy largely to deal with the fact that the federal government had not increased the broadcaster's approximately $1b parliamentary appropriation for more than a decade. In fact the Liberal government had cut funding for the CBC in the mid-1990s, leading to layoffs that even then significantly reduced the size of local radio and TV newsrooms across the country. In response the CBC centralized more activities in Toronto and the corporation began to integrate radio, television and subsequently internet operations and journalists, mirroring the private sector. CBC television relied more and more on advertising revenue to cover operating costs and over the last decade increasingly focused on programming such as reality television shows designed to boost ratings and bring in more advertising dollars. The result today is a public broadcaster on television virtually indistinguishable from its private sector competitors.

Convergence may have been a great theory but in reality it has been a disaster, setting the stage for the problems that have recently emerged in the Canadian media. In the real world, reporters for the *Globe and Mail* for instance fought hard to avoid giving their exclusive stories to the nightly *CTV National News*—owned by the same parent as the *Globe*—so that CTV could put the *Globe's* exclusive on the air the night before the paper hit the street. Not surprisingly, the end of competition in the boardroom has not meant the end of competition between newsrooms.

Despite the dreams of owners, it also remains true that different skills are required for reporting for different media. Some journalists can cross over and do strong work in both print and broadcast (though not at the same time) but that is the exception. Most print reporters face serious challenges trying to adapt to the rigours of writing for television or radio and understanding the emphasis required on pictures in television storytelling. In the initial few years, though, media owners thought those problems were just temporary. News organizations used their new converged, conglomerate status to lay off journalists in television and print newsrooms across the country. Despite a booming economy, newsrooms were shrinking under the mantra of convergence, all designed to ensure the industry maintained annual profit margins of more than 20 per cent. That kept shareholders happy and provided the cash for the media corporations to make interest payments on the huge debts they had incurred in consolidating and converging.

All this had several impacts on the relationship between centres and peripheries as played out in the media and the coverage they provide the country with of itself. That's because the editorial centres of each of the major media corporations and the CBC were all in Toronto (although Canwest's nominal headquarters was in Winnipeg). During the past decade across all the companies, the centre increasingly dictated format and sometimes content to the peripheries, where there was less and less flexibility in both what local newspapers and television stations produced and who produced it. That translated into less ability to reflect the local community in the daily local newspaper or television newscast. The decline in local ability to shape coverage to community interests occurred in major cities as well as smaller centres across Canada. This happened in several ways.

First, newsrooms responded to demands to cut staff by eliminating specialist reporters. Beats disappeared and gradually everyone became a general assignment reporter. The result has been a loss of expertise, critical analysis and context in reporting. When combined with increasing demand to file for multiple outlets and multiple times a day, the result is reporters who know less and less about more and more. That means every day is covered as a self-contained unit in which things that happened that day are dealt with as if they have never happened before and will never happen again. In complex fields such as parliament, government and public policy, when reporters know nothing or very little about the background and details of an issue they can always focus on conflict or personality. As a result most political and public policy coverage has become just that.

Second, newsroom cuts, particularly in local television, meant that to fill each day's newscast required every reporter in the newsroom to file every day. So every story became a same day story. There is no time for research or context so the dominant stories are those that can be done easily and quickly—crime and courts, traffic accidents and weather. None require detailed research or expertise and all can be turned around quickly. Both quality and breadth in local news suffered precisely at a time when audience choices for news were expanding exponentially thanks to the internet.

In television, particularly at the CBC, and in print, in the past smaller centres were the places where young journalists began their careers and developed their skills under the direction of more experienced staff. Then those with greater ambitions moved on to larger, national or international postings and organizations. In most local newsrooms those veteran teachers have taken redundancy payments or been laid off, so there is no one left to spot the talent and do the on-the-job teaching and training. Reporting quality clearly suffers as a result.

Third, news organizations, both public and private, imposed centrally designed templates on all their outlets again to cut costs and augment or maintain profit levels. Canwest newspapers across the country increasingly looked identical in design. All their newspapers shared the same web-page design and individual newspaper websites were centrally controlled, giving each paper virtually no ability to tailor web pages to local tastes.

Each network's local evening television newscasts were increasingly indistinguishable in look and content from city to city—again all mandated from the centre. Even the CBC hired a US consultant to redesign all its supper hour local newscasts across Canada in the fall of 2009 so they would look identical and match the content and approach of US private television. The result was a numbing sameness from community to community, limited, if any, opportunity for individual distinctiveness to match local tastes and interests (and Canada is a very large country) and no room for initiative, inventiveness or imagination.

Fourth, more and more production has been centralized as a further blow to the autonomy of individual newspapers and television stations located outside Toronto. Canwest produces certain sections for all its daily papers in Hamilton, Ontario, and satellites them to individual newsrooms each night across the country. Even CBC's local television newsrooms are not staffed sufficiently to produce an hour of local news every night. Lost in all this again is individual distinctiveness, initiative and an ability to shape local publications and programmes for local communities.

Fifth, even in a new medium like the internet that thrives on creativity and inventiveness in presenting content, centralization means standardization. At Canwest the websites for all its newspapers are centrally controlled and have identical appearances—one which is designed to ensure national advertisers get the same spot on every web page in every paper across the country. This has completely stifled entrepreneurship on the internet precisely at a time when it should be overflowing with creativity and new ideas. Instead of eleven Canwest papers competing with each other to try new ideas online, they all do the same thing as ordered from headquarters.

All these developments are byproducts of a decade or more of concentration, conglomeration and centralization. The result is local newspapers and television newscasts in communities across Canada have less breadth, are less comprehensive, less distinctive and more unable to provide communities with the local coverage that audiences and readers want.

In the world of public broadcasting, the CBC has gone back and forth, trying to eliminate local television news before 2000, killing late night local newscasts, then merging local shows into a hybrid local/national early evening newscast, then returning to hour-long local shows without the resources to staff them properly. Now in the face of a new round of cuts to deal with budget shortfalls, CBC is changing yet again, as its local newscasts now run, depending on location, at 5:00 pm, 5:30 pm and 6:00 pm—essentially the same newscast repeated three times every evening. The only consistency in this approach is the lack of consistency. Things change every two years or so—hardly a model that builds audience loyalty and CBC's low local television news ratings reflect that.

At the same time the internet has been gaining strength as an alternative source for news and information, whether through the websites of existing news organizations or through blogs, community websites, social networking sites and whatever else anyone wants to post. Unlike the United States where the decline in audiences and influence of the mainstream media has been underway for several years and debated for just as long, there has been little discussion of the issue in Canada, in part because newspaper circulation had not been declining anywhere near as quickly as in the U.S.

The 2008-09 recession in Canada changed some of that as the drop in advertising revenue hit both television and newspapers hard. Television networks responded to the fall in advertising by looking for another source of revenue with a proposal that has been rejected twice before. The over-the-air broadcasting system is broken, they proclaimed, and the way to fix it is to give the networks "fee for carriage" for their over-the-air local stations. In other words they argued the CRTC should force cable and satellite distributors to pay the over-the-air channels up to $300 million a year for the local television signals they currently rebroadcast for free. The networks launched an extensive national advertising campaign to back up their demands and shamelessly turned their newscasts into promotions for their point of view.

The cable and satellite distributors responded by claiming that fee for carriage would add up to $10 a month to every customer's TV bill which in many cases was already $70-80 a month. Nonsense, said the broadcasters. Cable companies should pay for the over-the-air signals out of their exorbitant profits, not demand more money from customers. If the broadcasters have financial problems, replied the cable and satellite companies, they should cut the $750 million they spend annually to buy foreign (almost exclusively U.S.) programming for broadcast in Canada. So it went, back and forth for most of 2009, with the claims and counterclaims reaching a climax at a CRTC hearing in late fall 2009 to consider the issue one more time. The CRTC had turned down fee for carriage twice before. In a country with cable and satellite penetration of more than 90 per cent, the CRTC said if the public had to pay for local TV they now get for free, the broadcasters must guarantee the new money they would get would be spent on local programming, a commitment the broadcasters refused to make.

This time, though, the broadcasters upped the stakes. Canwest put five stations in smaller markets up for sale then temporarily pulled back as there were no buyers. CTV said it would shut down three stations in smaller communities or sell them for $1 each. After more manoeuvres, Global did sell stations in Montreal and Hamilton, Ontario, to small specialty channel operator-broadcaster Channel Zero, which soon announced plans to substantially alter the content of the stations, focusing on local news and information as well as movies. In Victoria, B.C., Global sold the local station to a group of station employees and local investors. It operates as an independent station but in the spring of 2010 entered into an arrangement to carry CBC local news from Vancouver. There were no buyers, though, for CTV stations in Windsor, Ontario and Brandon, Manitoba. While CTV continued to operate Windsor, it closed its Brandon station in October 2009. In August that year Canwest shut down a Global station in Red Deer, Alberta, half way between Edmonton and Calgary.

In March 2010 the CRTC announced its decision on the fee for carriage issue, rejecting the broadcasters' demands yet again and urging them and the cable and satellite distributors to sit down and strike a deal. The regulator's backbone was stiffened on the issue as the Conservative government had made it clear that it would overrule the CRTC if it approved fee for carriage. Instead the CRTC offered a variety of inducements to encourage the two sides to negotiate including allowing broadcasters to withdraw their signals from cable and satellite companies if there was no agreement and also to withdraw any US entertainment programming simulcast on both Canadian and US channels carried by the cable/satellite company. Cable and satellite distributors received the power to move channels on the dial to cluster together the over-the-air and specialty channels owned by the same conglomerate. The Commission hoped the two sides will negotiate, as happened in the U.S., and strike deals that involved trade-off other than cash between the two. The balance in the broadcaster-cable war had also shifted as Global Television, formerly owned by now bankrupt Canwest and an advocate of fee of carriage, was now owned by Shaw Communications, the most vociferous opponent of fee for carriage among Canada's cable and satellite companies.

At the same time the CRTC said its proposed solution would not apply to the CBC. Under the Broadcasting Act the public broadcaster could not withhold its signal from anyone so it had no bargaining power for a negotiation. The CBC claimed this was discriminatory and would do it huge damage but the Commission said the issue of cable/satellite companies paying for CBC signals should be deferred until the public broadcaster's license renewal hearing in 2011.

The broadcaster-cable dispute, though, focused attention on only part of the issues facing Canadian media. The recession did hurt but, as was noted earlier, it was never very severe and is quickly coming to an end in Canada. It is clear that things are changing for the better on the advertising front and media conglomerates have not been hurt as badly as they predicted or feared. What is not changing is that television and newspapers are simply not as attractive to the public—particularly those under 30—as sources of news and information as they once were. Today there are many more choices for readers, listeners and viewers and in Canada the existing mainstream television networks and newspapers have not done much to adapt to the changing world of the media and the internet.

The financial problems of the television industry are not quite what they seem either. Over-the-air television did suffer an advertising drop with the recession but specialty channels are still doing very well with profit margins of more than 20 per cent. They are owned by the same conglomerates as own the over-the-air channels. At the same time in 2009 over-the-air broadcasters increased their spending on foreign programming to about $850 million from $775 million the year before. In this dispute the broadcasters wanted the government and the public to look at only part of the pie and bail them out by allowing them to collect millions of dollars for nothing more than what they provide now, based on problems only in the over-the-air slice of their business.

Curiously this whole debate instigated by the media through pressuring the government for money and by frequent reporting about the crisis facing local television and the decline of newspapers ("the business model is broken", the media regularly proclaimed) has taken place without any discussion at all of the content of what television and newspapers produce. In fact the changes the industry introduced during the preceding decade meant their product is simply not as comprehensive or good as it was, thanks largely to years of cuts. It no longer reflects the breadth of what is happening in communities the way it once did. As everyone knows, the mainstream media are no longer the gatekeepers they once were, with the power to decide what the public will know and when it will know it. In Canada the media have not figured out how to adapt to that decline in status and influence. The solution begins with a renewed emphasis on content. By starting with that there are ways to begin to turn the situation around to maintain newspapers and television stations in smaller communities in Canada.

There are a few important principles forgotten in the Canadian media's self-proclaimed tale of woe.

People will continue to pay for information that engages, enlightens and entertains them; that informs them about the world around them; that tells them about the triumphs and risks in their communities and that helps them make better choices and decisions about their families, their lives, their work, their possessions, their savings, their communities and their futures.

That information can be collected, edited and distributed more easily and widely than ever before because the equipment which journalists use to gather, edit and distribute news to audiences has never been cheaper to purchase; has never been lighter or easier to transport and never been easier to use. At the same time the quality of the images and sound this equipment produces has never been better.

It has never been cheaper and easier to communicate from anywhere in Canada (or around the globe for that matter) and the capital costs of producing and distributing the finished product to audiences—a newspaper or television newscast—whether it is text, video, audio, images or graphics, have never been cheaper thanks to the internet. All these costs are going in one direction—down.

There are a few other points missing from the media's debate in Canada about its future as well.

The internet is a major and growing distributor of news and information. The Pew Internet and American Life project found that a majority of Americans went online in 2008 to follow the Presidential election—doing everything from watching video to forwarding political material to friends to posting their thoughts on blogs and comments pages and message boards and using social media and networking sites to engage in political debates. Those under 25—precisely the group the mainstream media want to attract to guarantee their future—were particularly active in using social networking sites to debate politics.

Yet the Canadian media have yet to recognize that the internet requires content designed specifically for it. In Canada, with few exceptions such as the *Globe and Mail,* the media use the Web primarily as a means to display and distribute content originally designed for and distributed some other way—in print or broadcast. The CBC has taken a lead at various points on the Web but has suffered from the same lack of consistency as it has displayed in local television news. It has alternated between being vigorously proactive and cutting back. At the local level it has minimal sites which largely replicate what is on radio and television. The general lack of creativity in the public and private sectors—and lack of understanding or recognition of social networking sites beyond the superficial—is the result of the stifling influence of conglomerate ownership on innovation, the demand for uniformity, the possibility that editorial staff are now too demoralized by years of cutbacks to think of doing things in different ways and that most newsrooms are conservative, set in their ways and just too old to get what is happening on the Web.

The fact that Canadian television networks spent 2009 pleading for a government bailout is proof of their failure. The public in smaller communities are very anxious to retain their television stations but there is no outpouring of support for the media conglomerate owners of those stations.

What is needed is a rethinking of how the media tell stories and engage audiences and a much greater willingness to allow those audiences to participate in the media in creative ways. Journalists need to approach each story by asking what is the ideal way to combine all the formats available on the internet to best tell that story. Content does matter and is important to readers, listeners and viewers and that means it should be important to advertisers as well. That has been forgotten in the past decade.

Local differences also matter. The centre cannot simply dictate to the periphery. The push to hyper-local web sites by the mainstream media in some communities in the United States and links between newspapers and such local sites in others is one response. People do want to read about their communities and what is happening in them, yet newspapers and television in Canada have largely forgotten that. They stopped covering school boards, much of municipal government and in most cases even provincial legislatures and governments. More broadly, one size does not fit all and when an owner forces uniformity on all its papers, television stations or websites the result is bland, lacking in local character and, at its extreme, inconsequential. Readers, listeners and viewers quickly figure that out and they respond, now that they have the choice provided by the internet, by looking elsewhere for information and news they find relevant that helps them with decisions in their lives.

What do those Canadian readers, listeners and viewers want, what devices will they use to receive, read and view the news and how much will they pay for news they get?

None of these are impossible questions to resolve and some organizations think they already have answers. Certainly a lot is going to be driven by technology and maybe products which are still in the near future or just emerging—versions of iPads, Kindles and smart phones and distribution systems like iTunes for instance. That is just a start with undoubtedly more to come.

It is most likely that in the future there will be no common answer across the media to these questions. Attempts by conglomerates to force one answer on everyone will fail, just as they have failed up to now, particularly if their answer is really more of the same. The survivors will be those that focus on content, place a premium on experimentation and innovation in matching the appropriate media in which to tell the story to the type of story being told. They will also need to be flexible both in the way they distribute information received by consumers and in how they price it. The public would benefit if many competing content and business models emerge, each offering something different to consumers.

Within this new world, there is a real opportunity in Canada for the peripheries to break free from the centre and respond in their own ways, trying their own ideas and testing what works within their distinctive community. It requires investors with a willingness to accept reasonable rates of return that are likely to be smaller than in the past. It is also time for a revival of the principle that there is a degree of civic responsibility in owning a media outlet whether in a large city or small community, even if the owner also uses it as a platform for his or her own views.

The public broadcaster in Canada could play a role here that it does not play now. The CBC could go into communities and develop local news websites which combine video, audio, text, graphics, citizen contributions and still photos with a strongly local focus linked to that community and telling the stories about the people who live there. Overall, the limited capital costs required for such a media start-up, whether by the public broadcaster or private sector, creates opportunities for new entities to enter a business that has become the preserve of conglomerates and oligopolies.

In Canada, media concentration has meant abandoning the country, retreating to a few major centres. Journalism and public perceptions of and confidence in the media have all suffered as a result. However the failures of the past several years have opened the door for new media models returning to a focus on the communities their predecessors once served. They will take the place of tired and outdated conglomerates, converged and concentrated media. When that happens both journalists and the public will be the beneficiaries.

JOURNALISM IN THE USA: THE NATIONAL, THE LOCAL AND THE ONLINE CHALLENGE

MICHAEL PARKS

To read the front page of *The Times-Picayune* in New Orleans or that of *The Oregonian* in Portland is to know that you are not in Washington, DC, and to watch the news on WGN-TV in Chicago or on News 8 Austin in Texas is to know you are far, far from New York City. Not only does the continental vastness of the United States give "peripheries" a different scale, but it also gives a new meaning to the concept of "centers"—and to the definitions of news and the priorities they are assigned.

The centers are Washington for news of government, politics and foreign relations, New York for business and finance, and New York and Los Angeles for entertainment, the arts and lifestyle. And the rest of this country of 310 million lives in the peripheries, and not everyone— actually, not many at times—would agree that the news from those centers matters beyond the centers themselves.

A presidential press conference in Washington, for example, might merit staff-written stories of 650 or perhaps 800 words and a place on Page 1, and even an additional news analysis in *The Washington Post* and *The New York Times*, while editors at excellent regional newspapers like *The Times-Picayune* and *The Oregonian* will, depending on the issue, use a much shorter report from a wire service and place it somewhere on a national news page inside the paper. In the newsroom meetings where the front page is laid out or the evening's broadcast lineup decided, there is almost always a debate over what news that day matters most to the paper's readers or the station's viewers, but usually it is what is closest. The tension between the national news agenda, particularly the framing of the most important issues, and local interests is part of the daily life of every top editor and executive producer.

The United States is not unique in having multiple centers: Australia, Brazil, Canada, Israel and even China, where Beijing and Shanghai vie in many ways, are other examples. For Americans, however, the importance of the local usually overrides that of the national, and at the start of the 21st Century the local—sometimes even the hyper-local or micro-local—again became the focus for newspaper editors and television news directors in the hope that it would prove to be their competitive edge in the battle for audience attention. At the same time, Americans are turning in increasing numbers—about 46% on a daily basis—to the internet or mobile digital sources for news (Pew 2010, 1). That raises anew the question of which media set the agenda in national news, whether it is governmental, political, financial or lifestyle, and how it resonates through the country.

This essay will assess the roles and the relationships of the centers and the peripheries of American journalism in recent years and the impact that the accelerating digital transformation of media, particularly the news media, appears to be having on them.

Technological development enabled the stage-by-stage emergence of a national news agenda in the United States. With the completion of the country's telegraph and railroad systems in the late 19th Century, the United States at last was "running on the same clock of awareness and existing within a homogenous national space" (Carey 1998, 28-29), something that had come earlier in most of Europe's nation-states. Prior to that, newspapers carried as much news from the capitals of Europe as they did from Washington, and sometimes more; newspaper publishers in New York, Boston and Baltimore competed through most of that century to give readers the latest news from London and Paris by sending out fast boats to meet inbound ships from Europe in order to get hold of those cities' papers so they could reprint their news.

After the US Civil War (1861-1865), the country's population more than doubled over the next three decades as waves of immigrants landed and more population spread inland. Each town began to have its own daily or weekly newspaper so that the number of daily papers quadrupled, and by 1915 there were more than 2200 dailies across the country (Stephens 2007, 194-198). With the growth of The Associated Press, a non-profit news cooperative founded in 1846 as a way of sharing the costs of transmitting stories and later of news gathering itself, a coherent national news agenda emerged, particularly around major events such as the Spanish-American War in 1898, World War I and later the Great Depression. In the eyes of editors, these events interested everyone, and the AP made it possible for newspaper readers far away from the major cities of the East to read the same story on the same day. This shrank the distance that Americans felt from decision-making centers, and gradually strengthened the power of journalists in those centers in framing the stories that constituted the national news agenda.

Establishment of commercial radio stations, state by state, starting in 1920, and then their grouping into networks later in the decade, accelerated this change as Americans, for the first time, could get the same news simultaneously coast to coast. Television news, which began as scheduled broadcasts in 1948, brought everyone from the farthest reaches of the country into contact with news-generating centers with a vividness that surpassed radio, which already had transformed the country's understanding of itself.[1] In contrast to Britain, most of Europe, Japan, Australia and Canada, public service broadcasting on radio and television on a national basis came only in 1970.

The remaining element in the development of a national news agenda, begun in some ways by the early 20th Century newspaper empires of William Randolph Hearst, Joseph Pulitzer, E. W. Scripps and others, was the growth of large media companies, many of them coming to own scores of newspapers, magazines, radio and television stations as a result of increasing media consolidation—and most of them looking for ways to share content among their properties. Ben H. Bagdikian, former dean of journalism at the University of California, Berkeley, warned in his influential 1983 book *The Media Monopoly* that this pronounced concentration endangered the role that the press should play in American democracy by homogenizing the viewpoints available to citizens and reducing the number of voices that would be heard. In the book's sixth edition in 2000, Bagdikian summarized the situation this way: "As the United States enters the twenty-first century, power over the American mass media is flowing to the top with such devouring speed that it exceeds even the accelerated consolidation of the last twenty years. For the first time in US history, the country's most widespread news, commentary, and daily entertainment are controlled by six firms that are among the world's largest corporations, two of them foreign" (Bagdikian 2000, viii).

Yet, this consolidation also has had the effect of pulling the most remote corners of the country onto the same media landscape so that the concept of peripheries is far less one of geography and much more one of mentality, and for some perhaps political ideology.

In contrast to many other countries, only three newspapers circulate nationally in the United States—*The Wall Street Journal, USA Today* and *The New York Times*—and only 9% of those who say they closely follow the news read a national paper, according to a 2008 Gallup Poll (Gallup 2008). The influence of *The Times* and *The Journal*, however, greatly

---

[1] For a short, analytic history of American journalism, including its expansion across the country and its growth from newspapers to the internet, see Schudson and Tifft (2005).

exceeds their actual circulations because of their elite readership and because of their agenda-setting roles for other news media at the country's journalism centers and broadly across the United States. The overall number of daily newspapers has declined significantly over the past 25 years, but there are still more than 1400; their reporters, again diminished in numbers, remain the largest news-gathering force in the country with their work shared through The Associated Press. The overall drop in newspaper circulation has been severe—down 25.6% from 2000 to 2009, according to the Project for Excellence in Journalism. Although some of the loss has been a strategic choice by newspapers to cut unprofitable circulation, most has come as readers moved to news websites (Project for Excellence in Journalism 2010). Nonetheless, 40% of those surveyed by Gallup in 2008 said they still read a paper every day, and a further 40% of those interviewed said they read one several times a week or, depending on the news, at least occasionally (Gallup 2008).

Even as the national news agenda developed in the United States, the American proclivity to see the world first in terms of their towns or states has remained very strong, perhaps reflecting the long-standing American suspicion of authority.[2] Interviewed for the biennial 2008 study of news consumption by the Pew Research Center for the People & the Press, those who said they follow the news closely ranked local news higher in interest, often much higher, than national news, and those interests put crime, education, community, environment and local government ahead or equal to news from Washington or about politics—and that was in a presidential election year (Pew 2008, 39, 52-53). Interest in international news is relatively low—only 16% said they followed it closely. However, the weather outdrew everything, and little is more local than weather! (Pew 2008, 39).

Despite the role that network television played in shaping American understanding of the events of the final decades of the 20th Century—wars in Vietnam and the Middle East, the assassination of President John F. Kennedy, the astronauts' landing on the moon, the fall of the Berlin Wall, and the US civil rights movement among them—the audiences for the flagship evening newscasts on ABC, CBS, and NBC have declined from 62% of those Gallup surveyed in 1995 to 34% in 2008 on an everyday basis, and those who responded that they never watched the network newscasts jumped from 3% in 1995 to 23% in 2008 (Gallup 2008). Taking the place of the broadcast networks have been cable news companies— CNN, Fox News Channel and MSNBC. Forty percent of those who said

---

[2] For a full discussion of the origins and impact of this strong American trait, see Huntington (1983) and Lipset (1997).

they follow the news told Gallup they watched cable news daily, and a further 16% said they watched several times a week (Gallup 2008). Two of those cable companies, Fox and MSNBC, have perceptible tilts in the way they frame the news—Fox to the right, MSNBC to the left—and have drawn audiences that align with the recent social and political polarization in the United States (Pew 2010).

Studies by Pew and other researchers[3] have shown vast changes in the way Americans now get their news but also in the news that they get. In a 2008 survey, 57% of American editors told Pew they were publishing less national news than before even though it was in an election year; 64% said they were publishing less international news despite US involvement in two major foreign conflicts. In contrast, 62% said they were publishing more community news and 50% were carrying more state and local news. The survey also showed there is less news about science, the arts and other specialized subjects (Marshall 2008, 1). Analyses of local television news broadcasts have shown similar trends.[4]

When the proportion of Americans watching local television news and that reading daily newspapers are analyzed together, the preference for a local perspective on the news of the day is readily apparent, for the content of both of those media is overwhelmingly local.

For nearly fifteen years, however, news consumption as measured by the amount of time Americans spent each day getting news from all sources on all subjects has been in decline; readership of daily newspapers and audiences for all television news, network programs and local, were down sharply. Putnam saw the decline in newspaper readership and overall interest in the news as both evidence of the loss of social capital in the United States and as contributing elements in the diminution of civic engagement (Putnam 2001, 216-246).

Due primarily to increased use of internet news sources, however, the trend appears to have been reversed. In 2010, Americans reported

---

[3] See also Hamilton (2005). The best year-to-year snapshot of the US news media and its changing audiences is the Annual Report on American Journalism prepared by the Project for Excellence in Journalism in cooperation with the Pew Internet & American Life Project at the Pew Research Center, all of which are in Washington, DC. It can be viewed at http://www.stateofthemedia.org. And the Gallup Poll in its continuing national opinion surveys asks respondents how closely they follow the news, what their media use is and for their evaluation of the credibility of the American news media. See "Media Use and Evaluation",
http://www.gallup.com/poll/1663/Media-Use-Evaluation.aspx
[4] See the studies, for example, based on materials at the Lear Center Local News Archive developed at the Annenberg School for Communication & Journalism at the University of Southern California.

spending an average of 70 minutes a day, a jump of 13 minutes from 2008 and the highest total since the mid-1990s (to put that time commitment in perspective, it is slightly more than the amount of time the average American spends eating and drinking every day, according to the US Bureau of Labor Statistics). With the inclusion of online news, most of which comes from the websites of traditional media, the proportion of Americans who said they had gotten some kind of news the previous day was 83%, almost the same proportion as a decade before (Pew 2010, 1-4).

"There are many more ways to get the news these days", Pew commented, summarizing its 2010 survey results, adding:

> and as a consequence Americans are spending more time with the news than over much of the past decades. Digital platforms are playing a larger role in news consumption, and they seem to be more than making up for modest declines in the audience for traditional platforms ... Roughly a third (34%) of the public say they went online for news yesterday—on a par with radio, and slightly higher than daily newspapers. And when cell phones, email, social networks and podcasts are added in, 44% of Americans say they got news through one or more internet or mobile digital source yesterday (Pew 2010, 1).

For the past four years, Pew has also tracked public attentiveness to national news and has found strong continuing interest in such issues as health care reform, the economic downturn, the election of President Barack Obama and his administration, the oil spill in the Gulf of Mexico, and accidents and disasters of all sorts.[5]

Pew's research also showed, however, that 17% of those surveyed said they had got no news the previous day (Pew 2010). The proportion was unchanged from previous Pew surveys, suggesting that one in six

---

[5] The Pew Center for The People & The Press's weekly News Interest Index can be found at http://people-press.org/news-interest/. In an analysis of the prevalence of various issues across media platforms over a 12-month period, the Project for Excellence in Journalism at Pew found that the stories and issues that gained traction in social media, including blogs, YouTube and Twitter, differed significantly from those that led the mainstream press, but that they also differed from each other. Bloggers tended to focus on issues of ideological passion, individual or group rights and politics broadly. Blogs dealt more frequently with politics and government than did the traditional press and carried more on foreign events, science, technology, and the environment, less on the economy and less on health and medicine. Twitter passed along breaking news and focused on technology. YouTube's most watched videos seemed to have a sense of serendipity along with visual appeal (Project for Excellence, *New Media, Old Media* 2010).

American adults feels that he or she knows all that is needed without the news media. In journalistic terms, this may be the new periphery in American life. What makes this even more remarkable is that fully 82% of Americans are now internet users and spend an average of 19 hours a week on line (Center for the Digital Future 2010, 35-39).

As Pew reported, the most notable trend today is the way that those who follow the news closely blend traditional and online sources of news depending on the topics, the time of day, the ease of access and other factors. Assessing the results of its 2010 survey, Pew said:

> Instead of replacing traditional news platforms, Americans are integrating their news consumption habits. More than a third (36%) of Americans say they got news from both digital and traditional sources yesterday, just shy of the number who relied solely on traditional sources (39%). Only 9% of Americans got news through the Internet or mobile technology without using traditional sources (Pew 2010, 2).

The time spent on a website was short, but several were typically viewed.

An audience segment that the Pew researchers dubbed "Integrators" in its 2008 news consumption study said that television was the main source for news but that they went online on a typical day, many updating themselves while at work. Pew estimated that they constitute 23% of the public, were well-educated, affluent, and middle aged. They spent more time keeping abreast of the news than those who relied on either traditional or internet sources. They were also heavier consumers of national news, especially about politics, government, and Washington, than most and were avid sports fans (Pew 2008, 1-3). A smaller, second segment, "Net-Newsers," as Pew called them, were younger, even better educated, and had moved largely to the web for their news. Many more watched internet news clips than nightly network news broadcasts (30% vs. 18%), and twice as many read an online newspaper than a printed one (17% vs. 8%). Their use of news websites increased sharply during the day as they sought to keep up to the minute while at work—website operators see usage spikes first thing in the morning, before and after lunch and toward the end of the day—but these "Net-Newsers" also watched late-evening news on television (Pew 2008, 2-3). Estimated at 13% in 2008, this group appeared to have grown in the 2010 Pew study, though researchers did not employ the same segmentation that they used in their earlier analysis.

The integration of traditional and internet sources also has accelerated the earlier trend toward specialized niche publications and cablecasts. With the digital transformation of the media, news consumers increasingly are able to ask for "my news, my information when I want it, in the way I want it delivered and presented". Lee Rainie, director of the Pew Internet & American Life Project, said the most recent surveys the project has carried out showed that 67% of news consumers now follow only the specific news that interests them and that internet users increasingly are using customized news pages, web browsers, and RSS feeds to get that news (Rainie 2010). Despite the proliferation of blogs, however, only 9% of those surveyed in 2010 told Pew they used them the previous day for news, and only 11% of those who get their news from the internet principally went to a blog the previous day (Pew 2010).

With the shrinkage of both the space and time in which news is delivered, there may now be no peripheries in the geographic sense, but there clearly are centers where decisions are made—and where journalists carry out the news media's agenda-setting functions, not only in the traditional arena of public affairs but across a wide range of fields, including business, culture, entertainment, and lifestyle.[6]

The power of the Washington press corps—reporters, television correspondents, columnists and commentators—has been well studied, though mostly to assess the interplay between government and politics on the one hand and the news media on the other more than the impact those journalists' work has on their readers and viewers across the 50 states.[7] The influence of the business press, both in terms of agenda-setting on economic issues and in the shaping of corporate reputations, has also been examined closely, including half a dozen books about *The Wall Street Journal* alone.[8] And scholars in media and cultural studies have analyzed the influential roles of arts and entertainment critics, fashion writers and even restaurant reviewers in shaping both opinion and markets.

What is striking about most of the journalists working for traditional news media in these centers is the relatively small differentiation among them. While Washington reporters will compete to get inside information or to get news of a decision first, they are notably docile as they troop into government briefing rooms for an announcement that can also be viewed on CNN or C-SPAN. Financial coverage usually follows the lead set by *The Wall Street Journal* and *The New York Times*, even though Bloomberg or Thomson-Reuters news services might have had the scoop. Some

---

[6] For a succinct discussion of the American news media's role in the framing of issues, see McCombs (2005). Shoemaker and Vos (2009) synthesize recent research on framing and agenda-setting in the US news media.

[7] See, for example, Graber (2009 and 2010).

[8] See Ellison (2010) for a recent account of the takeover of the *Journal* by Rupert Murdoch and the changes he undertook at that institution.

scholars have seen this as the consequence of the professionalization of journalism (Tuchman 1978), others as the inevitable result of media consolidation and the decline of competition (Bagdikian 2000; McChesney 2000).

Occasionally a Washington journalist wonders whether they have lost relevance in widened access to news at the centers of power, the proliferation of the sources of news, and the speed with which information travels. Analyzing the critical commentaries about President Obama's lackluster Oval Office speech on the Gulf oil spill, a *New York Times* correspondent asked, "Does it really matter if you lose the pundits?" According to Adam Nagourney:

> There was a time when the after-action takes of big commentators were sought out by Americans trying to assess the latest news coming out of the capital … They helped drive public opinion. But tracking influences on public opinion has become greatly complicated now that once-exclusive club has been joined by the vast multitudes blogging or posting Twitter updates or otherwise opining online … It is not just the number of commentators or the abundance of platforms that is diluting the influence of the mainstream media, but their speed (Nagourney 2010).

One ironic result of these trends has been the reduction in the number of news organizations with their own correspondents in Washington; even when all the newspapers of the large chains are counted, the number of papers with bureaus in the capital has declined in the last twenty-five years from slightly more than 600 to fewer than 300. The longest serving White House correspondent, Helen Thomas, bluntly blamed her news media colleagues for becoming more lapdogs of the Washington political establishment and forgetting their watchdog roles (Thomas 2007). Whatever the causes, a major result has been that news coverage of the issues that matter particularly to one state or region, the classic geographic peripheries, are unlikely to get coverage. At the same time, more than 250 newsletters focused on issues such as national politics, consumer protection, climate, energy, food safety, the federal budget and taxes have their own Washington bureaus, reflecting the growth of niche publications (Project for Excellence in Journalism 2009, 1-7).

All that said, however, the development of a national news agenda, the consolidation of the media, the sameness in the coverage and the shrinkage of both the space and time in which news is delivered have not resulted in a homogenization of opinion across the United States. Distinct regional differences can be seen on a variety of political, economic and social issues in national polling. Attitudes to such issues as the wars in Iraq and

Afghanistan, health care reform and same-sex marriage vary significantly region to region as reported by Gallup's State of the States and other tracking polls. Studies of gay rights, a touchstone social question, and local newspapers, in disparate regions of the country show a far higher correlation with voting patterns in national elections rather than with the papers' coverage, the prominence of the placement or frequency of the stories (Pollock et al. 2006, Pan et al. 2010). Even if the question is about the strength of the American economy and asked in the midst of a recession, opinions will range widely, reflecting experience "out there" more than the views reported from Washington and New York. Gallup's Economic Confidence Poll, which is based on a daily tracking survey, has a theoretical optimistic-pessimistic range of +100 to -100, and in the first half of 2010 residents of Iowa, Minnesota and North Dakota were relatively less pessimistic at -13, -14 and -15 than West Virginia at -46 and Idaho at -41; the national average at the time was -26 (Jones 2010). More than half of the residents polled by Gallup in Wyoming, Mississippi and Utah, for example, identified themselves as politically conservative in the first half of 2010, making those the most conservative states in the country, and not by far; the District of Columbia and four New England states had the highest percentage of liberals (Jones 2010). The biennial elections to the 435-member House of Representatives almost always produce quite distinct political characters reflecting their disparate districts even when those elections do not lead to actual shifts in power between the two major parties.

One reason for this contradiction between Americans' news consumption, which provides wide access to journalism of the centers and is on the rise, and the opinion formation and voting patterns in the peripheries is that relatively few people believe what they read in the newspapers, see on television or hear on the radio. This is a well studied trend, probably attributable to that deeply rooted American suspicion of authority, and the most recent surveys by Pew, Gallup and others show no change except perhaps a continued erosion of the news media's credibility (Gallup 2010; Morales 2010; Pew 2010). Only two in ten of those surveyed by Pew in 2010 said they believed most of what they saw on the three broadcast networks, roughly the same proportion who believed what they read in national or local newspapers. Those who said they were Republicans or more conservative politically were the most skeptical—except when it came to Fox News, where 41% said they thought it was highly credible. Democrats or politically liberal showed strong preferences for CNN, *The New York Times*, National Public Radio, C-Span, and MSNBC and gave the lowest marks to Fox (Pew 2010). Broadly speaking, however, the credibility of the US news media is far lower than most journalists, whether they work for national or local media, want to believe. An open question for journalists and scholars is whether the rapidly growing use of the internet for news and information across most demographic and social groups will increase or further undercut the news media's credibility, as users find the information they want, developing trust in certain sources— or deepening skepticism.

In the past, technological change has altered the journalistic relationship between centers and peripheries in the United States, and speculation began in the early 1990s that the digital transformation of the news media would do so again. There has been extensive research on the way that news consumers are using the internet, including that by Pew and the Project for Excellence in Journalism, which has been cited, and there has been much serious discussion on how it will transform journalism.[9] The most tempting conclusions have been that the decline in the use of traditional news media will continue, perhaps at an even faster rate; that with the economic and legal barriers to publishing or broadcasting all but removed on the internet, news websites will proliferate, again even faster, with the participation of numerous citizen journalists, and that the new journalistic model will be from-many-to-many, fundamentally recasting the relationship between the news-making centers and the peripheries.

Some of this does appear to be happening, some does not. The use of traditional platforms for delivering news seems to have stabilized; at least the erosion has slowed as news consumers have recognized that every platform has its own strengths and weaknesses. Use of online and mobile sources is growing. The speed at which news is delivered is increasing, and new delivery techniques and devices are being invented almost annually. Content is changing so that it is increasingly customized and searchable. The role of a news aggregator or a search engine is quite different than the agenda-setting power that newspapers and newscasts have had. And news organizations have come to understand that the public participates and is no longer only an audience.

Studies of major online news websites have found, however, that they do not provide as much news as daily newspapers, that even the best blogs and citizen journalism websites do not have the staff or resources to replace local papers, that political blogs were heavily dependent on mainstream media rather than original reporting of their own and that traditional media in the decision-making centers continued to exercise an

---

[9] Among the most recent books are Doctor (2010), Jones (2009), King and Jarvis (2010) and McChesney (2010).

agenda-setting function across new and social media (Lacy 2010; Leccesse 2009; Maier 2010).

There is another way to view the ongoing changes and to use the metaphorical prism of centers and peripheries. In 1998, Carey argued that the internet, and the information and news that it would carry not just across the country but around the world, would inevitably displace the national system of communications that the United States had developed from the end of the 19th Century and, by implication, displace the national news agenda as well. On what would replace it, Carey took a global view, anticipating worldwide migrations over national borders, the use of the internet for new social and transnational groupings and a struggle over new forms of identity. But Carey warned that predictions were uncertain, for the future was truly uncertain, and that the new trends in communication would take decades to work out. He summarized his assessment this way:

> The Internet is at the center of the integration of a new media ecology which transforms the structural relations among older media such as print and broadcast and integrates them to a new center around the defining technologies of computer and satellite. The economic struggle among firms attempting to control and dominate this complex is the outer and visible edge of deeper transformations in the structure of nations and other forms of social relations .... The end point of all these changes is quite uncertain. The outcome will not be determined by technology alone but by an actual political struggle in which alternative visions of the future, which are much more than "interests," get translated into the laws and regulations that will govern our lives (1998, 34).

That anticipated struggle can be seen in the tough international negotiations over information and telecommunications services, in the debates over internet technical standards and in restrictions imposed by some governments on the flow of news, information and ideas across their national borders. What Carey was imagining in some ways was a radical redefinition of centers and peripheries, one that in some ways is prefigured now in the United States with everyone, regardless of geography, able to receive and in some new ways even to participate in the journalism of the country's multiple centers.

Acknowledgements

The author would like to thank Jessica Griffiths for her extensive research into changing dynamics of American journalism for this essay.

Works Cited

Bagdikian, B. H. 2000. *The Media Monopoly,* 6th ed. Boston: Beacon.

Carey, J. W. 1998. The Internet and the end of the national communication system: uncertain predictions of an uncertain future. *Journalism & Mass Communication Quarterly,* 75 (1): 28-34.

Center for the Digital Future. 2010. *2010 Digital Future Report.* Los Angeles: USC Annenberg School for Communication & Journalism.

Doctor, K. 2010. *Newsonomics—Twelve Trends that Will Shape the News You Get.* New York: St. Martin's Press.

Ellison, S. 2010. *War at the Wall Street Journal: Inside the Struggle to Control an American Business Empire.* New York: Houghton Mifflin Harcourt.

Gallup Poll. 2101. Media Use and Evaluation. http://www.gallup.com/poll/1663/Media-Use-Evaluation.aspx. Accessed 1 May 2010.

Graber, D. A. 2009. *Mass Media in American Politics,* 8th ed. Washington: CQ Press.

—. ed., 2010. *Media Power in Politics,* 6th ed. Washington: CQ Press.

Hamilton, J. T. 2004. *All the News That's Fit to Sell: How the Market Transforms Information into News.* Princeton: Princeton University Press.

—. 2005. The Market and the Media. In *The Press,* edited by G, Overholser and K. H. Jamieson. 351-371. Oxford: Oxford University Press.

Huntington, S. P. 1983. *American Politics—The Promise of Disharmony.* Cambridge, Mass.: Harvard University Press.

Jones, A. S. 2009. *Losing the News: The Future of the News that Feeds Democracy.* New York: Oxford University Press.

Jones, J. M. 2010. Economic Confidence Highest in D.C., Iowa, Minn., N.D; W. Va. Scores lowest on Gallup Economic Confidence Index. State of the States Poll. Washington: Gallup Poll, July 28, 2010 newsletter. http://www.gallup.com/poll/141587/Economic-Confidence-Highest-DC-Iowa-Minn-ND. aspx. Accessed 15 August 2010.

—. 2010. Wyoming, Mississippi, Utah Rank as Most Conservative States. Washington: Gallup Poll, August 2, 2010 newsletter. http://www.gallup.com/poll/141677/Wyoming-Mississippi-Utah-Rank-Conservative-States.aspx. Accessed 15 August 2010.

King, E. and J. Jarvis. 2010. *Free for All: The Internet's Transformation of Journalism.* Chicago: Northwestern University Press.

Lacy, S., M. Duffy, D. Riffe, E. Thorson and K. Fleming. 2010. Citizen Journalism Web Sites Complement Newspapers. *Newspaper Research Journal*, 31 (2): 34-47.

Leccesse, M. 2009. Online Information Sources of Political Blogs. *Journalism & Mass Communication Quarterly*, 86(3): 578-594.

Lipset, S. M. 1997. *American Exceptionalism—A Double-Edge Sword.* New York: W.W. Norton.

Maier, S. R. 2010. Newspapers Offer More News than Do Major Online Sites. *Newspaper Research Journal*, 31 (1): 6-19.

Marshall, G. T. and Project for Excellence in Journalism. 2008. *The Changing Newspaper Newsroom.* Washington: Pew Center for The People & The Press.

McChesney, R. 2000. *Rich Media, Poor Democracy: Communication Politics in Dubious Times.* New York: The New Press.

—. 2010. *The Death and Life of American Journalism: The Media Revolution that Will Begin the World Again.* New York: Nation Books.

McCombs, M. 2005. The Agenda-Setting Function of the Press. In *The Press,* edited by G. Overholser and K. H. Jamieson. 156-168. Oxford: Oxford University Press.

Morales, L. 2010. In U.S., Confidence in Newspapers, TV News Remains a Rarity. Washington: Gallup Poll, August 13, 2010 newsletter. http://www.gallup.com/poll/123365/Americans-Remain-Distrusting-News-Media.aspx. Accessed 15 August 2010.

Nagourney, A. 2010. Does It Matter if Obama Loses the Pundits? The New York Times, June 19, 2010. http://www.nytimes.com/2010/06/20/weekinreview/ 20nagourney.html?_r=1&scp=1&sq=%22does%20it%20matter%20if %20obama%20loses%20the%20pundits?%22&st=cse. Accessed 20 June 2010.

Overholser, G. and K. H. Jamieson, eds. 2005. *The Press.* Oxford: Oxford University Press.

Pan, P.-L., J. Meng and S. Zhou. 2010. Morality or equality? Ideological framing in news coverage of gay marriage legitimization. *The Social Science Journal*, 47 (3): 630-645.

Pew Research Center for the People & the Press. 2008. *Key News Audiences Now Blend Online and Traditional Sources: Audience Segments in a Changing News Environment.* Washington: Pew Research Center.

—. 2010. *Ideological News Sources: Who Watches and Why—Americans Spending More Time Following the News.* Washington: Pew Research Center.

—. 2010. News Interest Index, 2007-2010. Washington: Pew Research Center. http://people-press.org/news-interest/. Accessed 10 September 2010.

Pollock, J., L. de Zutter, S. Schumacher and E. Mitchell. 2006. Gay Rights: Nationwide Newspaper Coverage of Gay Adoption, Gay Marriage, and Gays in the Boy Scouts: A Community Structure Approach. Paper presented at the annual meeting of the International Communication Association, Dresden, Germany, June 16, 2006. http://www.allacademic.com/meta/p91306_index. html. Accessed 10 August 2010.

Project for Excellence in Journalism. 2010. *New Media, Old Media: How Blogs and Social Media Agendas Relate and Differ from the Traditional Press.* Washington: Pew Research Center.

—. 2009. *The New Washington Press Corps: As Mainstream Media Decline, Niche and Foreign Outlets Grow.* Washington: Pew Research Center.

Project for Excellence in Journalism and the Pew Internet & American Life Project. 2010. State of the News Media 2010. Project for Excellence in Journalism. http://www.stateofthenewsmedia.org/2010/. Accessed 1 May 2010.

Putnam, R. D. 2001. *Bowling Alone: The Collapse and Revival of American Community.* New York: Simon & Schuster.

Rainie, L. 2010. How News Consumption Has Changed Since 2000. Presentation to the S. I. Newhouse School of Public Communications, Syracuse, N.Y. http://www.pewinternet.org/Presentations/2010/Jun/How-Media-Consumption-Has-Changed-Since-2000.aspx. Accessed 30 July 2010.

Schudson M. and S. E. Tifft. 2005. American Journalism in Historical Perspective. In *The Press,* edited by G. Overholser and K. H. Jamieson. 17-47. Oxford: Oxford University Press.

Shoemaker, P. J. and T. P. Vos. 2009. *Gatekeeping Theory.* New York: Routledge.

Stephens, M. 2007. *A History of News,* 3rd edition. New York: Oxford University Press.

Thomas, H. 2007. *Watchdogs of Democracy? The Waning Washington Press Corps and How It Has Failed the Public.* New York: Scribner.

Tuchman, Gaye. 1978. *Making News: A Study in the Construction of Reality.* New York: Free Press.

THE ALHAMBRA PROJECT: A THEORY-BASED STRATEGY FOR THE CONSTRUCTION OF A CITIZEN JOURNALISM WEBSITE

NANCY NIEN-TSU CHEN, SANDRA BALL-ROKEACH, MICHAEL PARKS AND JIN HUANG

Introduction

The Alhambra Project was conceived in the midst of a number of intersecting processes that were rapidly changing the landscape of journalism in the United States. The advent of the World Wide Web, the evolution of interactive communication tools, and the growing number of citizens who are technology-savvy have created many problems for traditional journalism, but also unlimited possibilities for its reinvention. The composition of the markets for news products is also shifting, as local communities in an increasing number of countries become more diverse ethnically, culturally and linguistically under the forces of globalization. The interacting processes of technological evolution and globalization have enabled and called for greater collaboration between professional journalists and lay citizens in order to produce news that is relevant and useful to today's news consumers. The Alhambra Project represents one of the first attempts at developing a journalistic model for such collaboration that is informed by both theory and empirical observations. It is one of several initiatives of the Annenberg School for Communication and Journalism at the University of Southern California that seek to meet the evolving information and communication needs of citizens and communities in the 21st century.

Alhambra is a medium-size city located in the San Gabriel Valley region of Southern California. Slightly more than half of the city's 85,000 residents are Asian, mostly Chinese (US Census Bureau 2009). Latinos make up approximately one-third of the population and constitute the second largest ethnic group in Alhambra, followed by Anglos who account for about 10 percent of the residents.[1] Alhambra has a city council with elected members who make decisions on local policy issues. It also has over a dozen educational institutions, including nine public elementary schools, three public high schools as well as a number of private schools. In terms of recreation, there are many parks, sports facilities, Asian restaurants, Latin dance clubs and supermarkets that sell ethnic grocery and other goods that satisfy the needs of Alhambra's diverse residents.

Despite its many resources, Alhambra lacks a vibrant local media. In this regard, Alhambra represents a larger problem with respect to the need for local news that facilitates civic engagement. The only news publication that provides regular coverage of the city is *Around Alhambra*, a monthly English-language newspaper published by the business-oriented Chamber of Commerce. This publication has a circulation of approximately 50,000, and it is delivered monthly to all households and commercial business venues in Alhambra. The regional newspapers in Los Angeles County rarely cover the city. Alhambra also largely falls under the radar of the *Los Angeles Times*, the county's major metropolitan newspaper, which is owned by the Chicago-based Tribune Publishing Group, the second-largest newspaper publisher in the US in terms of revenue. The San Gabriel Valley Newspaper Group publishes two titles, the *Pasadena Star-News* and the *San Gabriel Valley Tribune*, that cover the San Gabriel Valley region of which Alhambra is a part. The *Pasadena Star-News* used to have a beat reporter for Alhambra, but it no longer does. There are also a number of county-wide ethnic newspapers in Chinese, Spanish and Vietnamese that occasionally report on Alhambra.

This absence of local media is consequential. A long line of research has demonstrated that local news is essential to community building and civic engagement (Ball-Rokeach, Kim and Matei 2001; Finnegan and Viswanath 1988; Friedland and McLeod 1999; Janowitz 1952; McLeod, Scheufele and Moy 1999; McLeod et al., 1999). In fact, studies have revealed that compared to six other residential communities in Los Angeles, residents in Alhambra and its neighboring suburb Monterey Park have the lowest level of community belonging, a critical component of civic engagement (Ball-Rokeach et al. 2001). The voter turnouts for local elections in Alhambra have also been consistently low, at an average of

---

[1] In the US, the term "Latinos" refers to the country's white or black residents of Latin-American descent, whereas the term "Anglos" has been expanded to refer to those white Americans of not only English heritage but more generally non-Latin ancestry.

45%, unless they were combined with a presidential election, which helped boost the turnouts to more than 77% in 2008 (Alhambra City Clerk's Office, personal communication, 22 April 2009). In comparison to voter turnouts in other Los Angeles neighborhoods, Alhambra's low turnouts are not particularly notable. However, it is the composition of the voters in Alhambra that is indicative of the city's distinctive civic participation patterns. Among the residents who voted during the 2008 presidential primary election, one third were Latinos, which was proportional to their representation in the total population of Alhambra. On the other hand, Asians made up only 34% of the voters although they constituted half of the Alhambra population. Anglos, however, were significantly over-represented in the turnout and made up almost one third of the voters (William C. Velasquez Institute, personal communication, 20 April 2009). In fact, the Asian community generally has a high propensity to acquire citizenship—and even voter registration—but low voting participation in the US. Research by the Asian Pacific American Legal Center (Ichinose and Kao 2006) indicated that across Los Angeles County in 2006, 52% of all registered voters voted, whereas only 41% of Asian registered voters cast their ballots.

The low levels of civic engagement among Alhambra residents and the limited local news coverage of Alhambra provided the impetus for the Alhambra Project. This project's not-so-immodest vision is for Alhambra residents to have a space where they can tell Alhambra stories and receive information about their neighborhood so that they will gradually form a sense of community across lines of ethnicity and become civically engaged. Put briefly, the envisioned local news venue will allow residents to "imagine" Alhambra as their community through shared narratives (Anderson 1983).

Groundwork has been carried out in Alhambra to assess the possibility of constructing a local news product that is based on a model of citizen journalism, where professional journalists work with local residents in neighborhood storytelling. The support and participation of residents, their major community organizations, and their media are especially important because the envisioned "Alhambra storyteller" is expected to be self-sustaining after an initial phase of financial support from the University of Southern California. Sustainability will be a function of how well this news product engages: (1) residents' community interests and concerns; (2) community organizations and institutions that residents connect with in their everyday lives; and (3) the media that residents connect to in their everyday lives. Of course, the involvement of local businesses is also critical, as advertising provides an important source of revenue to sustain the operation of this news venue.

Unlike most commercial news media, which begin with a set of preconceived ideas and features that are subsequently tested and fine-tuned through market research and then actual publication, the Alhambra project is not based upon any preconception about what type of news venue will be constructed. Rather, the project is guided by feedback from the residents, community organizations and local media as to what they would find most helpful and attractive. In other words, participation of and partnership with local residents and organizational stakeholders are what differentiate the Alhambra Project from the conventional strategy of developing a news product.

Communication infrastructure theory as a guide to exploratory research

Since 2008, the Alhambra Project team has been conducting research to assess the needs and wants of the residents and key community players in Alhambra. Informing the research is the Communication Infrastructure Theory (CIT), a theory developed on the basis of empirical studies conducted in a dozen communities across Los Angeles County to explicate the conditions under which civic engagement thrives (Ball-Rokeach et al. 2001; Kim and Ball-Rokeach 2006a; Kim and Ball-Rokeach 2006b; Kim, Jung and Ball-Rokeach 2006). Communication infrastructure is defined as "a neighborhood storytelling network set in its communication action context" (Ball-Rokeach et al. 2001, 396). Neighborhood storytelling encompasses stories that focus on a specific residential area and its residents. Research has indicated that such stories are circulated through multilevel networks. Macro-level storytelling networks are made up of large governmental and non-governmental organizations as well as the mainstream media, which tell stories primarily about a whole city or nation. Meso-level storytelling is performed by agents that focus on a particular area—in this case, these are community organizations and local media. The micro level is residents' personal networks in which residents talk to one another about issues, events or even gossip in their neighborhood. Research based on CIT has found that despite their marginalization in macro-level storytelling networks, neighborhoods can have a high level of belonging and civic participation when their meso- and micro-level storytellers, namely the local media, community organizations and residents, have strong and integrated connections to one another (Kim and Ball-Rokeach 2006a; Kim and Ball-Rokeach 2006b). In other words, civic engagement is high when there is a strong storytelling network of residents, community organizations and local (often ethnic) media, where each storyteller can prompt the others to begin and carry on a conversation about the community.

The communication action context constitutes the second layer of the indigenous communication infrastructure. It refers to the physical, psychological, sociocultural, economic or technological factors that facilitate or constrain open communication in a neighborhood. For example, ethnic diversity is one sociocultural factor that may constrain open communication in a neighborhood because language and cultural barriers are not conducive to regular conversations across ethnicities. Indeed, research has shown ethnic diversity or class heterogeneity in a neighborhood is negatively related to the residents' levels of civic engagement (Kim and Ball-Rokeach 2006c; Rice and Steele 2001; Rotolo 2000; Wilson 2006). However, it is the conviction of the Alhambra Project that diversity need not be a hindrance to civic engagement in a neighborhood if residents of different backgrounds have the chance to engage in frequent communication about their common interests and concerns. It is therefore the project's goal to promote cross-ethnic communication by creating a local news product with tri-lingual capabilities that is accessible to most residents in Alhambra.

Communication infrastructure theory guides the present work by helping the Alhambra Project team determine its research and implementation strategy. In the initial stages, the research effort has focused on getting to know the three major local storytellers, namely the residents, active community organizations and local media, both English-language and ethnic. Their community-related interests and concerns were identified, and the current interaction patterns among these storytellers were investigated. Empirical observations have also been made with regard to the communication action context of Alhambra—that is, features in the environment that either facilitate or constrain the activation of a local storytelling network. These observations indicate that, at present, ethnic diversity tends to act as a constraint to civic engagement in Alhambra as observed in previous literature. However, there is also evidence of some degree of inter-group communication and contact in certain community institutions, such as public schools. The implementation plan must subsequently rely upon the sustained and expanded activation of this discursive network.

Connecting to the literature on citizen journalism

In addition to using CIT as a theoretical framework guiding the Alhambra Project, the developing literature on, and practice of, citizen journalism has also influenced the project's direction. New communication technologies have provided individuals who are not professional journalists with a platform and a toolkit for telling stories about their community. Consequently, local storytelling utilizing an electronic platform has begun taking root in many neighborhoods across the US, giving rise to a new communication model that has been variously termed the placeblog (Williams 2009), hyperlocal media (Miel and Faris 2008), or in our preferred terminology, locally-oriented citizen journalism.

For some, this new model involves nothing more than bloggers who do little to no original reporting but nonetheless make an impact as part of the conversation about national and community events (Reynolds 2006). For others, citizen journalism is at its core a replacement for what traditional journalism is failing to provide. Here, we see the stirrings of a new kind of journalism that remains independent of the traditional distribution and production models of the mainstream press.

The citizen journalism initiatives that have won the most renown in the US, by those concerned about the future of traditional journalism and the vitality of civil society, are hyperlocal news websites, many started by former professional journalists (Deards 2009; Snyders 2009; Westphal 2009). Some of the well known examples in this category include the *Voice of San Diego, Minn Post, New West, St. Louis Beacon* and *Forum of Deerfield* (Miel and Faris 2008; Westphal 2008). These journalism sites have some things in common: they are run as non-profits; they are committed to local journalism as crucial to the health of civil society; and they rely on citizen-generated interactivity. Each site has a different level of professionalism; the *Voice of San Diego, New West* and *Minn Post* operate much like traditional newsrooms in that they have paid staff reporters, though some of these sites make use of blogs and reader feedback through comments on the site to enhance citizen participation. On the other hand, the *Forum of Deerfield* is primarily run through contributions from citizen journalists (Amjad 2008). In recent months, media giants have also begun to get involved with citizen journalism initiatives. For example, AOL acquired *Patch*, a network of hyperlocal news websites, in 2009 (Gomlak 2010). While AOL might be primarily interested in *Patch*'s ability to attract online advertising dollars from small communities in the US, the company's drive to expand the network by launching more hyperlocal news sites with interactive features could result in better local coverage and greater user involvement with news content.

In the language of CIT, most of these efforts focus upon one node of the storytelling network, namely the residents. This is a risky strategy because it is difficult for residents to carry the entire burden of storytelling in their communities, especially in the long run. Research has found that a major constraint on residents' civic engagement, a constraint that holds across ethnicity and class, is work—working too many hours, commuting too far, or having more than one job (Ball-Rokeach et al. 2001). The limits of residents' capacities to carry a sustained storytelling role give rise to the need to engage meso level storytellers—specifically, community organizations and institutions and local media.

Another important limitation of extant efforts to deploy new media to reinvigorate journalism and its role in prompting community-oriented engagement is the tendency to engage in ethnically-bounded storytelling among the computer literate and civically engaged. For example, case studies of the *Chi-Town Daily News* and *Forum of Deerfield* suggest that their readership and contributors are computer literate, mostly white, and already engaged in their community. These cases highlight major challenges to the Alhambra Project's effort to create a grounded local news venue that is inclusive of people from different ethnic, linguistic, and cultural backgrounds and to do so in a community where many residents are not civically engaged at present. Currently, the New American Media Foundation's *LA Beez* website probably comes the closest to a citizen journalism effort designed to give voice across a wide spectrum of race and class concerns. On a weekly basis, it publishes English translations of selected articles from Los Angeles-based ethnic and trade presses. While the *LA Beez* site may increase the accessibility of ethnic media stories to English speakers, it does not have the kind of citizen and community engagement in the production process that we are striving to attain; that is, it does not engage indigenous storytelling networks.

The challenge in a nutshell

The many challenges identified in the literature suggest that if the Alhambra Project is to have a chance of success in creating a local news product that serves as a storytelling network for civic engagement, a great deal must be learnt about Alhambra, its residents, its community organizations and institutions as well as the practices of extant local media. An unnerving difficulty felt as the project team set out on this course of inquiry was the possibility that nobody really wanted to know or tell Alhambra stories. For example, it could be that Alhambra is just not a place that residents identify with because they orient their social and economic lives elsewhere. Or it could be that only one segment of the population cares about Alhambra stories, thus preventing the kind of cross ethnic bridges that need to be built to have an inclusive community building storytelling network.

Research methods: Exploring the present state of the communication infrastructure

In order to gain a comprehensive understanding of Alhambra, the multilevel, multi-method and multilingual research methodology developed by Matei, Ball-Rokeach, Wilson and Hoyt (2001) has been deployed to identify: (1) residents' local concerns and attitudes toward Alhambra; (2) the community organizations and institutions that are the sites of civic action and community activities that engage residents; and (3) the storytelling practices of local and ethnic media that engage residents. Efforts have also been made to explore the communication action context, including those local businesses that residents patronize and which might be willing to pay for advertising with our local news product.

The process of uncovering the indigenous storytelling network begins with getting to know the area through field observations and interviews with knowledgeable persons. The motto for the next steps is "Let the residents be your guide". This means that residents inform the project team about the community organizations and institutions that matter to them in their everyday lives and the media that they connect to for understanding their worlds. This grounded strategy is intended to frame Alhambra in the eyes of the residents whom the project is trying to engage and reach through a local news venue.

The residents

A series of multilingual focus groups were conducted with a total of 91 Alhambra residents in May 2009. The design of the focus group protocol was informed by year-long preparations that involved analyses of secondary data (e.g. census data), interviews with key community informants, systematic field observations in Alhambra, and media monitoring of Alhambra-related news in the regional and ethnic media. These initial explorations of Alhambra suggested that the schools were an important discursive site, and this led to the decision to focus on an age group which was likely to have children in the home. Chinese, Latino and

Anglo residents of Alhambra between the ages of 25 and 45 years were recruited through random-digit-dialing to share their views on the following subject areas: (a) residents' community interests and concerns; (b) the nature and scope of interpersonal discussions among neighbors; (c) the presence and scope of communicative relationships among residents of different ethnicities; (d) community organizations that residents connect with in their everyday lives; (e) residents' current levels of civic engagement; (f) existing local news sources in Alhambra and residents' assessments of them; and (g) local news channels preferred by residents and the type of content that interests them.

Focus group discussions corroborated previous research findings on the low levels of civic engagement in Alhambra. When focus group participants were probed about the reasons behind their lack of community involvement, the most frequently cited reason was that residents did not know what was going on in their neighborhood because local news and information were not readily available. A number of participants explicitly expressed their desire to become more civically engaged but stated that they did not how to reach and communicate their concerns to local officials.

Residents' local media and their limitations as an Alhambra storyteller

Residents from different ethnic backgrounds all nominated *Around Alhambra*, the free monthly newspaper published by the Chamber of Commerce in English, as a common source from which they obtained limited and mostly business-related information about their community. However, both Latino and Chinese residents considered themselves underserved with information in their ethnic languages, even though ethnic Chinese in Alhambra were comparatively better served with a richer collection of ethnic newspapers, such as *China Daily, World Journal* and *Sing Tao Daily*. Each of these publications carried around two to three stories about Alhambra each week, and a number of focus group participants said that they bought the print version of these publications daily or simply accessed their content online when needed. Altogether, the majority of the focus group participants thought that the existing news sources provided insufficient information about Alhambra, which made it difficult for the residents to become more involved in their community despite their desire to do so. The lack of local coverage was also evident from informal media monitoring carried out by the project team members.

Focus group participants suggested that they would like to gain more information on local education, traffic and safety issues, on the availability of social and health care services in their community, and on shopping, dining and entertainment deals as well as recreational and cultural events that took place in Alhambra. The participants also proposed their preferred channels for receiving local news, and the internet was nominated by the largest number of individuals as a preferred channel. A number of the participants specified that they would like to receive an electronic newsletter via email on a weekly basis, and this newsletter should contain simple headlines and synopses of key stories of the week with links on which the reader could click for more comprehensive coverage. These findings were reassuring as they suggested receptivity to an Alhambra storyteller in the form of a citizen journalism website. The findings also appeared consistent with national trends, as recent research found that the internet has surpassed newspapers and radio in its popularity as a news platform, and only television was nominated by a higher percentage of American adults as a regular news source compared to the internet (Purcell et al. 2010).

All in all, there is very little imagining of Alhambra as a community in the news media that residents connect to in their everyday lives, and the most prominent ethnic media are only accessible to those residents who can read Mandarin or Spanish. Consequently, a key challenge to the Alhambra Project is to build upon these established connections to media in order to increase storytelling of Alhambra. For example, the abovementioned focus group findings could be distributed to media producers to document the residents' desire for more local coverage. Also, working relationships could be established with these media through links to our local news website which translates and disseminates their stories and offers a venue for them to expand their coverage and reach.

Residents' community organizations as potential storytelling sites

Focus group participants also identified a number of community organizations with which they were most connected. These organizations have the potential to become key storytellers in Alhambra, although there is little indication that these organizations are currently active storytellers of the community or operate sites where such storytelling occurs. The organizations include fitness centers and sports clubs, churches, charities, and schools. It is therefore critical for the project to engage and activate these organizations as Alhambra storytellers. The goal is to transform at least some of these potential sites into active sites of community storytelling by involving them as participants in the new media venue.

In sum, the Alhambra Project seeks to build upon associations that residents already have to create meso level storytelling which can be sustained. Residents come and go, but community organizations and local media are likely to have a longer tenure and a more stable storytelling capacity once they are involved.

Engaging businesses: Looking to future economic sustainability

Sustainability can be threatened by a lack of resident interest and involvement of meso level storytellers, but economic sustainability is another obvious challenge. The Alhambra Project has financial support from the University of Southern California for the launch of a local news website and its operation for a year, but other sources of revenue will be necessary thereafter. Therefore, the project team members are presently engaging business owners in focus group discussions and individual interviews to ascertain their interest and ability to pay for advertising on the site. As the experience of many other citizen journalism sites has demonstrated, the survival of a local news site for Alhambra will probably depend on a combination of revenue sources.

Next steps: Developing an "Alhambra storyteller" website

The Alhambra Project's CIT guided research activities have led to five conclusions:

(1) Low levels of civic engagement in Alhambra can be understood as a logical outcome of a weak communication infrastructure for imagining Alhambra as a community. Other factors surely play a part, but absent an integrated communication infrastructure, residents' present discursive environments discourage development of a sense of "belonging" and other aspects of civic engagement.

(2) Nonetheless, the requisite conditions for a successful community-building local news website are in place if the media and community organizations are able to follow the residents' leads and desires. Success is likely to require attention to how a local news website can be embedded in established relationships and associations, especially in the forms of community organizations and media that offer the potential to activate an Alhambra storytelling network. Furthermore, prior knowledge of the interests and concerns of residents and their preferred ways of accessing

community-relevant information is essential in developing an effective local news source.

(3) Communication infrastructure theory suggests the need for an expanded definition of citizen journalism that includes community organizations and institutions as well as local and ethnic media along with residents as the desired participants.

(4) The Alhambra Project faces an enormous challenge when it comes to building a storytelling bridge between ethnic groups. Ethnic diversity is probably the chief feature of the communication action context that constrains present Alhambra storytelling and the project's efforts to create a citizen journalism venue for future storytelling. Focus group discussions with Alhambra residents and other research observations (e.g. field observations of the presence or absence of naturally occurring cross-ethnic interactions) have suggested that the ethnic communities of Alhambra basically live in different storytelling networks. Most important in this regard is that they connect to different media in their daily lives, media that are accessible only in Mandarin, Spanish or English. Even when there is linguistic competence in English, people often prefer media that communicate in their native tongue, and English is the native tongue of a minority of residents in Alhambra. This phenomenon is not unique to Alhambra, but is, or is likely to be, a challenge for journalists and social researchers in communities around the world. In the context of Alhambra, it is clear that a tri-lingual site needs to be constructed, and the site must engage residents from the community's three primary ethnic groups as well as their respective community organizations and media.

(5) Collaborations between journalists trying to reconstruct models of journalism and social researchers who share a concern for reinvigorating civil society and who recognize the essential role of journalism in this endeavor can be worth the effort of working across disciplinary boundaries. As the Alhambra Project moves forward to construct a citizen journalism website, the application of communication infrastructure theory in advance of and during site construction is expected to provide sufficient and constant guides to how this site can better serve the purposes of civic engagement and constructive cross-ethnic communication while also meeting the challenge of sustainability.

As this chapter goes to press, the Alhambra project team is working with a website developer to construct a local news website with the following features to facilitate cross-ethnic understanding, conversations and interaction among residents and community organizations in the neighborhood:

(1) Aggregation of Alhambra-related stories from the Chinese, Spanish and English media on a daily basis, with several editor-selected stories from each type of media being manually translated into the other two languages on a weekly basis. An automatic online translation tool will be available on the site for translation of the remaining stories.

(2) Originally reported stories from professional journalists and local residents, with website users being able to add their comments to each story. During the past six months, a professional journalist from the Alhambra Project has been training Alhambra High School students with an interest in journalism in basic reporting skills. These students have already produced original print and audiovisual reports of various city meetings and events under the guidance of the supervising journalist. Such training and professional guidance are expected to be expanded to other Alhambra residents interested in telling stories about the community in the near future.

(3) A multi-ethnic calendar of community events with information supplied by community organizations, local businesses and residents themselves.

(4) A mapping tool that invites local residents, community organizations and businesses to visually narrate the physical establishments and social lives of their community. This mapping tool provides an alternative way through which visitors to the website can easily locate stories and information about various spots in Alhambra.

Our Alhambra local news website will always be a work in progress. After its launch, the site will be modified continuously, based on feedback from the community contributors and users, and the project team will carry on with monitoring and outreach activities to ensure that the website serves its purpose as a platform that enables residents and community organizations to share stories and engage in conversations about their neighborhood.[2]

Works Cited

Amjad, K. 2008. *The forum, Deerfield, NH: Seeking sustainability in hyperlocal journalism.* Cambridge, MA: Harvard University Berkman Center for Internet and Society.

Anderson, B. 1983. *Imagined communities: Reflections on the origin and spread of nationalism.* London: Verso.

---

[2] After nearly two years of research and preparation, the Alhambra Source (www.alhambrasource.org) was officially launched on August 29, 2010, to provide local news and stories in English, Chinese and Spanish.

Ball-Rokeach, S. J., Y.-C. Kim and S. Matei. 2001. Storytelling neighborhood: Paths to belonging in diverse urban environments. *Communication Research,* 28: 392–428.

Deards, H. 2009. MinnPost: Still in action in Minnesota. March 5. http://www.editorsweblog.org/multimedia/2009/03/minnpoststill_in_ac tion_in_ minnesota.php. Accessed 20April 2009.

Finnegan, J. R. and K. Viswanath. 1988. Community ties and use of cable TV and newspapers in a Midwest suburb. *Journalism Quarterly,* 65: 459–63.

Friedland, L. A. and J. M. McLeod. 1999. Community integration and mass media: A reconsideration. In *Mass media, social control, and social change: A macrosocial perspective,* edited by D. Demers and V. Kasisomayajula. 197–226. Ames: Iowa State University Press.

Gomlak, N. 2010. AOL seeks to fill need for local news with online news site Patch. *The Washington Post.* May 3. http://www.washingtonpost.com/wpdyn/content/article/2010/04/30/AR 2010043001632.html. Accessed 1 June 2010.

Ichinose, D. and D. Kao. 2006. *Asian Americans at the ballot box.* Los Angeles, CA: Asian American Legal Center of Southern California.

Janowitz, M. 1952. *The community press in an urban setting.* Glencoe, IL: Free Press.

Kim, Y.-C. and S. J. Ball-Rokeach. 2006a. Civic engagement from a communication infrastructure perspective. *Communication Theory,* 16: 173-197.

Kim, Y.-C. and S. J. Ball-Rokeach. 2006b. Community storytelling network, neighborhood context, and civic engagement: A multilevel approach. *Human Communication Research,* 32: 411-439.

Kim, Y.-C. and S. J. Ball-Rokeach. 2006c. Neighborhood storytelling resources and civic engagement: A multilevel approach. *Human Communication Research,* 32: 411-439.

Kim, Y.-C,. J.-Y. Jung and S. J. Ball-Rokeach. 2006. "Geo-ethnicity" and neighborhood engagement: A communication infrastructure perspective. *Political Communication,* 23: 421-441.

Matei, S., S. J. Ball-Rokeach, M. Wilson and E. Gutierrez Hoyt. 2001. Metamorphosis: A field research methodology for studying communication technology and community. *The Electronic Journal of Communication,* 11. http://www.cios.org/ www/ejcrec2.htm. Accessed 20 September 2009.

McLeod, J. M., D. A. Scheufele, P. Moy, E. M. Horowitz, R. L. Holbert, W. Zhang and J. Zubric. 1999. Understanding deliberation: The effects of discussion networks on participation in a public forum. *Communication Research*, 26: 743-774.

McLeod, J. M., D. A. Scheufele and P. Moy. 1999. Community, communication, and participation: The role of mass media and interpersonal discussion in local political participation. *Political Communication*, 16: 315–336.

Miel, P. and R. Faris. 2008. *Media Re:public: News and information as digital media come of age: Overview*. Cambridge, MA: Harvard University Berkman Center for Internet and Society.

Purcell, K., L. Rainie, A. Mitchell, T. Rosenstiel and K. Olmstead. 2010. Understanding the participatory news consumer: How internet and cell phone users have turned news into a social experience. http://www.pewinternet.org/Reports/2010/Online-News.aspx. Accessed 1 June 2010.

Reynolds, G. 2006. *An Army of Davids: How markets and technology empower ordinary people to beat big media, big government, and other Goliaths.* New York: Thomas Nelson.

Rice, T. W. and B. Steele. 2001. White ethnic diversity and community attachment in small Iowa towns. *Social Science Quarterly,* 82: 397-407.

Rotolo, T. 2000. Town heterogeneity and affiliation: A multilevel analysis of voluntary association membership. *Sociological Perspective,* 43: 271-289.

U.S. Census Bureau. (2000). United States Census 2000. http://factfinder .census.gov/servlet/nDatasetMainPageServlet?_program=DEC&_tabId =DEC1   &_submenuId=datasets_1&_lang=en&_ts=282966586325. Accessed 17 September 2009.

Snyders, M. 2009. The MinnPost model: Is it sustainable? Joel Kramer wants your money for his grand journalism experiment. 2 March. http://www. citypages.com/2009-03-04/news/the-minnpost-model-is-it-sustainable/. Accessed 20 April 2009.

Westphal, D. 2008. Well-known news sites to use Knight money to deepen reporting. *Online Journalism Review,* 19 December. http://www.ojr.org/ojr/ people/davidwestphal/200812/1606/. Accessed 20 April 2009.

—. 2009. Recession? Local news sites are hanging tough. *Online Journalism Review.* February 26. http://www.ojr.org/ojr/people/davidwestphal /200902/1660/. Accessed 20 September 2009.

Williams, L. 2009. What is a placeblog? http://placeblogger.com/content/what-is-placeblog.

Accessed 28 September 2009.

Wilson, Peter. 2006. Ethnic diversity "breeds mistrust." The Australian. October 10.
http://www.theaustralian.news.com.au/story/0,20867,20554070-5001561,00 .html. Accessed 20 September 2009.

SOMEONE ELSE'S PERIPHERY? JOURNALISM IN NEW ZEALAND

LINDA JEAN KENIX

Introduction

The accepted centre of all New Zealand media, whether mainstream or "alternative", remains in Auckland, the principal site of production. This makes logical sense on one level, given that almost half of all New Zealanders live in the Auckland region. However, the centre of New Zealand media ownership, particularly in relation to newspapers, actually resides far outside the country. Media conglomerates owned largely by Australian interests control most of the media in New Zealand. There is perhaps no other developed country on earth that has so little stake in its own mediated representations. The implications of this are far reaching. New Zealanders find themselves in the rather strange position of relying on those who live beyond their shores to select and tell news stories about them. However several alternative media have now developed from within both the geographic media centres and also the provincial peripheries with the aim of seeking to counterbalance the mainstream representations found in the corporately produced news of New Zealand.

Geography versus ideology

The main centre of journalism in New Zealand may today be in Auckland, but this has not always been the case. Early media centres were predicated on economic development in the area. *The Otago Daily Times,* based in Dunedin on the South Island, was the first newspaper in New Zealand. It began in 1861 by reporting on the goldrush that had swept through the Otago region (Ovens and Tucker 2008, 349). It took two more years until *The New Zealand Herald* was created in 1863. This paper quickly became the national voice of the mainstream media in New Zealand.

The New Zealand Herald, based in Auckland but distributed throughout the country, has the largest circulation by a wide margin and is read by an average of 530,000 people on a typical day (*Herald Readership* 2005), more than double the readership of any other daily newspaper in the country (*The Print Edition* 2007). Given that just over 4.3 million people live in New Zealand (*Top Statistics* 2009), the *Herald* readership constitutes a substantial portion of the population. However, the proportion of New Zealanders who actually subscribe to the *Herald*—and all mainstream newspapers in New Zealand—has continued to decline. Circulation for the *Herald* has gone from 195,000 in 2007 to 174,000 in 2009 (The New Zealand Audit Bureau of Circulations 2009).

While the *Herald* has come to dominate mainstream news coverage, there are several smaller centres of media that radiate out across the country. The larger centres of news inform the provincial peripheries of media content and the reverse is also true. *The New Zealand Herald* draws content from these smaller metropolitan dailies and they in turn pull stories from *The Herald.* Today, the major metropolitan dailies outside of Auckland are based in Wellington (*The Dominion Post*), Christchurch (*The Press*) and Dunedin (*The Otago Daily News*). Many stories from within these major metropolitan dailies are circulated and recycled around the smaller centres, not least because these newspapers are generally owned by the same company.

Thus far, the discussion has focused on geography as the central driving force behind media centres and provincial news outlets. However, as indicated in the introduction, very few of New Zealand's media companies are actually owned by New Zealanders. The Australian media conglomerate Fairfax Media Publications owns the two Sunday newspapers, *The Sunday News* and *The Sunday Star Times*, both principally located in Auckland. Only one major metropolitan newspaper, *The Otago Daily Times* based in Dunedin, is outside of major corporate control. It is owned by Allied Press, a New Zealand company that was formed in 1975 as the result of a merger between two of the oldest newspaper companies in the country, the Otago Daily Times Ltd and the Evening Star Company Ltd (*Allied Press History,* 2010). In addition to *The Otago Daily Times,* Allied Press owns several smaller provincial papers across the South Island. However, between them APN News and Media (APN) and Fairfax own sixteen (72%) of the twenty-two peripheral provincial newspapers ("Industry Overview" 2006). APN is an Australian-based subsidiary of Independent News & Media, which is itself based in Dublin and headed by the media mogul Tony O'Reilly. If provincial and metropolitan outlets are combined, only 8.6% of all mainstream newspapers are independently owned (Lealand 2008). Roughly 63% of daily and weekly newspaper circulation is owned by Fairfax and 28.5% is owned by APN (Lealand 2008). This means that out of roughly 4.3 million people "only about 60,000 readers still have an independent daily newspaper—10,000 less than in 2001" (Rosenberg 2008, 2). APN also owns *The Listener*, *New Zealand Women's Weekly* and a third of The Radio Network, not to mention *The New Zealand Herald*.

Of the seven free-to-air television channels, five are based in New Zealand and run by TVNZ, the state-owned broadcaster. The two that are not based in New Zealand are TV3 and Prime. However, almost all of the channels (apart from the state-funded Maori Television Service) rely on American, British and Australian programming for most of their content and still depend, at least partially, on commercial revenue. Pay television in New Zealand is provided by the Sky Network which is exclusively owned by Australian interests (78% by Independent News Limited, which is itself 44% owned by Rupert Murdoch's News Corporation, and 8.39% by the Commonwealth Bank of Australia) (Lealand 2008). The free-to-air broadcast channels which are state-owned exist under government charter. This charter in its current form was created by the Labour coalition administration of 1999 and stipulates that content must "feature programming across all genres that informs, entertains and educates New Zealand audiences" and should "provide shared experiences that contribute to a sense of citizenship and national identity" as well as ensuring "in its programmes and programme planning the participation of Maori and the presence of a significant Maori voice" (*TVNZ Charter* 2010). There has been a long and contentious debate about the effectiveness of the charter and whether it is based on fundamentally elitist ideals. Due in large part to that debate, there is the distinct possibility that the charter will be revoked under the present National government, which was elected in 2008.

New Zealand's largest radio network, The Radio Network, is a subsidiary of Australian Radio Network (ARN), which is itself owned by Clear Channel Communications, based in the United States; APN News & Media Radio Works, a component of Mediaworks (currently owned by the Australian based equity firm Ironbridge Capital), also has a substantial market share (Lealand 2008). Radio New Zealand, with a smaller market share, is the sole public radio provider and is funded through the governmental organisation New Zealand On Air. However, in February 2010 the Broadcasting Minister Jonathan Coleman stated that the Radio New Zealand board will be removed if they do not shift to a business model and increase revenues. He has stated publically that Radio New

Zealand must consider reducing their hours on air, possibly finding sponsorship for programmes, and even shifting to an AM frequency. It should be noted that there are a small number of community radio stations, but they struggle against the power of the commercial duopoly of The Radio Network and RadioWorks.

Paul Norris, the previous head of one of the leading broadcasting training institutions in New Zealand, has argued that foreign ownership in the country is "without parallel in the Western world" (Norris 2002, 36). There is a monopoly in pay television, duopolies in print and radio media, and "only three significant competitors in free-to-air television including the state-owned channels" (Rosenberg 2008, 1). In fact, every "major media company in the private sector is foreign-owned" (Norris 2002, 36). There are no cross-media ownership regulations in New Zealand. There is no legislation—or even recommendations—prohibiting any level of vertical and horizontal integration across media delivery systems or supply chains. There are no quota requirements for local or national content. This has led to a situation in which there may be geographical centres of media in the country, but the ideological centres of news content are to be found within the Australian and other foreign media conglomerates. Local ownership does not of itself guarantee diversity in content. However, foreign ownership does intrinsically result in "heightened commercialism, since success in commerce is what has given the media transnationals the ability to dominate their international markets" (Rosenberg 2008, 64). There is little to no concern about local culture or identity. Rather, commercial success is the primary focus. Such an emphasis on economic returns renders problematic the proper functioning of civil society in New Zealand (Murdock 1997). Furthermore the organizational roles, structure and policies stemming from ownership have an impact on reporting. As is the case in many media organisations, ownership can affect editorial policy, and ultimately content. On the commercial level the strategy appears for now to have worked: APN News and Media recently reported a net profit of NZ$120 million and underlying revenue of NZ$1.32 billion (One News 2010). However, this stake in ownership does not appear to have prevented the continual loss of circulation and viewership of mainstream media in the country.

The decline of mainstream centres

New Zealand may have the most deregulated media market in the world (Norris 2002). However, the mainstream media in New Zealand have experienced the same drastic decline found around the world. Some would argue that this reduction in mainstream circulation has much to do with technological advances in access to information. However it may have just as much to do with what has been called a "crisis of faith" (McGregor and Comrie 2002, 7). A recent *Readers Digest* poll in New Zealand found that journalism as a profession was rated 34th out of thirty-nine professional careers (*New Zealand's most trusted professions list* 2008). Journalists were placed just ahead of psychics/astrologers, real estate agents, politicians, car salesmen, sex workers and telemarketers who rounded out the bottom of the list.

The internet has irrevocably changed how information is shared. There is now an expectation, particularly among younger people, that news should be free and readily accessible. This open access to information has contributed to the decline of mainstream media consumption. A tendency to sample news media across a wide spectrum of choices online has translated into a reduction in focused attention on any one news source. Instead, most online users "surf" the internet for a variety of content. The desire of individuals to access diverse information almost instantaneously has in New Zealand led much mainstream journalism toward a style of reporting that resembles a series of unreflective soundbites. These soundbites are designed to grab the attention of quickly moving readers who are perpetually navigating through internet content. In committing to a model of journalism that produces information quickly but without much context or meaning, mainstream centres of journalism have also unwittingly led citizens to perceive (whether rightly or wrongly) an erosion of the values and ethics previously thought to be so central to mainstream journalism. Technological advances have influenced shifts in the style, format and process of delivery. However, the driving force behind these changes remains the commercialization of news, which technological developments have allowed mainstream news centres to exploit.

Furthermore, the forces of commercialism have downgraded local news as a central location of information and education to such a degree that there is widespread pessimism (Gardner, Csikszentmihalyi and William 2001) about mainstream centres of journalism in New Zealand. Current journalistic practices may be attributed to technological shifts, but they are also driven by commercial interests. For example, modern mainstream commercial radio news operates around "centralized processing, with fewer reporters on the ground around the country" (Norris 2002, 48). This means that broadcast news, like much print journalism, tends to be put together in a centralized location which has little direct, physical contact with the subject and setting of an actual news story. Such an approach is frustrating to anyone who wants immediate, relevant, local news. But the practice, which is now increasingly possible because of technological changes, cuts costs.

The drive towards a corporate, conglomerated media system in New Zealand has also resulted in a younger workforce, principally because older people simply cannot live on the wages paid by cost-cutting media conglomerates. The government has recently published average earning scales for journalists: starting pay begins at NZ$25,000 a year ("Journalist: Pay and progression" 2009). That is NZ$1,000 less than what one would earn on the minimum wage of NZ$12.50 per hour. Financial pressures do not extend only to salaries. New Zealand journalists acutely feel the pressure to change how and what they write in accordance with the commercial interests of media owners. In 2007, over half of 213 New Zealand journalists agreed that newsrooms had been pressured to do a story because it related to an advertiser, owner or sponsor (Hollings, Lealand, Samson and Tilley 2007). One hundred and eleven of the New Zealand journalists surveyed felt that inadequate resourcing was the primary reason that journalism could not fulfill its watchdog role. In August 2008, Fairfax told the Australian Stock Exchange that they would be cutting 550 jobs from their Australian and New Zealand newspapers. This meant a much larger reliance on outsourcing and rotating employment rosters between newspapers owned by the company. Attributing the cuts to losses in advertising revenue, the announcement was titled "Business Improvement Program" and caused Fairfax shares to jump fourteen cents (Overington and Lyons 2008).

The positioning of mainstream news centres in New Zealand as capitalistic enterprises first and foremost frustrates readers who have historically turned to newspapers as the centres of truth. Within a liberal pluralist model of democracy, an objective "fourth estate" is meant to defend the public interest by reporting the unbiased "truth". Mainstream journalism is still heralded as a source of factual information, but the concept of objectivity has become increasingly problematic. Because of the compounding and complex influences within each newspaper story, media scholars and practitioners have come to realize that objectivity in the mainstream press should be seen as an organizational goal, rather than a template for practice—at least if one equates objectivity with neutrality. A further complication in the media situation in New Zealand is that there is the explicit responsibility to address bicultural issues due to the Treaty of Waitangi, which is the founding document of this nation and guarantees equality for all New Zealanders. However, a survey of New Zealand journalism schools in 2005 found that more than 85 percent of students were Pakeha/European (Tully 2008).[1] The 85% of Pakeha journalism students is in contrast to 67.7 percent of the New Zealand population identifying as European, 14.6 percent as Maori and 9.2 percent as Asian. The over-representation of Pakeha in newsrooms is problematic as "news stories are constructed in ways that repeat traditional patterns of understanding. If the overwhelming majority of journalists are Pakeha, for example, a corresponding worldview holds dominance" (Tully 2008, 236).

If the dominant media leave many struggling to be heard—or seen—minority groups look elsewhere to have their stories told and to create their own social capital. The almost exclusively commercial drive for profit in New Zealand has damaged perceptions of truth and credibility in the news and has led to a reduced sense of national identity. However, alternative media centres have developed as an antidote to the mainstream media conglomerate.

Growth of Alternative Media Peripheries

Alternative media in New Zealand, like the mainstream press, principally originate from Auckland. But they are far more diffuse than mainstream media and stretch across the less populated areas of the country as well as the metropolitan centres. The internet is the principal reason that a wide range of contributors can now participate in alternative media across New Zealand. As more and more people go online, the opportunity for average citizens to be exposed to a variety of media messages has increased.

The growth of independent, unique, alternative messages online has exploded in recent years. Globally, over twenty hours of video were uploaded every minute onto YouTube in 2009 (*Broadcasting ourselves* 2009). This number was up from six hours of video every minute just two years prior. In the words of YouTube, this is the "equivalent of Hollywood releasing over 86,000 new full-length movies into theaters each week" (*Broadcasting ourselves* 2009). The social networking site Facebook reported 469 million global monthly unique visitors in 2010 (Inside Facebook 2010), which roughly equals about 600,000 new members every single day. In 2010, there are roughly 133 million blogs in the blogosphere (Intac 2010) and 50 million tweets every day in the world (Twitter Blog 2010). The most popular blog in New Zealand is kiwiblog, which attracted 2.68 million visits in 2009 (Kiwiblog 2010). The site is based principally

---

[1] In New Zealand Pakeha is a widely-used Maori term that refers to a New Zealander of European descent.

on the thoughts of one man, David Farrar, located in Wellington. In one week, the site brings in 121,000 page views—roughly a third of the most popular blog in the United Kingdom, but in a country with about one fifteenth of the UK's population. This suggests a very strong interest in alternative, non-corporate and non-commercial perspectives in New Zealand—particularly online.

Alternative media have been traditionally very hard to categorize (Downing 2003). Situated along a continuum, they can be defined as "any media that are produced by non-commercial sources and attempt to transform existing social roles and routines by critiquing and challenging power structures" (Atkinson 2006, 252). The existing social roles and routines that alternative media seek to critique generally stem from capitalism, consumerism, patriarchy and the nature of corporations. It is this foregrounding of social critique that has historically placed alternative media in diametric opposition to the mainstream media. This opposition allows for an independent "alternative communication" that constructs different social orders, traditions, values and social understandings (Hamilton 2000). Alternative media offer an independent platform for groups and individuals which have been marginalized by the mainstream media (Atton 2002) and provide much needed context. Mainstream media have often been criticized as maximizing audiences through pack-journalism that is conventional and formulaic, resulting in content that can be overly simplistic (McChesney 1999). In contrast, alternative media often advocate programmes of social change through the framework of politicized and in-depth social commentary (Armstrong 1981; Duncombe 1997).

It is important to note that mainstream and alternative media are not diametric opposites. However, one can characterize mainstream media by the stories they tend to cover and the stories they ignore. It has been argued that conventional media can "omit or bury items which might jeopardize the socio-cultural structure and man's faith in it" (Breed 2004, 419). Conversely, alternative media can highlight topics which mainstream publications have avoided. There are many early examples from New Zealand of alternative publications which illustrate how marginalized groups aimed to fill such an informational gap. The early twentieth century New Zealand Protestant magazine *The Nation* argued against what it perceived as the pervasive proliferation of Catholic ideology throughout society, while the late twentieth century and long-running Women's Electoral Lobby *Newsletter* argued that "all the good works and achievements of those in the feminist movement are daily undermined by the images of women, children and Maori shown on television" (McLeod

1988). The *Newsletter* produced images and stories about these marginalized groups that aimed to counter the negative representations found in the mainstream press. *Te Karere Maori* published British news in Maori complete with Maori language advertising as far back as 1870, only thirty years after New Zealand became a British colony (Ovens and Tucker 2008, 351). The early history of New Zealand media also involved popular labour newspapers such as *The Workingman's Gazette* (began in 1887) and *The Labour Advocate* (began in 1880).

Other alternative magazines such as *Earwig* (1970s) documented a specific cultural moment in time and illustrated the struggles of alternative media in relation to their mainstream counterparts. *Earwig* in particular served as exemplar to many other alternative publications because of its success in gaining access to the global Underground Press Syndicate (UPS)—the only New Zealand magazine to do so. Like other historical and contemporary alternative media, *Earwig* was both an open forum for artists and a centre for generating alternative current events. It originated in the relatively provincial town of Palmerston North and had only one requirement: material must have the indefinable "CHOMP" (Kenix 2010): the term is never defined in the magazine, but is understood as something uniquely different with power and strength. This indefinable uniqueness within the media landscape is still what separates alternative media peripheries from mainstream conglomerates. Alternative media have the capacity for "transforming spectators into active participants of everyday dealings and events affecting their lives" (Tracy 2007, 272). Indeed, alternative media often view their role as "one of educating and mobilizing the 'masses' in the service of the cause or movement" (Hamilton 2000, 359) and generally avoid one-way forms of communication. The frequent solicitation by alternative media outlets of feedback from audiences is purposeful, and the aim is to ensure that an "egalitarian relationship" can be formed between the media outlet and these audiences (Rodriguez 2001). Often the social change desired within alternative media is strikingly opposed to mainstream culture. Many alternative media outlets draw from the anarchist principles of nineteenth century Europe (McElroy 2003) in their dependence upon decentralization and the self-sufficiency of their readers (Brecher, Costello and Smith 2000; Starr 2000).

For example, the online *Nikolai Organization* (*The N.O.*) based in New Zealand is made up of "agents" who "execute missions" geared towards positive change. They rely strongly on user participation and have achieved laudable goals, such as planting a world record number of 22,400 trees in only a few hours (*The N.O.* 2010). They combine "escapism and networking with the aim of positively shaking up the existing order"

(*Secret agents plant 22,400-tree forest on Motuihe* 2009). Information on "missions" is provided on the website and participants document evidence of their actions through video or photographs. Within such an alternative media space, the reader is fully engaged in the process of creating an event and also on the reporting of that event. Amateur, citizen reporting for *The N.O.* stretches across the entirety of New Zealand.

Another example comes from *NZ Atheist Campaign* ("NZ Atheist Campaign" 2010), a website devoted to sharing information about atheism and raising money for advertisements on metropolitan buses throughout New Zealand. These ads have no background image and display only text that reads "THERE'S PROBABLY NO GOD. NOW STOP WORRYING AND ENJOY YOUR LIFE". The first campaign began in London with the work of one woman, Ariane Sherine (*F.A.Q.* 2010). The popularity of this original effort spread throughout the globe and as of May 2010 the NZ campaign had raised NZ$23,000. The organization urges readers to link to the NZ Atheist website on their own blogs and websites, donate money for future campaigns, become a fan of the NZ Atheist Bus Campaign on Facebook or follow the organization's tweets on Twitter. While the name may suggest that the bus campaign is the central reason for this organization's existence, it also argues strongly for developing interpersonal relationships to increase awareness about atheism, and argues that simply talking about atheism with "your workmate, neighbour or barista" (*Support* 2010) will cause social perceptions on atheism to shift. The organization argues that "there's perhaps no better way than good old fashioned word-of-mouth" (*Support* 2010) for the process of social change to begin.

One of the central goals of alternative media is to subvert the "hierarchy of access" (Atton 2002) which often dictates who is sourced in mainstream media content according to perceived credibility. Non-professional, citizen reporting practices like those demonstrated by *The N.O.* "emphasise first person eyewitness accounts by participants; reworking of the populist approaches of tabloid newspapers to recover a 'radical popular' style of reporting; collective and anti-hierarchical forms of organization ... an inclusive, radical form of civic journalism" (Atton 2003, 267). Amateur reporting is completely open to the reader as a welcome and inviting text without any coded language which might not be understood. Amateur reporting can also be seen in alternative radio broadcasts, such as *Spectrum*. This programme is a documentary series that has been transmitted on the public broadcaster, Radio New Zealand, throughout the past thirty years. It has thrived by functioning as a "training ground for novice producers" (Radio New Zealand 2010) across the country. Contributions are generally "quirky and colourful" and drawn from small provincial areas as well as large metropolitan centres. The show is ongoing, but because of its quality and its wide range of contributions, it has now "become recognised as one of New Zealand's most valuable libraries of oral history" (Radio New Zealand 2010).

Another popular alternative media for news in New Zealand is the online publication *Scoop*. It claims to give voice to "perspectives not being addressed through traditional media" (*Introducing Scoop* 2007). The organization argues that it is "unique, independent and necessary in NZ media" (*Scoop's Mission* 2007). It is the leading independent news publication in New Zealand with averages of 450,000-500,000 unique readers a month (*Scoop's Mission* 2007). *Scoop* aggregates unedited information from a variety of sources which range from traditional, professionalized institutions to small, individual contributors. The organization argues that it gives "voice to perspectives not being addressed through 'traditional media' sources" under the banner of "freedom, expression, ideas, information, empowerment, transformation" (*Scoop's Mission* 2007).

Conclusion

Foreign corporate conglomerates own almost all of New Zealand mainstream media. This takeover is unparalleled in the entire developed world. Profitability has soared within these organisations. However, increased revenue streams have not prevented the continued decline of mainstream media circulation and viewership in New Zealand. Conversely, alternative media have continued their relative growth—particularly online. Mainstream centres appear to be losing their grip as the sole source of information, while alternative media peripheries stretch their networks across this country. Whereas mainstream media continue to centralize and conglomerate into major centres of "objective" information and knowledge, alternative media continue to fragment and draw upon participant contributions to form peripheral networks of "subjective" information. Time will tell which kinds of information New Zealanders will eventually choose. In all likelihood, it will be a rich combination of both alternative and mainstream from both media centres and provincial sources.

Works Cited

Allied Press History. 2010. Dunedin: Allied Press Limited. http://www. alliedpress.co.nz/history.php.

Armstrong, D. 1981. *A trumpet to arms: Alternative media in America.* Boston: South End.

Atkinson, J. 2006. Analyzing resistance narratives at the North American Anarchist Gathering. *Journal of Communication Inquiry,* 30 (3): 251-272.

Atton, C. 2002. *Alternative media.* London: Sage.

—. 2003. What is 'alternative' journalism? *Journalism: Theory, Practice and Criticism,* 4 (3): 267-272.

Brecher, J, T. Costello and B. Smith. 2000. *Globalization from below: The power of solidarity.* Cambridge: South End.

Breed, W. 2004. Mass communication and socio-cultural integration. In *Mass Communication and American Social Thought: Key Texts 1919-1968,* edited by P. A. Simonson. 417-425. Lanham: Rowman and Littlefield.

Broadcasting ourselves. 2009. Youtube. http://youtube-global.blogspot.com/2009/05/zoinks-20-hours-of-video-uploaded-every_20.html.

Downing, J. 2003. Audiences and readers of alternative media: The absent lure of the virtually unknown. *Media, Culture & Society,* 25 (5): 625-645.

Duncombe, S. 1997. *Notes from underground: Zines and the politics of alternative culture.* London/New York: Verso.

F.A.Q. 2010. New Zealand Atheist Bus Campaign. http://www.nogod.org.nz/ faq/.

Gardner, H., M. Csikszentmihalyi and D. William. 2001. *Good Work.* New York: Basic Books.

Hamilton, J. 2000. Alternative media: Conceptual difficulties, critical possibilities. *Journal of Communication Inquiry,* 24 (4): 357-378.

Herald Readership. 2005. The New Zealand Herald. http://www.nzherald.co.nz/info/advertising/print/ad-herald-circulation. cfm. Accessed 13 October 2005.

Hollings, J., G. Lealand, A. Samson and E. Tilley. 2007. Profile 2007. The big NZ journalism survey: Underpaid, under-trained, under-resourced, unsure about the future - but still idealistic. *Pacific Journalism Review,* 13 (2), 175-197. http://www.pjreview.info/issues/docs/13_2/PJR13_2sep2007nzsurvey_ pp 175 _197.pdf. Accessed 6 February 2010.

Industry Overview. 2006. Industry Overview. Auckland. Newspaper Publishers Association. http://www.npa.co.nz/statistics.php. Accesssed 8 February 2010.

Inside Facebook. 2010. *Nielson: Facebook led 2009 social media traffic growth in the US and abroad.* http://www.insidefacebook.com/2010/02/23/nielsen-facebook-led-2009-social-media-traffic-growth-in-the-us-and-abroad/.

Intac. 2010. *Breakdown of the blogosphere.* http://www.intac.net/ breakdown-of-the-blogosphere/.

Introducing Scoop. 2007. Scoop Independent News. http://www.scoop.co.nz/about/. Accessed 17 April 2007.

Journalist: Pay and progression. 2009. New Zealand Government: Career Services. http://www.careers.govt.nz/default.aspx?id0=60103&id1=J32331. Accessed 22 February 2010.

Kenix, L. J. 2010. Resistance narratives in radical, alternative media: A historical examination of *Earwig. Equid Novi*, 31 (1): 89-113.

Kiwiblog. 2010. *Kiwiblog's 2009 stats.* http://www.kiwiblog.co.nz/ 2010/01/kiwiblogs_2009_stats.htmlœ.

Lealand, G. 2008. Media in New Zealand, July 2008. New Zealand Ministry of Education. http://www.tki.org.nz/r/media_studies/different_aspects/media_owners hip_e.php. Accessed 15 February 2010.

McChesney, R. 1999. *Rich media, poor democracy: Communication politics in dubious times.* Urbana: University of Illinois Press.

McElroy, W. 2003. *The debates of liberty: An overview of individualist anarchism, 1881-1908.* New York: Lexington Books.

McGregor, J., and M. Comrie, eds. 2002. *What's news? Reclaiming journalism in New Zealand.* Palmrston North: Dunmore Press.

McLeod, P. 1988. National Co-ordinator's Letter (May). *Women's Electoral Lobby.*

Murdock, G. 1997. Public broadcasting in privatised times: Rethinking the New Zealand experiment. In *Keeping it ours: Issues of television broadcasting in New Zealand*, edited by P. Norris and J. Farnsworth, 9-33. Christchurch: Christchurch Polytechnic.

The N.O. 2010. http://www.theno.org.nz/.

New Zealand's most trusted professions list. 2008. Readers Digest. http://www.readersdigest.co.nz/content/new-zealands-most-trusted-professions-for-2009/.

Norris, P. 2002. News media ownership in New Zealand. In *What's news? Reclaiming journalism in New Zealand*, edited by J. McGregor and M. Comrie, 33-55. Palmrston North: Dunmore Press.

NZ Atheist Campaign. 2010. New Zealand Atheist Bus Campaign. http:// www.nogod.org.nz/. Accessed 14 May 2010.

One News. 2010. *APN sees signs of improvement*. http://tvnz.co.nz/business-news/apn-sees-signs-improvement-3379103.

Ovens, J. and J. Tucker. 2008. A history of newspapers in New Zealand. In *Intro: A beginner's guide to professional news journalism*, edited by J. Tully, 349-368. Wellington: New Zealand Journalists Training Organisation.

Overington, C. and J. Lyons. 2008. Fairfax sheds 550 jobs and quality journalism. *The Australian* (27 August).

The Print Edition. 2007. The New Zealand Herald. http://info.nzherald.co.nz/advertising/print/. Accessed 4 September 2007.

Radio New Zealand. 2010. *About Spectrum*. http://www.radionz.co.nz/national/programmes/spectrum/about.

Rodriguez, C. 2001. *Fissures in the mediascape: An international study of citizens' media*. Cresskill: Hampton Press.

Rosenberg, B. 2008. *News media ownership in New Zealand*. canterbury.cyberplace.org.nz/community/CAFCA/.../mediaown.pdf.

Scoop's Mission. 2007. Scoop Independent News. http://www.scoop.co.nz/about /mission.html. Accessed 17 April 2007.

Secret agents plant 22,400-tree forest on Motuihe. 2009. Scoop. http://business.scoop.co.nz/2009/05/18/secret-agents-plant-22400-tree-forest-on-motuihe/#more-7386. Accessed 10 February 2010.

Starr, A. 2000. *Naming the enemy: Anti-corporate movement confront globalization*. London: Zed Books.

Support. 2010. New Zealand Atheist Bus Campaign. http://www.nogod.org.nz/ support/. Accessed 7 February 2010.

The New Zealand Audit Bureau of Circulations. 2009. New Zealand Herald. Wellington. http://www.abc.org.nz/audit/press.html?org=npa&publicationtype=News&publicationid=215&memberid=124&type=9 Accessed 8 February 2010.

Top Statistics. 2009. Auckland: Statistics New Zealand. http://www.stats. govt.nz/top-statistics.aspx.

Tracy, J. F. 2007. A historical case study of alternative news media and labor activism: The Dubuque Leader 1935-1939. *Journalism & Communication Monographs*, 8 (4): 267-343.

Tully, J., ed. 2008. *Intro: A beginner's guide to professional news journalism.* Wellington: New Zealand Journalists Training Organization.

TVNZ Charter. 2010. http://tvnz.co.nz/view/tvnz_story_skin/111535?format=html. Accessed 2 February 2010.

Twitter Blog. 2010. *Measuring Tweets.* http://blog.twitter.com/2010/02/measuring-tweets.html. Accessed 1 February 2010.

AFTERWORD

DAVID HUTCHISON AND HUGH O'DONNELL

There is much to feel positive about in the parts of the world examined in this book but it is also the case that many of our contributors are concerned about the resources currently available to finance high quality journalism. That is clear from Christopher Waddell's critique of the profit maximisation strategies which have been pursued in the Canadian press and broadcasting, from the sense in Tom Thomson's chapter that some way must be found to ensure that those who access newspapers online make a contribution to the cost of producing them, and from the anxiety Sue Wallace articulates about the survival of regional television news in England. These contributors, and others, are worried about how good journalism can continue to be financed, particularly, though not exclusively, in its print form.

In this context the internet might be viewed as a potentially lethal threat. However, as several other contributors make clear, it is also an opportunity, for example, in the Alhambra project discussed by Nancy Nien-Tsu Chen and her colleagues, in the hyper-local online strategy pursued by *Gazettelive* in the north of England examined by Andy Price, and in New Zealand, where Linda Jean Kenix finds cause for optimism in small online operations which offer an alternative to the mainstream media.

Some peripheries are remarkably vibrant—and, as can be seen from Isabel Soares' chapter, some are extremely sensitive about how they are portrayed elsewhere—but as Enric Castelló shows, even in Catalonia, which is often cited as one of the strongest and most successful examples of a "stateless nation", it is simply not possible to escape the Spanish framework; not only that, there are peripheries in Catalonia itself which resent the power of Barcelona. And, as Simon Gwyn Roberts points out, Wales too has peripheries which feel that the fragmented nature of the principality is not properly represented in print or in broadcasting.

There may be vibrant Welsh language publications—the *Papurau Bro* discussed by Glyn Mon Hughes, for example—but there is no national Welsh press. Reference was made in our Introduction to the decline of the indigenous press in Scotland and the growing power of the London-based titles. As the chapters by Farrel Corcoran and Greg McLaughlin make clear, this is not a phenomenon which is confined to Scotland. It might seem unsurprising that the indigenous press in the north of Ireland faces stiff competition from Fleet Street—and the south—but for London newspapers now to be selling almost as many copies as indigenous titles in the Irish Republic is surely remarkable, given the turbulent nature of Irish-British history.

France would appear to offer a striking contrast to these four situations since, as Raymond Kuhn shows, the regional press in that country continues to outsell the Paris-based titles. On the other hand, the newspapers and magazines of the capital do dominate the national political agenda making process. As Michael Parks demonstrates, in the United States the national agenda there too is set by several big city papers—and broadcasting organisations—but regional and local publications are remarkably persistent and popular. In Britain the London-based press dominates sales throughout the UK, as noted above, and also the national policy making agenda. But, as Howard Tumber shows, the London titles in their home territory offer their readers very sparse accounts of what is going on outside of England—and in some spheres even outside of the capital and the south east. And, as David Stenhouse reveals, ex-pat journalists from one of the devolved polities often seem to revel in presenting to metropolitan audiences a view of where they came from which is partial, to say the least. It would be an interesting and useful study which examined how Welsh and Irish journalists who are employed in London represent their home nations to metropolitan audiences, and which compared their work to that of their Scottish colleagues.

Marc Stanton's chapter explores another metropolitan characteristic, the tendency to present the developing world in a rather negative fashion. This phenomenon has been commented on before but it is very useful— and a little depressing—to see how little change there appears to have been in such representations over the years.

Peripheries do continue to have strong senses of themselves. Even in a country like England, which remains a centralised state with no apparent appetite for regional devolution, as Samantha Lay and Deirdre O'Neill find, television news audiences want higher local/regional content than they are currently being offered. Mike Cormack is struck by how localised the newspapers from the Scottish Highlands which he studies are, and how they demonstrate very little sense that the areas in which they operate are part of a larger region, the existence of which is trumpeted in the titles of innumerable public bodies. But the Gaelic current affairs programme

Eòrpa offers a remarkable contrast for, as Douglas Chalmers shows, it is the most European-oriented current affairs programme being transmitted in the UK at the moment.

There may well be a real desire for news media which reflect peripheries' senses of themselves, sometimes very localised senses, but at the same time the power of centres appears to be growing in many countries, and sometimes—as is currently the case in New Zealand and to a significant extent in the UK too—the centres of financial control can be located outside the country completely: News International, which is now the biggest company involved in the UK media, is either American or Australian but it is certainly not British; and the New Zealand media are owned mainly in Australia—and the Irish Republic.

As noted earlier, the internet might seem to be the obvious saviour of journalism on the periphery and several of our contributors explore what is going on in cyberspace, but time after time they come back to the importance of properly financed journalism which adheres to high standards—perhaps not quite as high in the Anglo Saxon world as those which German journalists appear to be committed to, according to the findings of Siegfried Weischenberg and his colleagues, but high enough for much of the time.

Whether small-scale online operations can ever muster the wherewithal to compete other than at the fringes must remain a matter of some doubt. And that is why well resourced public service oriented journalism in the private and public sectors remains crucial.

Greg McLaughlin emphasises the importance of BBC Northern Ireland and Glyn Mon Hughes that of BBC Wales and S4C, while Christopher Waddell stresses the role of the—currently beleaguered—Canadian Broadcasting Corporation. These organisations are funded in part or in whole by public money. As several of our contributors point out, if the Labour government in Britain had won the 2010 election—and had honoured a pre-election commitment—public money would have been made available to fund private sector consortia to provide regional news services on Channel 3 (ITV) which the franchise holders had declared were no longer financially viable. Whether these alternative news services can be financed on a secure basis into the future is now far from clear.

Direct public subsidy of the press—if not broadcasting—has historically been anathema in Britain and the US, although on the European mainland there are well-developed systems of subsidy, particularly in Scandinavia. The objective of such subsidy is the preservation of a plural press in order to ensure that there is a range of information sources and points of view available in the public sphere. The peculiarities of the situations in Norway and Sweden—highly regionalised presses and an accelerating decline in the number of areas with more than one newspaper—may have led to the decisions forty years ago to use public money in order to rectify the perceived deficiencies of the market.[1] But it is striking that in 2010 the Federal Trade Commission published a discussion paper which explored a range of potential support measures which the US government might embark on, using also public money, to help papers fund journalism deemed to be essential in an informed democracy (Federal Trade Commission 2010).

In Scotland in 2010 a proposal by local authorities to put statutory notices online, and thus save significant sums, was initially supported by the Scottish Government, but after newspaper companies protested, and after they and others gave evidence on the future of the Scottish press to one of the Edinburgh parliament's standing committees, the Government informed the local authorities that they would not be permitted to proceed with the proposal (Scottish Parliament 2010). Throughout the discussion press representatives were at pains to stress not only that not everyone had internet access but also how important local newspapers were in keeping citizens properly informed. They argued that without the revenue—the word "subsidy" was not employed—which local authority advertising provided, many papers would in current circumstances be substantially weakened and some of them might face closure.

The UK government had by this time also indicated that it was not prepared to see such advertising move online in England. So both administrations decided to reject arguments about financial efficiency in favour of public good considerations. It would be surprising if this trend were not to manifest itself in other parts of the world, and if the media in peripheral areas were not to find themselves enmeshed in the ensuing debates. The outcomes of these crucially important discussions will depend on a number of factors, including the force of the arguments deployed, the strength of citizen involvement and the willingness of politicians to think radically about how a vibrant public sphere—in both centres and peripheries—can be sustained in the digital age.

Works Cited

Federal Trade Commission. 2010. Discussion Draft: Potential policy recommendations to support the reinvention of Journalism. Washington:

---

[1] See, for example Skogerbo (1997) and Murschetz (1997).

FTC. www.ftc.gov/opp/workshops/news/jun15/docs/new-staff-discuss
ion.pdf. Accessed 9 September 2010.
Murschetz, P. 1997. *State Support for the Press: Theory and Practice.*
Dusseldorf: European Institute for the Media.
Scottish Parliament Education, Lifelong Learning and Culture Committee.
2010. Report on the Scottish local newspaper industry. Edinburgh:
Scottish Parliament.
www.scottish.parliament.uk/s3/committees/ellc/reports-10/edr10-
07.htm. Accessed 9 September 2010.
Skogerbo, E. 1997. The Press Subsidy System in Norway. *European
Journal of Communication,* 12 (1): 99-118.

CONTRIBUTORS

Sandra Ball-Rokeach is a Professor in the Annenberg School for Communication & Journalism at the University of Southern California. She has authored or edited seven books and published extensively in communication, sociology and psychology journals. Among her current research projects is the Metamorphosis Project, which advances a communication infrastructure perspective on urban community and its evolution under the forces of globalisation and digitalisation.

Enric Castelló is Senior Lecturer at the Department of Communication Studies of the Universitat Rovira i Virgili, Tarragona. His fields of research interests are media and discourse, political communication and national identities. He is the editor of the *Catalan Journal of Communication & Cultural Studies* and is co-editor (jointly with Alexander Dhoest and Hugh O'Donnell) of *The Nation on Screen*.

Douglas Chalmers lectures in Media and Journalism at Glasgow Caledonian University, and between 2005 and 2010 was a member of the BBC Audience Council Scotland, with a remit to monitor the BBC's Gaelic language output. He has written and researched widely on Gaelic arts and culture, and their relation to economic and social development.

Nancy Nien-Tsu Chen is a PhD student in the Annenberg School for Communication & Journalism at the University of Southern California. Between 2002 and 2005 she worked in radio and television news in Australia and Taiwan.

Farrel Corcoran is Professor of Communication in Dublin City University where he currently directs the MA in Political and Public Communication. He was Chairman of RTE, the Irish public service broadcaster, from 1995 to 2000 and has published a major study of Irish television in the age of cultural globalisation.

Mike Cormack is Programme Leader for the BA in Gaelic and Media Studies at Sabhal Mòr Ostaig, part of the University of the Highlands and Islands, Scotland. He has published many articles on the Gaelic media and on minority language media more generally. He is co-editor of the book *Minority Language Media: Concepts, Critiques and Case Studies.*

Jin Huang earned her Master's Degree in Strategic Public Relations from the Annenberg School for Communication & Journalism at the University of Southern California in 2010. She currently works in financial public relations in Beijing, China.

Glyn Mon Hughes is Senior Lecturer in Journalism at Liverpool John Moores University. He has worked extensively in journalism for the BBC as well as for newspapers and magazines in London, Cardiff, Birmingham and Manchester. He writes for a range of music journals and is presently working on a history of Welsh language journalism.

David Hutchison is Visiting Professor in Media Policy at Glasgow Caledonian University and has been involved with journalism education for over twenty years. Among his publications are *Media Policy* and *The Media in Scotland* (co-edited with Neil Blain). He is the chair of Regional Screen Scotland.

Linda Jean Kenix is currently Senior Lecturer in Media and Communication at the University of Canterbury in New Zealand. Since graduating from the University of Texas in 2001, she has published widely in academic journals. Her work has focused on the representation of politically marginalised groups in mainstream and alternative media.

Raymond Kuhn is Professor of Politics at Queen Mary, University of London. He has written extensively on French media policy and political communication. His books include *The Media in Contemporary France*, and *Politics and the Media in Britain*. He has also published articles in a wide range of academic journals.

Samantha Lay worked in journalism, then as a public relations executive for the Consumers' Association before moving into academic life. She has taught at the University of Bedfordshire and Salford University. She is the author of *British Social Realism—From Documentary to Brit Grit*. She is the founder and editor of Medianation.co.uk.

Maja Malik is Assistant Professor at the Institute of Communication Science at the University of Münster. Her teaching and research focus on media occupations and professions, the coverage of social issues, media journalism and self-criticism, journalism theories, and theories of public relations. She has published books and book chapters on journalism in Germany, on media criticism and survey methods in journalism research.

Greg McLaughlin lectures in media and journalism at the University of Ulster, Coleraine. He is the author of *The War Correspondent* and, with Stephen Baker, of *The Propaganda of Peace: the Role of Media and Culture in the Northern Ireland Peace Process* as well as a number of other articles on the media and conflict.

Hugh O'Donnell is Professor of Language and Popular Culture at Glasgow Caledonian University. He specialises in cross-cultural analysis of popular cultural products, focusing mainly on soap operas, mediated sport and representations of monarchy. His publications include *Good Times, Bad Times: Soap Opera and Society in Western Europe* and *Media* and *Monarchy and Power* (with Neil Blain). He is currently involved in the Framework 6 DYLAN Integrated Project on multilingualism in Europe.

Deirdre O'Neill has been teaching the practice and theory of journalism for over fifteen years at Leeds Trinity University College. She has a science background, initially working on medical and scientific publications before moving into more mainstream magazine journalism. She has published internationally—both collaboratively and on her own—on the British press, dealing with news values, trade union coverage and sources in local newspapers.

Michael Parks is a Professor in the Annenberg School for Communication & Journalism at the University of Southern California, and he was Director of the Journalism Program between 2001 and 2008. Prior to serving at USC, he was Editor of the *Los Angeles Times*, the largest metropolitan newspaper in the United States, from 1997 to 2000. His assignments as a journalist have taken him around the globe, and his comprehensive coverage of the struggle against apartheid in South Africa earned him the 1987 Pulitzer Prize for International Reporting.

Andy Price is the Assistant Director of the Institute of Digital Innovation at Teesside University and a Principal Lecturer in New Media. With a background in regional newspaper publishing and new media, he works closely with the media industry on curriculum and human resource development. His research interests include hyperlocal news, online journalism and media geography and technology.

Simon Gwyn Roberts is Senior Lecturer in Journalism at the University of Chester. His research centres on the role of the media in the process of political devolution across the EU: in particular, it examines the relationship between the wider media and questions of political engagement and cultural identity. Before re-entering academia in 2003, he was a practising journalist for ten years.

Armin Scholl is Associate Professor at the Institute for Communication Science in Münster, Germany. His research and teaching focus is on communication theory, journalism research and empirical methods. He has published several books, articles and book chapters on theoretical and methodological aspects and on empirical results in journalism research.

Isabel Soares is Assistant Professor at the Technical University Lisbon and her research interests relate mostly to literary journalism. She was founder of the International Association for Literary Journalism Studies, of which she is currently Research Committee Chair. She has published extensively on Portuguese literary journalism.

Marc Stanton is currently Senior Broadcast Journalism Lecturer at Edge Hill University, Ormskirk. Prior to entering academia he was a Producer for NBC News in Beijing and prior to that an undercover reporter for various independent companies, the BBC and ITN.

David Stenhouse is a Senior Producer at BBC Scotland, Visiting Professor of Journalism and English Studies at the University of Strathclyde and author of *On the Make, How the Scots Took over London* .

Tom Thomson is Group Managing Editor of the Herald & Times Group, one of Scotland's leading multimedia companies. He began in journalism with Scottish newspapers before a long career with Reuters, starting as a foreign correspondent in North America, the Middle East and southern Africa. Latterly he was Global Managing Editor based in London.

Howard Tumber is Professor of Journalism and Communication, and Director of the Centre for Law, Justice and Journalism at City University London. He has published widely in the field of the sociology of news and journalism and is the author, co-author/editor of eight books including: *Critical Concepts in Journalism, Journalists under Fire, Media at War: the Iraq Crisis, Reporting Crime* and *Television and Riots*. He is a founder and co-editor of the journal *Journalism: Theory, Practice and Criticism.*

Christopher Waddell is director of the School of Journalism and Communication at Carleton University in Ottawa. He is a former Executive Producer of news specials and Parliamentary Bureau Chief for CBC Television News, as well as past national editor, associate editor, Ottawa bureau chief and economics reporter for *The Globe and Mail* newspaper.

Sue Wallace is a Senior Lecturer in journalism at The Media School, Bournemouth University. She also has twenty years experience as a broadcast journalist with both commercial and BBC news organisations. Her research interests include Public Service Media, new technology in broadcasting, and journalists' working practices

Siegfried Weischenberg holds the chair in Journalism and Communication Studies at the University of Hamburg. From 1999 to 2001 he was chairman of the German Federation of Journalists. He has published more than 20 books and numerous articles on mass media and journalism. His main research areas are journalism, political communication, media ethics, media economy, communication technologies and news production.